BILLY CANNON

BILLY CANNON

A LONG, LONG RUN

Charles N. deGravelles

LOUISIANA STATE UNIVERSITY PRESS

Baton Rouge

Published by Louisiana State University Press
Copyright © 2015 by Louisiana State University Press
All rights reserved
Manufactured in the United States of America
Third printing, 2015

Designer: Laura Roubique Gleason
Typefaces: Sentinel, text; Constructa, display
Printer and binder: Maple Press

This book contains personal recollections. All names, dates, and events
herein are accurate to the best of the author's knowledge, and all opinions
expressed are the author's or those of his subject.

Library of Congress Cataloging-in-Publication Data

deGravelles, Charles, 1949–
  Billy Cannon : a long, long run / Charles N. deGravelles.
    pages cm
  ISBN 978-0-8071-6220-0 (cloth : alk. paper) — ISBN 978-0-8071-
6221-7 (epub) — ISBN 978-0-8071-6222-4 (pdf) — ISBN 978-0-8071-
6223-1 (mobi) 1. Cannon, Billy Abb, 1937–. 2. Football players—United
States—Biography. 3. Houston Oilers (Football team)—History.
4. Oakland Raiders (Football team)—History. 5. Kansas City Chiefs
(Football team)—History. I. Title.
  GV939.C365D44 2016
  796.332092—dc23
  [B]

                                                              2015018662

To Eliot and Ricki, Meg, and Will, Tiger fans to the bone;
to Benjamin, who wanted to know how the book was coming;
and to Elizabeth, who had other things on her mind.

CONTENTS

Illustrations follow page 80

PROLOGUE

THE LEGEND

The dentist easily recognizes the signs of fear. Below him, a prison inmate lies rigid in the long Naugahyde-covered dental chair. Neither reassurance from the dental assistant nor the anesthetic, injected into the soft tissue at the back of the inmate's mouth, has done a thing to quiet his panic; you can see it in his eyes as he squints up into the lamp. The dentist finds it sad and funny that a man should have to come to prison to be made to go to the dentist.

The dentist is dressed in a white coat. He puts a hand on the inmate's shoulder and bends down, inches from the inmate's face. He is smiling, and the smile makes deep crinkles around his eyes. "Open up, my man, and let's have another look." Still terrified but accustomed, after twenty years of incarceration, to following orders, the inmate complies. The dentist reaches upward to adjust the lamp and then bends down with a shiny stainless steel probe and a small mirror, one in each hand, and begins to pick and poke. His hands are big and spotted with age, but they work with speed and precision.

When the dentist stands back up, his smile has vanished, and the inmate notices for the first time how big he is. The dentist shakes his head in disapproval. "How long since you've had your teeth looked at?"

The inmate has to think. "I don't know, let's see . . . I was locked up in St. Tammany in '89 . . . and I got to Angola in '90 . . . uh, I'm not sure. A long time."

The dentist smiles again: "No kidding?"

As he works, the dentist does most of the talking, asking questions and then cracking jokes. He has an easy way that doesn't condescend. The inmate wants to talk football—he sees the Louisiana State University posters and pictures on the wall, and he wants to tell the man that his own team, the Florida Gators, is superior in every way, but when he tries, he can't speak for the obvious reason—his mouth is full of instruments. He makes a few guttural sounds which the dentist understands (he has been doing this a while). Even with his mouth wide open, the inmate manages to laugh from time to time, odd sputters from the back of his throat; this tall dentist has an excellent supply of one-liners.

For a few moments, the inmate has forgotten he's locked in a maximum-security prison. He remembers as a boy going with his mother to see the dentist in Tampa, coming out with a neat little pack that included a new toothbrush, toothpaste, and floss. But his mother died during the years he's been locked up for killing an off-duty police officer in Louisiana, and those better days are long gone.

When the dentist has finished filling a couple of cavities, he says it's time to stop. Others are outside in the waiting room. The inmate gets up from the chair. He realizes it's been a while since he felt the fear he came in with.

"You're going to need to come back. You know that, right?" the dentist asks.

"I ain't goin' nowhere," the inmate says, "though I wish I was."

"Make an appointment with Tonia on your way out."

"You gonna be the one to work on me?"

"If the levee holds and the river doesn't wash us both out of here," the dentist says.

"Wouldn't that be my lucky day?" the inmate says. "Hey, Doc, you're in the wrong profession, you know that?"

"That right? What should I be doing?"

"Stand-up comic. You're pretty good."

"Yeah, well, I don't know how much longer I'm going to be standing."

The inmate tries to estimate the man's age. Seventy? Seventy-five? "You know what," the inmate says, "you're probably not going to make it around here anyway."

"Oh, yeah, why's that?"

"Seems to me like you give a damn."

When he gets back to his dorm, the inmate tells his bunkmate about the dentist.

"You know who that is, don't you?" the bunkmate asks.

The inmate is dumbstruck. "You mean that guy is Billy Cannon? I could tell he liked LSU 'cause there was some pictures on the wall." He laughed. "Can you believe it? I tried to convince Billy Cannon the only real team in the SEC is the Gators."

Everybody in prison has a nickname. The inmate's is "Flash." Even though he didn't recognize Cannon, Flash has known about him for as long as he can remember. The man is a football legend, and those in the prison who know the story of the elderly dentist's early days call him by that name: Legend. He has earned it. With an amazing combination of speed, strength, skill, and determination, Cannon led every team he was ever a part of—in high school, at LSU, in the pros— to one championship after another. Gifted in each facet of the game, he could run, throw, kick, catch, block, and tackle. And could he run! One of the greatest running backs of his time, some would argue of all time, Cannon is still an object of worship among LSU fans.

In 1959, Billy Cannon became the only LSU player to win the Heisman Trophy. For over fifty years, on the anniversary of his most famous play, October 31, television and radio stations in Louisiana replay it—Cannon's fourth-quarter punt return against the University of Mississippi, an amazing effort in which he eludes defenders and breaks tackles to score the game-winning touchdown. When LSU hosts the Rebels in Tiger Stadium, the famous run is replayed, complete with the jubilation of adoring fans, on the stadium's giant video screen.

Cannon has, in fact, been at the Louisiana State Penitentiary at Angola nearly as long as Flash. He's not an inmate, as some believe, but started to work as a dentist in 1995, a decade after legal troubles of his own—a less glamorous part of the legend—ended a successful orthodontics practice in Baton Rouge. Warden Burl Cain, well known himself for taming the nation's largest and most difficult prison, considered Cannon a catch. The football hero brought attention to Cain's ongoing efforts to reform the massive prison, and Cain eagerly put him to work to further those efforts.

Cain and others have been encouraging Cannon for years to tell his life story. Many writers have approached him with the same idea, some of them with enticing financial offers. Cannon's answer has always been the same: "If somebody wants to tell my story, they're going to have to wait until I'm gone."

One writer didn't wait. Although Frank Deford vigorously denies that his 1981 novel, *Everybody's All American,* was based on Cannon, the similarities between the main character, Gavin Grey, and Cannon, are many. The connections became more apparent when the movie version was set at LSU and filmed in Tiger Stadium. Cannon rejected repeated requests to consult with the filmmakers. When he saw the movie, he was not a fan.

In spite of Cannon's well-known reticence, one man refused to give up on the idea of a Billy Cannon biography. Richard Thompson remembers how, after LSU's 1958 national championship season, Cannon visited his middle school in Shreveport. For Thompson and his fellow students, Cannon was a celebrity of the caliber of Elvis. Thompson got to shake the hand of his hero. He never forgot the moment.

Thompson spent much of his career in Louisiana government, including as an undersecretary in the Department of Corrections and Public Safety. He worked closely with Burl Cain. For years, he and Cain approached Cannon about a book—and met rejection—again and again. Last year, in 2014, Thompson's persistence was finally rewarded when Cannon agreed to a book—with one stipulation. The biography had to include the innovative improvements Warden Cain had instituted at the Angola Prison—changes that Billy Cannon had personally witnessed and of which he was a part.

Finding the right person to tell the story was not easy. Some of the best sportswriters in the country had covered Cannon for years—what new was there to say? And during the lowest times of Cannon's life, some of those same writers seemed to take pleasure in detailing his mistakes. Worse, some of what they wrote was untrue. When reporters were granted a rare interview with the football hero, they quickly learned there was much that he wouldn't discuss.

But Thompson mentioned a little-known writer who was different from others; in addition to experience as a journalist and writer, he had been a volunteer chaplain at Louisiana State Penitentiary, generally known as Angola, for twenty-five years, three of those as a spiritual advisor for a death-row inmate.

In April of 2014, four men—Cannon, Cain, Thompson, and I—met on the prison grounds for a lunch of stewed chicken and rice, potato salad, sweet tea, and homemade pralines. As inmate trustee "Big Lou" Cruze served us, we discussed what a biography of Billy Cannon might look like. When the lunch—and the meeting—were done, Cannon had agreed to tell his complete story, and I had agreed to write it.

ACKNOWLEDGMENTS

Thanks to Richard Thompson for initiating and putting the pieces of this project together and for support along the way. Thanks to John Hardy for his help and encouragement. Thanks to the Cannon family, especially Dot, Bunnie, and Elaine Cannon for help locating photographs and family documents. Thanks to my son, William de-Gravelles, a renaissance man of the twenty-first century, for his deep football knowledge and editing skills. Very special thanks to William Caverlee—fine writer, astute editor, and dear friend—for his many hours improving the manuscript; and to my wife, Angela—where would I be without her?

BILLY
CANNON

1

THE RECRUIT

The Visit

Decembers in Baton Rouge are notoriously indecisive. Days may be bitingly cold, or they may force you to peel off your jacket and roll up your sleeves. Other days—and it can be a Christmas Day—are better suited for T-shirts. But whatever else, December in Louisiana is going to be damp. A gray lid of low-hanging clouds drops over the state towards the end of the year, holding in the moisture, and the air—cold, cool, or shirtsleeve warm—feels soggy.

On a humid December day in 1955, Billy Cannon had his sleeves rolled up as he sat at his kitchen table. His mother, Virgie, had cracked the window for ventilation and adjusted the gas heater to low. The Cannons were hosting a special guest, and Virgie was anxious that everything be just right. She had spent the afternoon straightening and cleaning and, even now, as she tried to focus on their guest, she kept glancing around the room for an out-of-place potted plant or an undusted surface she might have missed.

And as it happened, Billy Cannon was himself drawn in different directions—frustratingly so for LSU head football coach, Paul Dietzel, the man who had come to court him. The star fullback from Istrouma High School had received promising offers from a number of prominent colleges, and he expected many more, but his mind was not made up. He enjoyed the uncertainty, and he intended to keep it that way for a while.

Billy could afford to play the waiting game since he was arguably the best high-school running back in the country, and his defensive play at safety was as good or better. He had recently ended his senior football season as a high-school All-American, leading the Istrouma Indians of Baton Rouge to an undefeated season and the state championship, and setting a state scoring record of 229 points, even though he often played only the first half of games. He would prove his speed and power again in the spring by winning both the 100-yard dash (9.65 seconds with a wind assist) and shot put (57 feet, 4 inches, a heave that beat the previous state record by almost two feet). In the East-West Prep All-America football game in Memphis in August, he would be named most valuable player.

The famous running back and his parents, Virgie and Harvey Sr., sat with Dietzel at the family's small kitchen table. The Cannons' neighborhood was working-class, their house a simple, wood-frame clapboard on Osceola Street. Billy would later call it, and the dozens like it for blocks in any direction, a "north Baton Rouge box." Dietzel had just finished his first season as Tiger head coach with a losing season and a ninth-place ranking in the conference. He believed that his future success depended on getting his state's best players, and he had already collected several key commitments, including crosstown players from fancier parts of the city. Dietzel was animated as he talked, his eyes moving from Billy to the parents and back. Elbows on the table, chin resting on his big clasped hands, Billy felt none of the urgency that Dietzel conveyed. His eyes lazily followed the adults at their talk.

Dietzel was only thirty-one years old, but he looked even younger—not much older, in fact, than Billy. His boyish look would be a lifelong trademark. He was also untested. He had worked under several top coaches—Red Blaik at Army, Sid Gillman at Miami, and Paul "Bear" Bryant at Kentucky—but LSU was his first opportunity as head coach. Handsome, well mannered, well spoken, he was already known for his preparation and communication skills; and here in the Cannons' kitchen, laid out his points with precision.

Dietzel assured the Cannons that Billy would be surrounded by excellent athletes. He ticked off a list of those he had already signed. Billy's Istrouma teammate, Duane Leopard, an excellent center, had been among the first to say yes to LSU. Billy had played against many on the list: Emile Fournet from Bogalusa, Carroll Bergeron from Terrebonne High in Houma, and three standouts from Istrouma's rival,

Baton Rouge High School—Warren Rabb, Don Norwood, and Gus Kinchen. One player, Johnny Robinson of University High of Baton Rouge, Billy knew only by reputation. But the name that stood out most was Max Fugler, an astute and relentless linebacker from Ferriday, the only other high-school All-American from the state. In Billy's only game against him, the North-South High School All Star Game, Fugler had dogged Billy all four quarters, stopping or slowing him down on nearly every run.

Dietzel laid his list on the table. In recent years, he said, many of Louisiana's top players had been lured by out-of-state teams. Two of the best, John David Crow of Springhill, the 1957 Heisman Trophy winner, and Bobby Marks of Warren Easton in New Orleans, had chosen Texas A&M and its talented coach, Bear Bryant. Dietzel's first priority in rebuilding LSU football, he told the Cannon family, was to keep the best Louisiana players at home. He looked straight at Billy. "I'm hoping you'll want to be a Tiger."

Dietzel didn't seem to be making much headway with the Istrouma star, but just because Billy was quiet didn't mean that he wasn't paying attention. He watched his parents carefully to gauge the impact of each of the coach's claims. He knew that he would make up his own mind, but what his father and mother thought made a difference to him. "This is going to be a first-class operation all the way," Dietzel concluded. Billy would later have the chance to remind Coach Dietzel of this promise.

The meeting was short, thirty minutes at most, and cordial, ending with handshakes at the front door. Dietzel had not signed Billy, but the young coach was already thinking of other ways to reach out to him. This would not be the last time during a hectic recruiting season that LSU would make a run at Billy Cannon.

The Hard Rush for Cannon

LSU was not about to let the Baton Rouge hometown hero slip away. Within days of the home visit, two of Paul Dietzel's assistant coaches, Carl Maddox and Abner Wimberly, met with Billy on the Istrouma High School campus in the office of head football coach, James "Big Fuzz" Brown. Billy was joined by his teammate and best friend, a talented 200-pound tackle named Luther Fortenberry. Determined to follow Billy wherever he went, Fortenberry was disappointed when, at the close of the meeting, Billy had still not made up his mind.

In the spring semester, LSU made yet another attempt to sign the running back. This time, Billy was invited to the campus to meet Athletic Director Jim Corbett. Having just left a position as public relations director for NBC Sports, Corbett was becoming known throughout college football as an innovator. Because of his background, Corbett understood better than his counterparts at many schools the growing potential of television in NCAA sports. (Before too long, LSU would get its first chance to play before a nationwide audience.) Corbett also understood the inextricable relationship between a football team's success and the revenue it could generate. At LSU, the athletic department had to raise its own funds, and ticket sales were crucial. Dietzel and Corbett barnstormed the state, promoting the football program as no one had done before. But ultimately, filling seats at Tiger Stadium depended on winning football games, which depended on great players. At this point in the 1950s, Jim Corbett wanted to play a direct part in the effort to recruit a winning team.

Coach Brown went with Billy to the meeting in the athletic director's office, located in the north end of Tiger Stadium. Gracious and welcoming, Corbett spoke to Billy about LSU's academics as well as its athletics, stressing the importance of a college degree. As he saw them out, he shook Billy's hand and told him, "Anything you need, my door is always open to you."

The meeting with Corbett impressed Billy, but something happened after the meeting that disturbed him. As Cannon and Brown walked out of the stadium office complex, the Tiger football team was straggling onto the practice field. Some players already lazed in the shade of oaks as they waited for their coaches. Others clustered in groups, idly talking. One player in particular looked completely unprepared for practice. His shoes were unlaced, his pants unbuckled, and his jersey untucked, hanging crooked over his shoulder pads. Coach Brown looked the team over and shook his head. On *his* team, players came to practice looking sharp, energized, and ready to play. Billy was shocked when his soft-spoken coach said, "I'd hate to coach a piece of garbage like that." The incident left Billy with a bad taste in his mouth.

Florida Gators and the Fast Flight Back

As talented and sought after as he was, Billy Cannon was still a boy from a working-class neighborhood. His world was small, a few blocks of frame houses, schools, businesses, and churches (the Baptist church, in Billy's case) collectively called Istrouma. Billy's father had worked in the Standard Oil Company complex, composed of a petroleum refinery and several associated plants, until he lost a leg in an industrial accident. Since the accident, Billy's mother had worked in state government as a secretary.

As he grew up, Billy's world widened bit by bit. At one time or another, he managed a paper route, loaded and unloaded trucks for a meat packer, and hawked programs and concessions at Istrouma, LSU, and Southern University games. He traveled with his dad on fishing trips to the countless waterways around Baton Rouge and with his family twice each year as far as Neshoba County, Mississippi, to see his grandparents.

But Billy's world widened the most through sports. On busses with teammates, he had traveled blacktop highways through rice fields and cane fields, over rivers and lakes. Elbow to elbow with teammates in South Louisiana diners, he'd sampled spicy boudin, gumbo, and hogshead cheese. Soft-shelled crab po'boys on the menu and Cajun music on the jukebox were within driving distance of Baton Rouge, but such items seemed to Billy and his teammates as exotic as fare from a South American country. On rare occasions, such as the state championship game in Shreveport, his team even spent the night in a hotel. But most of all, he'd competed—running, kicking, passing, catching—testing himself in Lake Charles, Houma, Bogalusa, as well as Baton Rouge, against players of widely varying abilities, the best of whom he would encounter later as opponents or teammates in college and the pros.

And now, because he was a national recruit, universities were offering to pay his way to their campuses if he would consider playing there, and Billy was excited to take advantage of the chance to travel and learn. He and his teammate Luther Fortenberry received airline tickets to Gainesville for their first out-of-town recruiting trip. Warmly greeted by University of Florida coaches, they were given a campus tour and spent the night in a college dorm. Taken to restaurants they could never have afforded back home, they were allowed to order anything on the menu (they both ordered steak). Billy and Luther stepped onto the field of Ben Hill Griffin Stadium, better known to Florida fans as The Swamp, and could hear in their imaginations the crowds roar from the empty stands that surrounded them. They were ushered in to meet the head football coach, Bob Woodruff, who explained how each of the boys would contribute to a winning football program. It was a template of events that subsequent trips would follow—heady stuff for two boys who'd grown up in the shadow of refinery stacks.

Fortenberry and Billy had been friends since the seventh grade. In the tightly bound world of their Istrouma neighborhood, they had sat together in class and played together whatever sport was in season—an annual rotation of football, basketball, track, and baseball. The following year, 1956, Luther would stand as best man in Billy's wedding. There was no question in Fortenberry's mind that Billy would elevate any of the teams that were recruiting him—among them Notre Dame, Rice, Georgia Tech, Oklahoma, and Texas. And if it were possible, wherever Billy played, Luther would be at his side.

Florida became Billy's top option the day he met Dick Jones, a recruiter for Coach Woodruff, and the team's top talent scout. During one game of Istrouma High School's 1955 championship season, Jones sat among the cheering fans, taking careful notes as Billy ran with the football; the following spring, he flew back to Baton Rouge to watch Billy run track.

Held at LSU at the end of the season, the state meet in 1956 drew the largest crowds of the year, and those crowds would come to a hushed standstill whenever Billy Cannon crouched into the starting blocks. When the gun fired for the 100-yard dash, Billy, known for his explosive starts, was first out of the blocks, and, as usual, he led the field the whole race, widening the gap with each step. But that day, as Billy leaned into the tape, he felt his hamstring tighten, and he limped to a painful stop. His coaches gathered round him and watched as he tested the leg, first walking, then jogging lightly. They all shook their heads. They agreed that Billy should pull on his sweats and sit out the rest of the meet. Another race would only make the injury worse and could jeopardize his football career. It wasn't worth the risk.

Head down in disgust and disappointment, Billy was leaving the stadium when a man called and waved him over. He introduced himself as Coach Dick Jones, a recruiter for the University of Florida. Jones questioned Billy about his injury and agreed with the coaches' decision that he should sit out for the rest of the meet. Jones was affable, relaxed, and knowledgeable, and Billy took to him immediately. He told the coach he'd seen the Gators play at LSU and believed that his own style of running would fit in nicely with their offense. Jones invited him to visit the Florida campus and program.

Weeks later, at the end of their trip to Gainesville, Billy Cannon and Luther Fortenberry boarded a Southern Airways plane and took their seats, steadily talking the whole trip back. Luther pestered Billy for an answer: Shouldn't we play for Florida? Shouldn't we give them an answer before the team roster gets filled? Billy waved him off; he wasn't going to commit until he'd seen what the others had to offer.

The first leg of the flight was a stormy one. It was the first time flying for both boys, and with every bounce, bump, and drop, they clenched their eyes and grabbed the arm rests, wondering if this flight would also be their last. When the plane finally landed in Montgomery, Alabama, an intermediate stop, the boys were wide-eyed but relieved.

New passengers boarded and buckled their seatbelts; the plane cranked its engines and taxied onto the runway. Billy and Luther never stopped talking, arguing the pros and cons of college programs and retelling stories of their undefeated season. Billy happened to look out the window and noticed lights on the tarmac. "Man, that was fast! Look, we're already back." Luther leaned over to see. He nodded. "And not a single bump the whole flight." When no one got up to exit the aircraft, the boys slowly realized that the plane had not left the ground in Montgomery. Area storms had kept them grounded. Finally, the other passengers did stand, and Billy and Luther followed them sheepishly down the aisle for an overnight stay at a nearby hotel. They eventually made it back to Baton Rouge, got into their cars, and drove home. "We thought we'd finally made it," Billy chuckled, "leaving Baton Rouge as big-time recruits, getting wined and dined by universities, and the truth is we didn't even know if we were in the air or on the ground. Luther and I laughed about it for years."

Alabama: Arrested Again and in a Foreign Land

Billy had seen Alabama play. Whenever he'd sold concessions at LSU, he always kept one eye on the action, mentally critiquing each team that came to campus. The Crimson Tide had been lackluster the last few years, but just as in the case at LSU, a new coach, Jennings B. "Ears" Whitworth, was promising hope for better times. And Billy knew two former Istrouma players who were playing for Alabama on scholarship. Earl Phillips, a tight end, and Howard Taylor, a tackle, had graduated a year ahead of Billy, and they were his guides for the visit. In fact they had been allowed to rent a new car to escort him. The three rode proudly through campus in a new rented car, stopping to introduce the Louisiana recruit to staff and supporters.

The boys laughed and talked about more than football. Both Earl and Howard were proud members of the ROTC program at the University of Alabama, and bragged that after college they were going straight into the Army. In 1956, none of the boys could have known that the growing U.S. presence in Vietnam would eventually take as many American lives as it did. Billy had his own reasons for shaking his head. "Not for me," he told them fiercely. "I'm going to keep playing football."

What the three wanted most that night was to drive. Poor boys from north Baton Rouge only had access to used cars—slow ones at that. In Billy's family, cars were handed down like clothes. The most recent model, almost always a used Plymouth bought at Moran Motor Company, belonged to his dad. Once the brothers could drive, no vehicle was ever relinquished before it made its way down the line—to Harvey Jr. and finally to Billy, ever the proud owner of the oldest—and slowest—clunker.

Thus, driving a new car—this rental was right off the lot—was as novel as an airplane ride. They wanted to feel what it was like to push a brand-new engine to its limits. That night in Alabama, after some arguing over who would drive first, Earl took the wheel. On a straight stretch of highway outside of town, he gradually accelerated. Sixty, seventy, ninety, ninety-five—with arms waving out the open windows like cowboys on a bronco, the boys hooted as they flew.

From the back seat, Billy heard the siren first. As they slowed down and pulled over, the swirling lights smeared the car's interior. Even as a high-school senior, he'd been pulled over more than once. He felt sick: "Arrested again," he thought, "and in a foreign land."

Thankfully (for Howard and Billy), the police arrested only Earl and for speeding, not DWI. It was a slow drive back in the new car. As they sat in the dorm room, not knowing what to expect, Howard wondered if they should call Coach Whitworth. "No!" Billy pleaded. The last thing he needed was his name associated again with something on the wrong side of the law.

In a couple of hours, the key turned in the dorm room door, and Earl came in. "They put me behind bars," he moaned. He had used his one call to phone the Alabama assistant coach for recruiting. "He didn't ask about me," Earl complained. "The first words out of coach's mouth were, 'Where's Cannon?'" When Earl assured him Cannon was safe and back at the school, the coach laughed. "I wished they'd locked him up instead," he said. "We wouldn't have let him out till we signed him."

Johnny Vaught: You Could Tell Why People Loved Him

Of the teams that truly interested Billy, the University of Mississippi at Oxford was by far the best. Head coach Johnny Vaught had led the Rebels to Southeastern Conference championships with a 9–2 season in 1954 and a 10–1 the season before Billy's visit. Eventually Vaught would earn six SEC titles. In 1961, his Ole Miss Rebels would be the national champions.

Billy's trip included an invitation to the team's awards banquet. In his sport coat and tie, he enjoyed a steak with all the trimmings among some of the greatest college players in the nation. It was easy to imagine himself as a star player, not a raw recruit. At the lectern, Coach Vaught reviewed a remarkable year. The Rebels had closed a nearly perfect season with a Cotton Bowl victory against Texas Christian University; Ole Miss quarterback Eagle Day had earned the most valuable player award. Day and many others were applauded as they left their seats to walk to the head table, shake Vaught's hand, and receive their awards. Suddenly Billy's own sports banquet, at which he'd been recognized as All-State, All-American, and much else besides, seemed small and far away.

Billy had a meeting with Coach Vaught the next morning. In a world where recruiters were hired pitchmen, often taking liberties with the truth, Vaught's low-key sincerity was a relief. "I really liked him," Billy remembered. "He had as many questions for me as I had for him. He was really interested, very honest, very frank. You could tell why people really loved him."

But would he be able to run sprints and throw the shot at Ole Miss? Billy considered these non-negotiable elements of any scholarship offer. Vaught conceded that the Ole Miss track program was not well developed. There was no full-time track coach, not even a track—runners and field athletes worked out on grass. These were serious issues for Billy. He wasn't ready to say no to Ole Miss, but he certainly wasn't ready to say yes.

Badmouthing and Disappointment

Billy's recruiting year had one major disappointment: Texas A&M hadn't invited him to its campus. In his first year as head coach, Bear Bryant had taken the Aggies from a 1–9 season in 1954 to 7–2–1 in 1955. Billy felt certain the team would continue to rise, and he wanted badly to be considered as a candidate. His instincts were right. Led by a Louisiana running back, John David Crow, a Heisman trophy winner the following year, the 1956 Aggies would jump to No. 1 in the nation with a record of 9–0–1. Cannon couldn't understand why A&M wasn't courting him. Years later, he would believe that Bryant already had his sights fixed on a move to Alabama, where he would continue his legendary career.

There was another possible explanation for the Aggies' lack of interest: LSU's new coach. Paul Dietzel had worked under Bryant at Kentucky and believed that the Bear was an aggressive recruiter who didn't mind breaking rules if he had too. Some called Bryant's Aggies the best team money could buy. Dietzel's first year in Baton Rouge had been a discouraging 3–5–2, and he was determined that he wouldn't have another losing season. He decided to telephone Bryant to discourage what he believed was Bryant's illegal poaching of Louisiana players. As he would later tell the story in his autobiography, *Call Me Coach,* Dietzel was blunt with Bryant: "'Coach, I'm very fond of you and grateful that you treated me so well when I was on your staff, but if you continue to use that private airplane to haul Louisiana athletes and their parents to College Station, I will turn you in.'" According to Dietzel, "we never lost another athlete to Texas A&M."

Even more disappointing than A&M's lack of interest was the hypocrisy of some of the colleges who courted him. Billy had done his best to be straight with recruiters, careful not to lead them on. If he knew he wasn't seriously considering a school, he would tell them up front. These recruiters invariably expressed regret and left the door open for Billy to change his mind. The problem was, after Billy had made his final choice and was no longer eligible, he began to hear through the grapevine that some of these same coaches denied recruiting him at all because, as they told it, "Cannon is a thug."

Trouble with the Law

Billy resented the hypocrisy of these coaches, but he knew where the slurs came from, and he acknowledged and regretted what he had done to earn them. In 1955, the summer before his final year at Istrouma, Billy had been arrested and prosecuted for a serious crime. A page-one story in the June 12, 1955, edition of the Baton Rouge *Morning Advocate* newspaper caught the city by surprise: booked for theft the night before was Istrouma High School football star, Billy A. Cannon, seventeen.

Billy had only just finished his junior year. As usual, he had earned high marks scholastically and, for the first time ever, had finished outstanding seasons in three sports—football, basketball, and track. His coaches had marveled as they watched him move from a benchwarmer to a star in a single school year.

Billy was not one to bask in his accomplishments or to sit idly. His summer would be as busy as his school year. Every Monday, Wednesday, and Friday he lifted weights at Alvin Roy's gym, continuing a training regimen the renowned weight coach had started at Istrouma High School the previous January. Whenever he was needed, he unloaded and loaded trucks on the night shift for Manda's, a meat distributor that had employed him the summer before. And yet with all this, Billy found time to get into serious trouble. He and a group of friends began to spend some of their summer evenings cruising pool halls and bars or waiting outside hotels and public restrooms known for illicit sexual activity. They were looking for easy money and excitement. They found both.

In addition to being a plant town, Baton Rouge was one of the largest inland ports in the country. Ocean-going tankers from all over the world navigated up the Mississippi River from the Gulf of Mexico to off-load everything from coffee beans to cars, then made their way back down, filled with grain or refined gasoline. For every church and school in Istrouma, there was a pool hall or bar where plant workers guzzled beer after coming off a shift, and sailors coming into port drank, gambled, and looked for love. The education a high-school boy could receive in such a milieu was far different from the one Billy had received in classrooms or the church sanctuary where Brother Sam Rushing preached the Good News on Sundays. And, for Billy, there was plenty to learn.

"Dixie" was the name locals gave to the district of stores and bars across from the Standard Oil plant complex where Weller Avenue runs into Scenic Highway. Anytime he walked down Weller, Billy could glance under the old-fashioned swinging doors of Hebert's Bar. "It looked huge to me," he remembered, "thirty or forty stools, seven or eight tables, and the place crowded with plant workers and sailors coming off the ships." Nearby was the Hotel Bruin, a pool hall, bar, and whorehouse. In his memoir, *Smiley! A Laughing Matter,* writer Smiley Anders, a classmate of Billy's, called the Hotel Bruin "the gateway to the Weller Avenue fleshpots. . . . The bars [in Dixie] had an especially raunchy character, and you could see virtually anything happen there during a typical evening. An aged B-girl hustling a sailor from Holland, the house drunk falling off the barstool, plainclothes detectives sitting around trying to look inconspicuous in their crew cuts and Sears suits and white socks. It was, indeed, a liberal education."

Even though they were only high-school boys, Billy and his friends already knew the places where sailors or working men would hook up for casual sex. Billy and his accomplices would wait in the street for such a man, leaving a liaison, to make their approach. Sometimes their quarry had been with a female prostitute in a hotel room, sometimes in a restroom with a man. The boys would surround their mark and demand anything of value—money, jewelry, watches. The embarrassment and fear of being exposed was usually incentive enough for a victim to give up his valuables without a fight, but if not, Billy and the others had no hesitation in taking what they wanted by force. After a night's work, they would try to sell what wasn't cash, or if they couldn't find a buyer, just split the booty.

Once, one of Billy's friends heard about a philandering deacon in his church, and they followed the man to his girlfriend's house. "We were waiting for him next to his car when he finally came out," Billy remembered. "He didn't want to put up any resistance, didn't want to fight. All he wanted to do was give up whatever he had on him—I think he had a watch and some money—and get out of there."

In the early morning of June 11, 1955, not long after midnight, police arrested Billy and three other boys. Officers patrolling Scenic Highway noticed a car pull over, the driver talking briefly to a man walking on the side of the road, then speed away. Questioned by the police, the man said that several boys were in the car and had offered to sell him jewelry and liquor. The officers followed, then stopped the car, and found a number of stolen items under the seats and stuffed in a canvas bag. Police detained all the boys (two were sixteen years old) and in the following days questioned others involved in what they termed "a gang."

The June 23, 1955, edition of the *Morning Advocate* reported the consequences of the crime: "Istrouma football star Billy A. Cannon and another Istrouma High School student, both pleaded guilty in District Court to theft charges and drew ninety-day suspended jail sentences."

The liquor and jewelry, it was determined, had been taken from a forty-four-year-old LSU professor. Billy had driven with the man to his apartment near campus, where he had roughed the professor up, stolen jewelry, cash, and bottles of whisky, and had then left with his cohorts, who had followed and were waiting in a car outside. At the sentencing, Judge G. Caldwell Herget "sternly remonstrated . . . the youths and warned them against any future occurrences before pronouncing sentence." As the judge noted in assessing a sentence, no weapons were used, and no one was seriously injured, but it was, nonetheless, an ugly stain on a budding career and a mistake Billy would regret the rest of his life.

Those who knew Billy only through the sports pages were astonished. Throughout his eleventh-grade school year, he had been in the newspaper nearly every weekend—accounts of dazzling touchdown runs in almost every game of a winning football season, starting on a basketball team which made it to the state playoffs, and consistently winning three events in track meets, including the state meet. His potential seemed limitless; many believed he could become an all-time great in college and professional football. Billy Cannon as gang leader was hard to imagine.

Those who knew Billy better found his predicament a little less puzzling. He was a good student, popular with his classmates, handsome, and, of course, an immensely gifted athlete, but Billy was also known to be impulsive, with a restless, even reckless, energy that rules didn't always restrain. Billy described himself as "outspoken, something of a clown." He loved to play pranks, to make others laugh, but sometimes the laughter came at someone else's expense, and he was routinely disciplined for acting up in class or getting into trouble. The basketball team photo in the 1955 Istrouma yearbook, *Pow Wow*, shows the customary rows of smiling players, but if you look carefully, you will notice that the middle finger of Billy Cannon's right hand is pointed out straight, as are those of players on either side of him. Inspired by Billy, they are grinning as they surreptitiously "shoot the bird" for the camera. A faculty advisor caught the photo and took it out, but another student was able to slip it back in before the yearbook made its way to the printer.

One man who knew well both sides of Billy Cannon was Clyde H. Lindsey, a coach and math teacher at Istrouma. Hired in 1947, Lindsey had been student body president at Kilgore Junior College and an LSU star athlete in his own right. And as Istrouma was soon to discover, he was an excellent coach. In Lindsey's first year as basketball coach, the team went undefeated. As a defensive football coach, he helped the Indians win state championships in 1950 and 1951.

Lindsey knew the Cannon family. Billy's older brother, Harvey Jr., had played on both of those championship teams. Harvey Cannon Sr. was a regular member of the Sideline Coaches Club, fathers who assembled to watch practice. Even before Billy got to high school, Lindsey knew him by reputation. Billy had failed eighth grade by skipping classes two or three days a week to ride around town with a friend on his motorcycle and to hang out at a local pool hall—behavior which forced him to repeat the academic year.

Nevertheless, in his second eighth-grade term and throughout high school, Billy's grades were excellent. When he got to high school, Billy took the accelerated classes the school offered—Lindsey's math class and others in chemistry, English, and social studies. Lindsey described Billy as "exceptionally smart, always near the top of the class." But good marks didn't mean Billy had totally changed or that his age of rebellion was behind him.

There was an element of Billy's character that resisted authority, that bent rules to the breaking point and beyond. Throughout his life, Billy acknowledged that strain, even if he never fully understood it. "The mind seems to run in circles," he later mused, "and one of my circuits rotates in the wrong direction. Every now and again, that circuit just seems to roll back around to the front." Once, someone compared him to the actor, James Dean, famous for his role as a tough young rebel. Cannon laughed as he remembered the old hand-me-down automobile he had driven in high school. "Yeah, James Dean with a slow car."

For all this, Billy didn't stand out to those around him as a bad kid but as a talented and sometimes unruly one who skirted the edge of propriety and the law just for the adventure of it. Those who knew him best were his strongest defenders. As a senior, the school year after his arrest, Billy was voted by his classmates "Best All-Around Boy." Track and field teammates witnessed Billy giving special attention to a youngster, disabled with polio, who came to meets to watch Billy run. Because he was unable to climb into the stands, the boy's father had made a seat for him in the back of the family pickup truck and backed it up near the south end zone, the final turn of the track. Billy made it a point to spend some time with the boy during every meet, especially as he waited at the anchor spot for the official's flag to signal that the race was ready to begin. "It was such a small thing," Billy remembered later, "but it meant a lot to that boy."

Others close to Billy saw the good in him. Robert Meador coached Billy in both football and basketball at Istrouma. After Billy's arrest, Meador described Billy for the local newspaper as "a typical youngster living in north Baton Rouge. By that I mean kids will be kids. They all get into mischief." Meador told the *Morning Advocate,* "Billy was always serious when he was dealing with his superiors. He was an intelligent kid, a good student. He adhered, generally speaking, to the rules of the school."

By Billy's junior year, Coach Lindsey had been promoted to assistant principal at Istrouma High. Lindsey was a strict disciplinarian who used the paddle when he thought it necessary. Lindsey knew very well the wayward side of Billy Cannon, just as Billy knew the sting of Coach Lindsey's paddle. "You could see in Billy a kind of fierce adventurousness," Lindsey remembered. "He wanted to see what life was like—from all angles. He wanted to try new things, things the other kids wouldn't even think about, and it didn't matter much to Billy whether some of those things broke the rules. But he was a good student, a great athlete. It may sound strange, but basically he was a good boy. You couldn't help but like him."

Lindsey remembered that Billy never denied a wrong-doing. "If you caught him at something, he'd admit it right away and apologize. You could tell he meant it too. He took his punishment without complaining. He knew he had it coming, and he took it." Lindsey smiled. "You just didn't know what he was going to try next."

After his arrest and the subsequent flurry of negative publicity, there was a group within the community who wanted to bar Billy from playing football and other sports. For Billy, while acknowledging his crime and feeling bad about it, such a consequence was unimaginable. "I decided that if they didn't let me play, I was going to go to Mississippi to a junior college to finish my senior year. There were some other kids who were doing that. I could have gone anywhere. This would give me three years playing junior college ball—my senior year and two more years. I would come out as a graduated sophomore and would still have two years of eligibility at the university level."

But to his great relief, Istrouma's administration and coaches—including Lindsey, Brown, and Brown's brother, the principal, Ellis A. "Little Fuzz" Brown—supported him. "God bless them," Billy said. "They would hear none of it, and I was allowed to play."

On the day of sentencing in 1955, Billy stood before the Nineteenth Judicial District Court and apologized for the robberies to the judge, to his own family, and to others in the courtroom. Coach Meador was in the courtroom that day. And as a fellow member of Istrouma Baptist Church, Meador was also in church on Sunday when Billy was allowed to speak. "He spoke from his heart to the full congregation of over 1,200 people," Meador said. "He knew that God was the only one that could provide the forgiveness." Years later, when asked about that summer, Billy called what he'd done "stupid, criminal."

Not everyone forgave Billy. During the following football season, the year of Istrouma's state championship season, opposing fans as well as players from across the line of scrimmage heckled him with screams of "jailbird." But according to his friend and teammate, Luther Fortenberry, the taunts only "pumped the whole team up to go out and beat them," he said. It was the kind of support in adversity Billy would be grateful to receive again much later in his life.

Looks Like We've Got an LSU Deal

Billy wasn't sure how his latest and more serious trouble would affect his dream to play football at the highest levels. Robbing and assaulting people had rightly earned him a felony conviction. His own school and neighborhood had rallied behind him, but would he be accepted by the colleges where he wanted to play?

For all his questions, Billy was sure about one thing: somehow, eventually he was going to play somewhere, and he was going to play well. One way or another, he *would* move up. After the trial, Billy told one of his coaches matter-of-factly that he would become a college All-American.

After Billy's conviction but before Dietzel's visit, the Cannons had received a more mysterious guest. Visitors to the Cannon home on Osceola were rare; thus, Billy was surprised one evening when someone knocked at the door. He was more surprised when his father opened the door to the East Baton Rouge Parish district attorney. J. St. Clare Favrot nodded as he shook Billy's hand. Only weeks before, Favrot had argued forcefully before Judge Herget to prosecute Billy for theft. But Favrot hadn't come to the Cannons to talk to Billy. Out of earshot, the D.A. and Harvey Sr. spoke quietly in the kitchen. The meeting didn't last long. When Favrot had gone, Harvey Sr. offered no explanation. Billy wondered if the visit might have had to do with going to LSU, but he didn't ask, and his father told him only what he had told him before, "It's your decision. You don't have to go to LSU if you don't want to."

Harvey Cannon Sr. did eventually have a hand in Billy's decision to play for the LSU Tigers. Since the family had moved to Baton Rouge, Harvey always bought his automobiles from Moran Motor Company, a Plymouth and DeSoto dealership on North Twenty-first Street. On plant-worker wages, a used car was all Harvey Sr. could afford—no air conditioner, no frills—but he needed a car he could depend on. Over the years, he'd bought three Plymouths. They had proven to be solid cars, tough enough to serve not only his needs but, down the line, those of Harvey Jr. and Billy as well. In the process, Harvey Sr. and Ralph Moran had become friends.

On Sunday, April 30, 1955, Harvey Sr. took Billy to see Mr. Moran in his office at the dealership. Moran and the elder Cannon traded stories easily. They spoke about the weather, the neighborhood, Billy's extraordinary season.

Mr. Moran turned suddenly to Billy. "I want you to go to LSU. I think your family wants you to go to LSU." Billy was struck by his directness. "If you go to LSU and there's anything you need," he said, "come to me, and I can help."

Billy understood he was not being offered money to play in Baton Rouge. This was not a bribe or a payoff. It was a pledge of long-term support. Here was someone in his own neighborhood, trusted by his father, who would stick by him through any eventuality. Feeling especially isolated and vulnerable after his scrape with the law, Billy was moved. "He was the only person who really wanted me to go to LSU and who promised support," Billy later remembered.

In particular, Moran promised to help Billy find good summer jobs. Billy had worked since he was a young boy; he took work for granted as a part of life. He'd expected to work between college semesters, doing what he'd done in a previous summer, unloading boxes of frozen chickens from the back of eighteen-wheelers for the Manda brothers. Now he had a vision of office work. Maybe he'd even sell cars for his dad's friend. "How much will I make?"

"More than you've made before," Moran promised.

Billy thought in silence for a moment. He had hesitated at every turn in the long process, but he had procrastinated long enough. Now it seemed so easy. "Looks like we've got an LSU deal," he said.

"Good," Moran said. "Don't move. Keep your seats." He picked up the phone to call Paul Dietzel. "We're going to do this today."

2

THE FARM

Raw Talent

Harvey Whittle Cannon Sr. was known for his prowess in sports. Born in 1904 on a farm in Neshoba County, Mississippi, by the time he was in high school, he stood over six feet tall. He relished anything physical. In one photograph, he poses shirtless, flexing his biceps in the manner of Charles Atlas, America's strongman of the time. In another photo, he strikes a boxer's stance. Harvey Sr. could pitch a baseball accurately at high speeds, but he was a good player at any position. He loved baseball so much he continued to play after he was married. His size and strength also served him well in basketball. A family photo features one of his teams. They are dressed in uniforms with caps, arms folded across chests, frowning in a cocksure challenge to all comers. The six team members include Harvey Sr., his brother Bankston, and two Cannon cousins, Howard and Johnny Breeland.

Another sport at which Harvey Sr. excelled was much older than basketball and baseball—and for most of the country, more obscure: the Native American game of stickball. Harvey Sr. grew up near a Choctaw reservation and learned the game from Indians. It had been played for generations, he was told, probably before the European settlers arrived, as a more peaceful substitute for war. It was not a peaceful sport. Two teams of competitors, each brandishing two sticks fitted with leather pouches, fought to move a small ball up and down the field. A point was scored when a team hit the ball against a tall vertical pole on the opposing side of the field. A minimum of rules, hurtling bodies, and flailing sticks produced many injuries.

Harvey Sr.'s size, strength, speed, and toughness proved more useful in stickball than in basketball and baseball. He boasted of a strain of Indian blood in his lineage. A Cannon family genealogy describes a long-missing tintype of a Cannon ancestor, Stirling F. Cannon, born in 1819, posing in Indian garb. It is believed that Stirling's mother, Cecelia Barton, the concubine of one William Cannon, was a Choctaw.

Many years later, as Harvey Sr. led his two sons, Harvey Jr. and Billy, through the crowded Neshoba County Fair, an old Indian tapped Billy on the shoulder and nodded towards the boys' father. He said, "Your dad was the best stickball player I've ever seen."

All this made Harvey Sr. a natural for the game of football. A Mississippi State recruiter thought so too. Because many rural high schools in the late 1910s and early 1920s didn't play the game, college football programs combed the counties for good athletes of any sport. After running a group of interested boys through a series of drills, a recruiter offered Harvey Sr. a scholarship to go to school in Starkville if he would play football. Harvey took the offer home, but after talking it over with his father, decided to decline. He was needed on the farm. It was a decision he often thought about, and he talked about the offer the rest of his life, following college football as a Bulldogs fan. Harvey Sr. would pass on his love of the game—and his athleticism—to his two sons.

The Doctor Will See You Now

When Virgie Cannon went into labor with her second child, she sent for Dr. Hand. With an office in Philadelphia, Mississippi, roughly ten miles to the north, he was the only physician in the region. For Dr. Hand, getting to the Cannon farm was no easy trip. The Cannons lived in a land and culture that would later become familiar to other Americans through the writings of William Faulkner and James Agee and the photographs of Walker Evans. This part of Mississippi consisted of sparsely populated hills and a patchwork quilt of cotton fields and forests through which dirt roads connected tiny crossroads communities like Tucker (the closest to the Cannon farm) and Union—each little more than a few houses, a post office, and a general store. The country was a mix of whites, blacks, and Indians, and life was a struggle for almost everyone. Neighbors were often miles apart.

Philadelphia, the county seat, was a real town; the charter was said to have been signed in 1841 by President Martin Van Buren. Its few streets laid out in a grid with a courthouse at the center, Philadelphia boasted a county board of police, a jail, a bank, a barbershop, schools, a drugstore, lawyers, and, of course, the office of Dr. Hand.

Philadelphia was in many ways typical of the rural Deep South in the first half of the twentieth century. The large number of blacks living along the country roads and in their own sections of villages and towns were second-class citizens, forced to use separate public restrooms and water fountains, and unable to eat in white restaurants. Jim Crow laws enacted at the turn of the century imposed voting restrictions such as literacy and property-ownership requirements that kept many African Americans from the polls. In 1964, Philadelphia became a notorious standard bearer for the racism of the Old South when three civil rights workers were murdered there. James Earl Chaney, Andrew Goodman, and Michael Schwerner, attempting to register African Americans to vote, were kidnapped and shot at close range on a country road in June of 1964 by members of the Mississippi White Knights of the Ku Klux Klan, the Neshoba County Sheriff's Office, and the Philadelphia Police Department. When the state refused to prosecute, the federal government charged eighteen individuals for the murders. Only seven were prosecuted, and they received relatively light sentences, but the Philadelphia murders helped inspire the Civil Rights Act of 1964 and the Voting Rights Act of 1965.

Virgie was at home with four-year-old Harvey Jr. when she felt her first contractions. As he did every morning, Harvey Sr. had left at sunup with his mules and chains for work. There was no easy way to reach him in 1937. Harvey Sr. was a "mule-skinner" and ran a portable sawmill for a lumberman, Abb DeWeese, making fifty cents per day. Harvey Sr. would hitch his team to trees felled by DeWeese's foresters and "skin" them of their branches as his mules dragged them through the woods to the portable mill where he would rough-cut the logs into planks. In the evenings and on weekends, Harvey Sr. farmed cotton on the forty acres he had bought and mortgaged after he and Virgie were married.

Virgie called to the young black woman who helped her around the house. Her instructions were simple and specific: get to Philadelphia and bring Dr. Hand. When the young woman made it on foot to the nearest neighbor, over a mile away, she borrowed the neighbor's wagon, hitched up the neighbor's mules, and continued her quest. As it happened, the neighbor was a midwife, and she headed directly to the Cannon place. The new baby was born that evening, not long after the midwife arrived, on August 2, 1937. Harvey Sr. decided to name their new son Billy Abb Cannon, the middle name in honor of his employer. The housekeeper returned sometime later with news that she had made it to Philadelphia and finally found Dr. Hand. "Tell them," the doctor instructed her, "that I'll get there as soon as I can."

By the time Dr. Hand got to the farm, Billy Cannon was three days old.

Life on the Farm

Virgie Lee Savell and Harvey Whittle Cannon Sr. were born only a little over one year apart and raised in the same county, but they never knew each other until they left home. Virgie graduated from Progress High School and attended the Philadelphia Business School. They first met at the East Mississippi State Mental Hospital in Meridian, Mississippi, where Virgie was working as a nurse and Harvey as a night orderly. A family photograph shows a large gathering of young nurses posing on the steps of an imposing brick building. Virgie Savell, serious and professional-looking in her starched uniform and cap, stands on the front row near the left. In the upper right of the photo, on the highest step and as far to the other side as it is possible to be, is a smiling young man in a suit, Harvey Whittle Cannon Sr. A Reverend Dubois married the couple on October 4, 1930, and they made their way back to Neshoba County. There Harvey and Virgie bought forty acres and a team of mules, and began a life together on their own farm.

As Virgie remembered it, life on the farm was good. She wrote of the period in a scrapbook and journal, "There isn't any mansion that held any more joy than the little white house on the hill." The small frame house sat between two oaks that she planted. It had a front porch with a swing. Here, Virgie minded the new baby, cleaned, and cooked while Harvey Jr., now four and with the pale skin and white-blond hair of the Cannons, played with the Indian boys from the next farm over. After a day of logging, Harvey Sr. would take little Harvey with him to do what was needed around the farm or in the barn that he had built of raw-cut timbers behind the house. With two jobs, he was making more than enough money to provide for his family.

Harvey's fortunes improved even more when he was given the chance to participate in a three-way land swap with the bank and the U.S. Department of the Interior. When the papers were signed, Harvey had acquired a new and bigger place, the 162-acre Beech Farm on the west side of Philadelphia. The young family wasted no time moving into their new home. The original Cannon farm became part of the Choctaw Indian Reservation. Even though America was in the middle of the Great Depression, with thousands from every region of the country destitute and out of work, the future for the Cannons seemed promising.

But the promise went unfulfilled. Two consecutive years of heavy rain and flooding ruined the cotton crop, and Harvey Sr.'s log-skinning income was not enough to meet the mortgage. He sold the farm to the bank, his equipment to neighbors, and paid off his farm hands. He was able to salvage enough cash to buy a used car, but there was still the matter of making a living and finding a place for himself and his family to live. By the time the Beech Farm became profitable again, the Cannons had moved out of Mississippi.

Itinerant Years

The worldwide economic depression had put millions of Americans out of work, and natural disasters such as the Dust Bowl droughts of the 1930s added to the number of itinerant men looking for work wherever they could find it. Harvey Cannon Sr. and his family joined a nation of migrants—out of work, out of money, and looking for a place to live and a means to survive.

Harvey Sr. was a skilled machinist from his days running the Abb DeWeese sawmill, and he was willing to take what employment he could find. Billy remembered the distinction his father made between a job and work. "People then weren't worried about getting a job," Billy said. "They weren't looking for a particular position. What you needed was an income, bread on the table. What you needed was work."

Harvey Sr. heard that there was work to be had in Memphis, so he set off in his used car. Once he found employment and a place to live, he sent for Virgie and the boys. It was a pattern the Cannons would follow for the next three years.

Billy recalled little of Memphis other than that his father worked on the docks. The only other testament to that period is a weathered photograph from a family album. In it, Billy follows his mother down a crowded Memphis street. Virgie looks grim and determined, gripping a package wrapped in butcher paper, perhaps a cheap cut of meat for a stew that night. Billy is looking up at what must have been a bewildering sight for a three-year-old from a cotton farm in Mississippi—multistoried buildings.

Billy's first real memories of these years are of his next home in New Albany, Indiana, where Harvey Sr. found work in a coal mine which was upgrading its equipment as America geared up for World War II. The family lived in one side of a duplex apartment in a working-class district. By the 1940–41 school year, Harvey Jr. was enrolled in a public school. To get Billy out from under her feet for a few minutes in the afternoons, Virgie would send him out to sit on the stoop and wait for his brother to come home. Other kids were coming home from school, too, and one in particular, a third-grader, began to bully the younger Cannon. "For some reason, this kid decided it was his God-appointed task to make my life miserable," Billy said. "Every time he could catch me, he'd beat the hell out of me. I begged Momma to let me stay inside, but I wouldn't tell her why. She wouldn't have it, and I'd be forced out again onto the stoop to meet my fate."

The Cannons next moved to Alabama. The Birmingham area had long produced steel, but World War II had created greater demands for the metal, and factories were upsizing and retooling to meet the challenge. Their first home was in outlying Childersburg, but eventually they found a place in the city. Pockets of black and white families lived in the same part of town, a racially mixed area of a kind they'd become accustomed to. "We were all poor, all working," Billy recalled. "Or if somebody wasn't working, he was looking for work."

A Campbell Soup factory near the Cannon's apartment spread a rich, appealing aroma through the neighborhood. Some days, word would spread, too: there was leftover chicken broth at the Campbell factory. Virgie and her boys would stand in line with a bucket. "Mom would cook with it," Billy said, "and so did a lot of other people."

By this time, Billy was old enough to make friends, and he and a black boy his own age roamed the neighborhood in search of things to do. Down the block from the Cannon apartment was a small church that became a major source of entertainment for Billy and his friend. On hot nights, church members would open the windows for ventilation, and the prayers and music drifted out as the two small boys peered inside from the shadows.

Billy dubbed it a "holy rolly" church. Lit up in the night like a lantern, with strange noises floating out, it had the appeal of magic. He didn't know its denomination, but it was an all-white congregation. "It seems like something was always about to happen," Billy remembered, "and we were always ready to see it and then run. One night, a woman fell out with the Holy Ghost. She started screaming and kicking and grabbing the air. She went down like a board. We were terrified. We broke and ran."

The boys would debate whether to go back, and every time the lure of the eccentric church won out. Best of all were the nights when the pastor brought out the snakes. "He kept a box of poisonous snakes," Billy remembered. "They'd get this particular drum beat going and start passing around those snakes and holding them up. Somebody near our window had one that twisted around and looked right at us—or so we thought. That was it. We took off running."

The Three Rs: Readin', 'Ritin', and the Road to Baton Rouge

By 1942, Harvey Sr. was looking for a better situation. His work in coal and steel, essential for the war, had kept him out of the army, and now word was spreading of more—and better—war-related work. He heard that Standard Oil, a petroleum refinery on the Mississippi River at Baton Rouge, was also expanding for the war effort, offering higher-paying jobs. Two of the plant's newest products, high-octane aviation fuel and synthetic rubber, were needed in abundance overseas. Once again, Harvey Sr. headed off alone to find work and a new place to live. By this time he'd traded his used car for a somewhat newer model, a maroon 1939 Ford. He returned with good news: the huge refinery and its many contractors were all hiring.

Virgie's brother-in-law, Chester Nelson, married to her younger sister, Rachel, was also looking for work. There was plenty for all in Baton Rouge. Billy later joked that back in Neshoba County, Mississippi, "anybody with a lick of sense knew the Three Rs: readin', 'ritin', and the road to Baton Rouge." Harvey Sr. first landed work with a contractor erecting flares for Standard Oil. When that project was done, he hired on with a plant located within the Standard complex, Solvay Process Company, maker of soda ash used in one of the many chemical processes.

Because Baton Rouge was a boom town, drawing workers from all over the country, apartments were hard to come by. Harvey and Chester approached the owner of an abandoned store on Scenic Highway near the plants in the north part of the city. It was dilapidated, and the lot on which it sat was overgrown with weeds. The owner was happy to rent it to them. The brothers-in-law partitioned the building, cleaned and fixed it up, and moved in. Uncle Check (Chester), Aunt Rachel, and their two children, Bobby and Evelyn, took the front. The Cannon family took the back.

The Number One Stomper

But in spite of the centrality of Baton Rouge for the Cannons, Neshoba County, Mississippi, continued to be an important part of their lives. The family traveled back to their original home as often as twice a year, usually in July during the time of the Neshoba County Fair, and sometimes during Thanksgiving or Christmas holidays.

Harvey Sr. would almost always drop Virgie and the boys off at her parents' home and then go on alone to see his own parents. John Robert Cannon, known to Billy and Harvey Jr. as Grandaddy Robert, was first married to Retha (Margaretha Magnolia Martha Tullos). Harvey Sr. was the fourth of their eight children. Retha was beautiful—tall and elegant with long red hair. It was said that her height and the lightness of her hair passed down to Harvey Sr., his two boys, and some of their children. When Retha died, Robert remarried a forty-nine-year-old "spinster" named Nancy Ford. Billy and Harvey called her "Nannie." (Virgie's mother they called Mama Nannie.) Nannie was known to take very good care of Grandaddy Robert, careful within their large family that he always enjoyed the best selections of meat and the biggest piece of pie.

Billy was particularly close to Virgie's parents, Willoughby Henry Savell (known to the grandkids as Papa Will) and Nancy Jane Kilpatrick (Mama Nannie). Papa Will was a cattle farmer, lean, tough, self-reliant, and hard-working. Mama Nannie was very pretty, with high cheekbones that may have come down to her from her great grand-mother Wright, an Indian. Because Virgie was one of twelve children, there were usually plenty of aunts, uncles, and cousins around when the Cannons came to visit.

Billy loved being at her house, surrounded by so many relatives. Saturday nights were especially memorable. After supper, Virgie and her sisters cleaned up quickly, washing dishes, wiping the table, and filling the slop bucket with leftovers for the hogs the next day.

Then Mama Nannie brought out the radio. It was portable, with a square battery. With much chatter and laughter, family members took their places around it. Mama Nannie tuned in and adjusted the volume. It was time for *The Grand Ole Opry*, "the Show that Made Country Music Famous," broadcast from Nashville, Tennessee. By the time Billy was born, the *Opry* was over a decade old and drew listeners from all over the country. Musicians such as Hank Williams, the Carter family, Bill Monroe, and Ernest Tubb were regulars, but Mama Nannie's favorite was the show's comedian, Minnie Pearl. The children and grandchildren loved Minnie Pearl too, but even more, they loved to hear Mama Nannie laugh. When the laughter finally died down, the radio was turned off and returned to its place, the coal-oil lamp was dimmed, and Billy and his family went to bed.

To Billy Cannon and his cousins, Papa Will seemed remote. Most mornings, he had already left for the fields by the time they woke. They saw and heard him mostly at dinner and supper before he turned in for another day. One morning, though, when Billy was about ten years old, he was awake when Papa Will was eating breakfast. He asked if he could go with his grandfather to work. To Billy's surprise, Papa Will nodded.

Billy watched Papa Will hitch two mules to the wagon. "They were huge." Billy smiled as he remembered: "They might not be huge today, but they were huge on that day."

Together they rode to the top of a hill from which Billy could see down into "the bottoms," a field where Papa Will had cut the hay with a mule-drawn sickle and stacked it into neat piles. That day, Billy was going to help him load it.

Billy wasn't prepared for the descent. "To a city boy from Baton Rouge, it seemed like we were going straight down. There was no brake, and to keep ahead of the wagon, the mules had to go faster and faster. By the time they got to the bottom, I felt like we were flying." Accustomed to the maneuver, the mules made a wide turn to slow down and pulled the wagon up to the first stack of hay.

The mules moved from stack to stack on Papa Will's command. Using a pitchfork, Papa Will threw the hay, one forkful after another, into the wagon. Billy's job was to maximize the load by spreading and stamping it down with his feet. "I was called the stomper," he said. The work was slow and tiring, but Billy loved it. He loved the physical exertion, he loved being in the open air, but most of all, he loved doing something with his grandfather.

They stopped only when the top was too high for Papa Will to reach with a pitch of hay. Any higher and the hay would have slid out the back when they made the climb back up the hill. Billy was looking down on his grandfather from what, to him, was a tremendous height. He was exhilarated. "I was working with Papa Will," he remembers. "I was part of the deal."

Now it was time to start up the steep hill that had so frightened him on the way down. Papa Will helped Billy down and put him on the seat of the wagon. The wagon began inching its way upward behind the straining mules. "The further up the hill we went," Billy recalled, "the steeper the grade. I watched them struggle. Their haunches were sweating. You could see every muscle. Sometimes they'd miss a step, and we'd slip back a little. I didn't think they were going to make it. Papa Will would talk to them, calling them each by name, and some-times he'd tap their backsides with the reigns. They never gave up, never quit. It was my first observation of giving it everything you've got. I thought I was happy when we got to the bottom of the hill after flying down, but it was nothing to how I felt when we finally got to the top."

When they finished stacking the hay in the loft, they got a drink of cool water from the spring. Papa Will told Billy he'd done a good job. Little else could have brought him such happiness. Then they got back on the wagon and headed back down to the bottoms for the next load.

Billy counted this day as among the most important in his life. It left him with a feeling he would remember and would sometimes recapture in his long athletic career, the feeling of being part of an undertaking in which people worked hard together, each doing his best, to achieve something good. "I was part of a process," he says. "I wasn't even sure then what the process was, but it was good, and I was part of it."

At the end of a long day, Billy and Papa Will walked back into the house. Harvey Sr. had spent the day with his own family, but now he was back. He looked over at his son and asked what he'd been doing. Billy told him, "Today, I was the number one stomper."

3

BATON ROUGE

Settling In

From the beginning, Baton Rouge felt like home to the Cannons. Their new life in Louisiana was the most comfortable they had known since driving away from their white-painted farmhouse on the hill back in Neshoba County, Mississippi. The old store on Scenic Highway was basic but roomy, and the family was used to making the best of a new place. Harvey Sr. and Chester did what carpentry and plumbing were necessary to convert the space into two separate units. The sisters, Virgie and Rachel, hung curtains, threw down rugs, unpacked, and arranged the familiar and cheerful rudiments of their many previous homes: a few pieces of furniture, along with photos and mementos.

Having Aunt Rachel, Uncle Check, and the cousins, Bobby and Evelyn, living on the other side of the partition of the converted store added to the feeling of home. The two young families often shared supper in the evenings, laughing and joking, trading news and stories of work, the war, and of friends and relatives back home.

But the Cannons' sense of being in the right place went beyond having family close at hand. There was security here. The Cannons had only to look out the door of their rented store to see a fuming, roaring complex of towers, stacks, pipes, tubes, and vessels. Standard Oil's Baton Rouge facility was an enormous and expanding oil refinery that made fuel, lubricant, and petrochemicals. It also made lots of money. Harvey Sr.'s wages were those of a laborer, but he had never made more. Billy remembers a Friday evening when his father proudly held up a check for a hundred dollars, the most he had ever made in one week.

The original Standard Oil, founded in 1870 by John D. Rockefeller, was a multinational corporation so large and powerful that by 1904 it controlled 91 percent of the oil production in the United States and hired tens of thousands of employees worldwide. When the U.S. Supreme Court, in accordance with the Sherman Anti-Trust Act, declared it an illegal monopoly in 1911, Standard was broken up into ninety independent "arms-length" companies, each with a different board of directors. The biggest two of those companies were Standard Oil of New York, which eventually became Mobil, and Standard Oil of New Jersey, which eventually became Exxon. The Baton Rouge operation was affiliated with the New Jersey company.

Standard Oil of Louisiana was big, by far the largest employer in Baton Rouge. When it opened in 1909, the plant employed 700 workers and could process 1,800 barrels of crude oil per day. During the war years, as other fuel-related companies such as Ethyl Gasoline Corporation and the Aluminum Company of America (Alcoa), were moving into Baton Rouge, the population of the city more than doubled—from 44,000 in 1940 to 110,000 five years later. For anyone looking, there was work and more work.

Well before it declared war in 1941, the United States was becoming increasingly involved in the events unfolding in Europe. In spite of the many who wanted to keep out of the conflict, President Franklin Roosevelt quietly steered the country into a position to help defeat Germany, Italy, and Japan. The Lend-Lease Act of 1941 allowed the president to send badly needed equipment at no charge to England, China, and the Soviet Union. At home, the country was quietly preparing to go to war. Two months prior to the December 7, 1941, Japanese bombing of Pearl Harbor, which ended the country's official neutrality, the U.S. Army Air Forces established a military base at Harding Field on eight hundred acres in northern Baton Rouge (the first federal military installation in the city since Reconstruction) as a maintenance and supply base and a training center for pilots.

Once war was declared, life in Baton Rouge changed quickly. Manufacturing facilities like Standard began operating at full capacity and beyond to supply war-related products. The Depression was unquestionably over, thousands like Harvey Cannon were finally back to work, and a common resolve drew people closer together.

The Cannons and their neighbors on the home front willingly shared the sacrifices of war. Periodic blackouts, collection drives, and rationing of basic items became commonplace. When Virgie needed sugar, butter, coffee, meat—and, of course, cigarettes for Harvey Sr.—she took the whole family to the distribution center on Third Street. Billy and Harvey Jr., each in his own line, ration stamps in hand, stood among the adults, pretending to be grown up.

They were not on the front lines, but Harvey Sr. and his fellow plant workers were contributing to the war effort all the same; without the refined oil, gasoline, aviation fuel, and synthetic rubber they helped produce, the Allies couldn't win. A sense of common purpose, of making a difference, pervaded the city.

For the first time, the Cannons lived in a neighborhood of which they felt a part. Their section of Baton Rouge, known loosely as Istrouma, was, in essence, the bedroom of Standard Oil. Someone in almost every household in Istrouma worked in "the plant," the 225-acre complex of refineries and chemical manufacturing facilities on the east bank of the Mississippi River. Scenic Highway (U.S. Highway 61), on which the Cannons' first home was located, ran on one side of the plant, running north, parallel to the river, up to Natchez, Vicksburg, Memphis, and beyond. Further east, Plank Road, running to the northeast, roughly parallel to Scenic, formed the other boundary of the neighborhood.

Streets in Istrouma were named for Indian tribes—Iroquois, Huron, Chippewa—an odd coincidence for a family that had come from Neshoba County, so heavily populated with Indians. The southern boundary of the neighborhood was, in fact, named Choctaw, the tribe that was a part of the Cannon lineage. But there were few Indians left in the Baton Rouge area by the 1940s, and strangely, none of the streets were named for some of the earliest tribes who inhabited the region prior to the coming of the Europeans: the Acolapissa, Quinapissa, Tangipahoa, and Opelousa.

In some ways, the Istrouma neighborhood was a hodgepodge of peoples—"rednecks" like the Cannons living side by side with French-speaking Cajuns from south Louisiana and other working-class families who'd made their way to Baton Rouge from different parts of the country, many representing other ethnic traditions. But in the most important ways, their Istrouma neighbors were families much like their own—new to the city, many from out of state, with blue-collar dads earning a basic but livable wage, and stay-at-home moms mind-ing young children and keeping house. Some neighborhood groups were formed by church affiliation, others by ethnicity, but everyone shared the same schools and an interest in seeing their children do well enough in school to leave the neighborhood for someplace better.

Chicken Droppings, Shots, and Dried Prunes

The first year that Billy lived in Baton Rouge, he was too young for school. Harvey Jr. came home every afternoon from the third grade, bubbling with tales of new friends and teachers. During the day, without his brother, Billy had to satisfy himself with exploring the neighborhood alone. At five, he was proud to be able to climb a neighbor's fence and balance along its boarded top. He was fascinated by the chickens on the other side. Virgie warned him about climbing the fence but to no avail. Even at five, Billy was going to do things his own way. One day, atop the fence, unsteadily stepping around the perimeter of the chicken yard, Billy lost his balance and fell inside. He hit the ground and began to squall as a sudden fury of black and white feathers swirled about—a big Dominicker rooster was all over him. He scrambled back over the fence to safety and ran home sobbing. Virgie was not sympathetic; she refused to let him in until she'd hosed off the dirt and chicken droppings in which he was covered.

On the brighter side, there was Mr. Judson Ourso's store across the street. It was here that Billy discovered the delight of dried prunes—an unlikely favorite for a young boy. Still, of all the other enticements Ourso's offered—licorice, candy corn, peppermint (Harvey's favorite)—nothing was better to Billy than prunes. It was here that Billy also learned the value of a nickel—the cost of one little bag of the dried fruit—and here that he first heard the local word *lagniappe,* Cajun French for "a little extra." Mr. Ourso would usually throw in an extra prune or two just to watch Billy smile.

The Rivalry

Pierre Le Moyne d'Iberville, who founded the French colony of Louisiana, explored the area and gave it the name Red Stick (Baton Rouge) in 1699; the first permanent settlement was French, dating from 1719.

The city grew up around a British fort, built in 1779 on high ground overlooking the Mississippi River from its east bank. Over the decades, the fort and the city changed hands numerous times, spurring the growth of the city along a straight stretch of the river below the fort. This growth was encouraged by ever-increasing river traffic, by becoming the state's capital in 1846, and, most of all, by the construction of the Standard Oil plant in 1909.

Standard Oil executives and mid-level managers lived well away from the noise and grit of the plant—and its laborers—in graceful neighborhoods bearing names such as the Garden District, Steele Place, and Hundred Oaks. Colonial Revival and English cottages were set in lawns of neatly trimmed St. Augustine grass on quiet streets lined with live oaks and crape myrtles. These elegant homes were miles away from the deafening hiss and clangor of vats, vessels, and thousands of miles of pipe. The eerie glare and shadow of flares, the inescapable stench of chemicals and steam, and the layers of grime that covered everything were the world of the working man.

Another engine of the city's growth was also located far from the maze of stacks and the miles of pipe of Standard Oil. Louisiana State University moved from the downtown area in 1925 to its current campus along Highland Road, south of town. Under the leadership of its greatest advocate, Governor Huey P. Long, the state's flagship university underwent a renaissance in the 1930s, drawing top faculty from around the country and expanding its facilities, including a vastly enlarged football stadium. Surrounding the campus were neighborhoods called the Lakes and University Gardens.

African American neighborhoods such as Catfish Town, Old South Baton Rouge (known as "The Bottoms"), and Eden Park bordered white sections of town, mostly in pockets of the lowest-lying, least desirable places in the city. North of the plants lay Zion City and Scotlandville, other African American communities, and Southern, the city's black university.

Unlike the racially diverse working-class section of Birmingham in which Billy and a black boy had become friends, Istrouma did not include people of color. The 1940s and 1950s in Baton Rouge, as in most of the South, were eras of strict segregation. Neighborhoods, businesses, and schools were separate but not equal. Billy Cannon would graduate from Istrouma High School and LSU without ever having a black classmate or teammate. Both institutions would remain segregated until the 1960s.

The proud working-class neighborhoods of north Baton Rouge and the upper- and middle-class neighborhoods on the other sides of town formed the ingredients for a perfect rivalry. Baton Rouge High School, located on Government Street at Eugene, was the premier public school in the city. But by the time the Cannons arrived, Istrouma schools were attracting good teachers and coaches and were providing a high-quality education as well. Many Istrouma graduates, including Billy and Harvey Cannon Jr., would go to college and earn postgraduate degrees.

The sport of football had come a long way, too, since the early 1920s when Mississippi State attempted to recruit Harvey Cannon Sr. right out of high school. By the time the Cannons moved to Baton Rouge in 1942, the sport had become so popular that there were few high schools that didn't have a program. And by the time Harvey Jr. and Billy began playing, in the late 1940s and early 1950s, there was an established football rivalry between the two parts of the city, represented by the Istrouma Indians and the Bulldogs of Baton Rouge High.

Young Billy Cannon and Sports

An early picture of Billy Cannon was taken in the back of the Scenic Highway house. Harvey Sr. is squatting between his two sons. With one hand he balances a football on its end as if he's holding it for a placekicker; a cigarette casually dangles from the other. Harvey Jr. is also squatting down. Like his dad in every way but the cigarette and the football, he seems a smaller replica of Harvey Sr. Beside them, Billy stands in a crisp shirt, shorts, and sandals, hands clasped behind his back, staring beyond the camera. He seems to be thinking about something other than football.

In truth, as he grew, Billy thought about little else but getting into some kind of game. By second grade, the Cannons had moved into a rental house on Linwood Street in Standard Heights, a nearby neighborhood just south of the railroad track. The move put the Cannon brothers into another school district. Too young to be on a team, and now having to make a new set of friends, Billy inserted himself into whatever game he could—be it tag, marbles, or tops.

At recess, boys of all ages played "one against all," a melee of kids fighting over a ball. "Whoever had it ran until the others brought him down," Billy remembered. "Then somebody else took it and ran. Everybody played, but not everybody got into the thick of it. Some kids would just kind of circle around the main cluster. I was just a skinny Mississippi towhead, not particularly tall for my age, but I wanted to be in the middle of it. That was the fun of the game."

The next year, Billy and his family moved back to Istrouma—literally across the tracks. It was their third house, located on Osceola Street, a simple wood-frame with a living room, kitchen, bathroom, and two bedrooms. For the first time, it was their own home, albeit mortgaged to the bank, and close enough to the Istrouma schools for Billy and Harvey Jr. to walk. Billy was in third grade now and would live in this house until he went to college.

In fifth grade, Billy played his first organized sport, a basketball team coached by a high-school student. "There were no games," Billy recalled, "only practice. We weren't tall or particularly good, but we didn't care. We were a team." Billy took advantage of a "no-cut" policy that covered all sports and all grades through high-school graduation: if a student joined, came to practice, and kept up his grades, he could be on the team. He might not play much, but he couldn't be cut. "It produced great camaraderie," Billy remembers, "and it kept a lot of kids like me playing while they got better over time."

In sixth grade, the sports scene improved somewhat for Billy: the basketball team played several games. On game days, players were to wear their "uniforms"—T-shirts and shorts. "All I had was a bathing suit," Billy said, "so that's what I wore. That night I told Mama I wasn't going to wear that suit again, that I needed regular shorts like the other boys. She talked it over with Daddy, and they decided to get me some."

The last game of the year was a "road trip." The boys rode their bikes up Plank Road to the Hollywood School while their coach followed slowly in his car. "We were used to playing in a gym," Billy remembered, "and this was a dirt court. We played a great game and we won. You'd have thought we'd gotten a gold medal in the Olympics."

One sport Billy chose not to continue was boxing. The training was rigorous, even for the sixth-graders. They hit the big bag and the speed bag. They jumped rope and they jogged the track, and sometimes a combination of the two. "If you've never run a quarter mile skipping rope, you need to try it," Billy said. "It's harder than it looks." One night after supper, Harvey Sr. called his youngest son over. "Let me see that knot on your arm." Billy proudly flexed his biceps as his dad had done for a camera many years before. "That's good," Harvey Sr. said.

Billy's only bout didn't go so well. His coaches matched him against a fellow teammate named Collins "Cossie" Stephens, two years older but about the same size. They were set to box three rounds. "We came out, the ref gave us instructions, and we bumped gloves." Billy grinned. "I was great up until then. But as soon as the bell rang, Cossie beat me from the top of my head to the tips of my toes. The best I can say is that I survived three rounds, nine long minutes of getting beat up. I didn't need the judges to tell me I'd lost that fight." Billy decided boxing was not his sport.

Billy's athletic career continued without particular promise, but he tried his hand at whatever was available. For Billy, the year was divided not by seasons of weather but by seasons of sports. Seventh grade and the years to come were a cycle of athletics. Without boxing, spring meant track and field, followed by baseball in the summer, football in the fall, and basketball in winter.

Middle-school track was practiced during physical education classes where classmates raced and jumped informally; there were no meets. Summer-league baseball, on the other hand, was well organized and offered plenty of competition. Formed by the American Legion, teams enlisted several hundred boys from across the city. Billy proudly wore a red T-shirt with the name of the team's sponsor—Hernandez Ice Company—on the back. Billy's defensive play earned him a starting spot at right field, and he hit and ran well enough to get on base at a fair clip. Ever emulating the best in the game, Billy decided to try chewing tobacco, a common vice for big-league ballplayers. On his way to practice, he stopped at a store and bought a packet of the cheapest available brand, Brown's Mule, for twelve cents. With a wad in his cheek, Billy swaggered to right field, already beginning to feel like a pro. Unfortunately, no one had taught him that the big leaguers spit out the juice. After several swallows, Billy began to feel sick. "I found myself face down in the grass, heaving," he recalled, "green as clover. I threw up not once but twice."

Billy continued to play as an outfielder in high school, but when pitchers got strong enough to throw curve balls, he began to see that he would have to give up the sport. "I couldn't hit a curve ball with a paddle," Billy remembered. His last "at bat" was as a junior. The Istrouma Indians were playing the Catholic High Bears at Baton Rouge's Red Stick Park. A former Hernandez Ice teammate, Blondie Meliet, now playing for Catholic, was pitching. "Blondie struck me out with three consecutive curve ball pitches." So ended baseball for Billy Cannon.

Billy was unquestionably athletic but short for his age and skinny, quick, with good speed, but not a standout in any sport. In basketball, he sat on the bench during many of the seventh-grade games, substituting for other players only during scrimmages, but he never missed practice, worked hard, carefully watched older and better players. The same determination that had him climbing and walking the neighbor's fence at five years old was by now entrenched in Billy's character.

There was no football team for middle-school students, so Billy hung around the after-school varsity practices. The Brown brothers—Big Fuzz and Little Fuzz, as they were known—had a well-developed program in every major sport, and Billy's brother, Harvey Jr., was a high-school sophomore, playing them all. One afternoon, Billy was watching the team practice. "The kicker, Paul Miller, had forgotten to bring out the tee, and he had no one else to hold it, so he called to me, 'Hey, boy, come hold the ball.' I couldn't get out there fast enough. He kicked the ball and he kicked my hand, but I wouldn't flinch and I wouldn't stop. It was a thrill to think of myself as part of the varsity squad, even if I wasn't. I told Momma and Daddy about it that night."

The Istrouma coaches were quick to utilize the natural size and speed of Harvey Jr., traits no doubt inherited from the Cannons and Savells. In football he was an excellent tight end, fast with good hands. In 1950 and 1951, he played on two state-championship teams. In track and field, he ran sprints, threw the discuss, and put the shot. Before Billy competed in either of these sports, he was watching Harvey Jr. on the field and on the track and was even helping him at home to practice.

Life in Istrouma

Billy wasn't the only one to love Istrouma sports. The school and its teams were a source of pride for the whole neighborhood. "Half of Baton Rouge was out watching a football game on a Friday night," Billy remembered. That included the other parts of town and their schools; rival Baton Rouge High, Catholic High, and other teams elsewhere in the area were playing too. "The only ones from our part of town who didn't make it to Istrouma games were those dads who worked the night shifts at the plant."

An unusual feature of Istrouma football games was a section in the stands reserved for African American fans. Segregated in other ways, the school welcomed black fans, many of whom were employed at the school, in the plants, or by companies that serviced the plants. They sat in their own area near the south end zone. Later, when Billy played on the high-school team, he was a particular favorite of black as well as white Istrouma fans.

When the Cannons moved into their Osceola Street home, further from the plant and closer to the Istrouma schools, eight-year-old Billy began sleeping on the porch. Like most houses in their part of town, the Cannon home had no air conditioning. Screened windows were left open to catch breezes during the hot summer months, but Billy found it easier to sleep on a rollaway bed in the relative cool of the back porch. He slept there until he was thirteen.

Portable window units that blew "refrigerated air" began to be available in the years after the war, but they could only cool a single room and were, in any event, too expensive for the Cannons. Instead, the family invested in an attic fan that would pull air through the whole house. On one of his days off, Harvey Sr. installed the big fan, Billy and Harvey Jr. helping their dad, and everyone looked forward to their first cool summer night.

By the time Billy brought his things in from the back porch into the brothers' room, Harvey Jr. had rigged up his own cooling system. It was a sheet, tied off vertically, somewhat like a sail, to divert all the fan-drawn air coming through their bedroom window directly over his bed. Billy carefully weighed his options. Harvey Jr. was seventeen, in size a full grown man. If he pulled the sheet down, his brother would only put it up again, or worse, he would start a fight. Taking his case to dad or mom always had its own risks. In the end, he said nothing, hoping there would be enough moving air on his side of the room to sleep comfortably. For Billy, it was a long, uncomfortable night. He woke up in the morning hot and out of sorts, but when he heard his brother coughing, he smiled at the unforeseen justice: Harvey had given himself a sore throat.

Discipline and Work

Ordinarily, the Cannon brothers got along well enough. Harvey, four years older and much bigger, could readily win any physical fight; such dominance was usually enough to keep a certain level of peace. Their age difference encouraged peace in another way—each had his own friends and interests so their time together was limited. But occasionally they did fight—Billy could be pushed only so far—and when they were caught, both would lose.

Discipline in the Cannon household was physical, not unusual for the time. Schools relied on paddles for punishment, and whippings were common among the families of Istrouma. Once, when Virgie broke up a fight between her boys, she sent them into the yard, each to find and cut his own "switch," a flexible branch from a bush or small tree with enough heft to leave a mark and a memory. Billy cut a fair-sized switch ("I guess I didn't know any better," he said), and his mother swatted his legs until the tears welled up. Harvey, hoping to lighten his penalty, handed her a small, flimsy switch. Virgie considered it for a moment, then told him the level of his punishment had just escalated: "You're going to have a talk with your father tonight," she said.

Virgie was tough. Harvey Sr. was tougher. A quiet, gentle man in many ways, he had little patience for foolishness. The worst punishment the boys could face was to be taken by their father out to the shed for a whipping, but Harvey Sr. could exact punishment anywhere. Once, when Harvey Jr. was in high school, he argued with his mother in the kitchen as she set the table for supper. According to Billy, Harvey Jr. was Virgie's favorite, a preference she didn't try to hide. But that didn't keep mother and son from arguing frequently. Billy remembered that the disagreement had something to do with a girlfriend of Harvey Jr. "They kept on at it and at it, even after we'd all sat down to eat. Daddy didn't say anything for a long time; he just sat there listening to them. His only warning of what was coming was when he said, 'Sonny Boy.' That's what he called my brother. When he said, 'Sonny Boy,' everything stopped. Harvey put his hands over his ears. He was telling Daddy he didn't want to hear what he was going to say. We all knew something was about to happen; we just didn't know what. A second later, Daddy hit Harvey Jr. so hard it knocked him out of his chair and up against the wall. That was it. It was over. Mamma was horrified. She told him, 'You could have hurt him, Harvey.' He looked at her and said. 'That's what I meant to do.'"

Billy got his worst whipping when he was in high school. One day, he and some friends skipped school to joyride in someone's "new" used car. When they passed some piles of scrap metal in an open field, they decided to load it and sell it for whatever they could get. By the time they finished selling the third load, school was over, and they went back and dressed out for practice. Coach Brown called Billy into his office to find out why Billy hadn't been at school. As he made up a story about staying at home to help take care of his sick father, Billy had no idea his father was in the next room listening, having come to the school to return a borrowed shot. At the end of Billy's elaborate story, Harvey Sr. stepped into the room and told the coach, "When you get finished with him, send him home to me."

After practice, alone in the shed with his father, Billy waited for the worst. Finding nothing else he could use, Harvey Sr. ripped a plank from an old wooden packing crate in the corner. "My only prayer," Billy says, "was that he didn't hit me with the side that still had the nail in it." With one hand, Harvey Sr. grabbed Billy by the arm; with the other he whaled away with the plank until Billy was on the floor. When it was over, Harvey Sr. was breathing hard. "Get up," he said. "And quit that crying before you go in. It makes your mother nervous."

Work—hard physical labor—was an expected, intrinsic part of life in the Cannon household; the boys took it for granted. Their father would go almost anywhere and do almost anything to provide for his family. As Billy discovered on trips back to the homestead, his hero and grandfather, Papa Will, had a reputation in Neshoba County, Mississippi, as an especially hard worker. "Money didn't grow on trees"; the brothers heard the old saw countless times. As soon as Harvey Jr. and Billy were old enough, they were expected to go to work.

Each of the brothers had his own paper route. In the dark before sunrise, they bicycled to a central location in Istrouma to fold and bag their newspapers. Then they were off to deliver to as many as two hundred customers. They had to collect payments too, a dollar or so per month from every customer on their route—the money usually left for the paper boy on the front porch or steps in an envelope.

Only once did Harvey Sr. have to intervene in his sons' business affairs. When a paper-route supervisor refused to compensate Harvey Jr. for a non-paying customer—as was the custom—their father put the boys in the car, drove to the supervisor's house, and held him by his shirt collar up against the wall. The terrified man immediately made good on his obligation.

But Billy discovered a means of earning money much more to his liking: selling concessions and programs at sporting events. At the time, the only high-school football field with bleachers was Baton Rouge High, and it was a busy place. Not only high schools but Southern University played there. Billy rode his bike from Istrouma across town to sell at Thursday- and Friday-night games, making a dollar or more per night. On Saturday home games, he would pedal even further to Tiger Stadium on the LSU campus.

It was not an easy task to walk through a crowded stadium with a tray of cold drinks, taking orders from customers, handling drinks without spilling them, making change, all the while keeping an eye on the playing field, but Billy soon became an expert. He was no longer only a lover of football; he became a student of the game as well. Working night after night, he came to know the names of the hundreds of high-school and college players, coaches, even the strategies and plays they ran.

Of the many great athletes he watched, Billy's favorite was Southern University running back Odie Posey. Originally from San Antonio, Posey led Southern to three Black College National Championships, four SWAC titles, and two bowl games. In 1949, he led black colleges in rushing with 1,399 yards. In that year, against arch-rival Florida A&M, Posey ran for an amazing 358 total yards. His pro career with the Los Angeles Rams in the NFL was interrupted by a military deferment. In the Navy, he made the All-Service Football team.

Billy was inspired by Posey's speed and agility, and his amazingly quick cutting ability. Needless to say, at twelve and thirteen years old, Billy already imagined himself in an LSU Tiger uniform, a football tucked under his arm, breaking loose from would-be tacklers and heading for the goal line—running to glory with Odie Posey's moves.

Posey returned to Baton Rouge to finish his degree and eventually owned a Gulf gas station near the Southern campus. "Over the years, I went out several times to talk to him," Billy said. "He was the running back I wanted to be."

The most lucrative of Billy's businesses was also tied to sports: selling tickets. Ben Peabody's full-service Esso gasoline station on Scenic Highway was a hub of social activity in Istrouma. You could buy fishing bait, snacks, and cold drinks. Men would gather to talk football and politics. A wide bulletin board advertised everything from used cars to lost pets, and tickets to high-school games were available at Peabody's for a pregame discounted price. Billy was friends with Peabody's oldest daughter and sometimes hung out there. Once, when Billy was in middle school, someone at Ben Peabody's offered Billy two tickets to an Istrouma football game at the discounted price of fifty cents each. "They knew I worked and had the money to buy them," Billy remembered. At first he declined—he didn't need tickets since he was working concessions and got into the games for free. But he quickly changed his mind. At the gate, tickets sold for seventy-five cents each. If he got to the stadium a little early, he could make his sales pitch to fans before they reached the ticket booth and resell the pair of tickets for their face value. Billy quickly and easily sold the two tickets and made a half-dollar profit.

Now he was inspired. Working through Ben Peabody's gas station, Billy began to buy as many tickets as he could afford, collecting them on Thursdays, selling them on game night for full price, and pocketing five to six dollars per game. What started out as a chance encounter developed into something of a career and would be Billy's main source of income for years to come; he eventually gave up selling cold drinks altogether. During high school and college, Billy's summer jobs came and went, but he never gave up his most reliable source of income. Even when he became college football's most famous player, Billy was still making money selling tickets.

4

THE ACCIDENT

The Accident

A decade before arriving in Baton Rouge, the Cannons were penni-less. Two years running, a rain-gorged river and its tributary creeks backed up, flooding their fields and their dreams of farming cotton in Mississippi. When the bank repossessed the farm, the Cannons left Neshoba County and traveled cross-country from one job to an-other—surviving by sheer persistence. The country itself seemed to travel with them—from depression through war to peacetime pros-perity. It was in Baton Rouge that the Cannons found modest suc-cess. They bought their own house. They joined a church. They made friends. They saved for extras like an attic fan. The schools were good, and the boys excelled. They learned to play instruments and played sports, made their own friends and, working at small jobs, earned their own money.

In 1949, the summer before Billy entered seventh grade, Harvey Sr. had an accident that changed everything. Virgie was at home that day, and the boys were off from school for the summer, when a man ran up the porch steps and banged on the door. There had been an accident at the plant, he said. He pointed to their car, not where it should have been, at work, but parked and running in the driveway. Harvey Sr. was in the back seat, the man said, hurt. Could Virgie drive her hus-band to the hospital? Virgie had never learned to drive, so she got into the passenger side as the man slid back behind the wheel. Harvey Jr. and Billy got into the back seat with their dad. They stared at him in terrified silence. Conscious, but doubled over and moaning, Harvey

Sr. barely acknowledged them. Billy felt sick. He closed his eyes and prayed. The car pulled off. Virgie gripped her purse and struggled to remain calm.

As they sped through the Indian-named streets of the Istrouma neighborhood toward the hospital, the man told Virgie all he knew of what had happened. Harvey Sr. had been perched on a makeshift scaffold, changing out the parts of a large piece of equipment. It was a typical Baton Rouge summer day, and heat from the sun radiated off the metal and engulfed him. Sweat saturated his T-shirt. It ran from under his hard hat into his eyes. It slid down his arms onto the wrench. As he wrestled to break loose a nut, locked in rust to its bolt, the wrench slipped, Harvey Sr. lost his balance and fell off the scaffold, cart-wheeling through a tangle of pipe to the ground. Laborers quickly gathered around him. Supervisors were notified. He was alive but groaning in pain, the bottom of his left leg mangled. It had slammed against a twelve-inch pipe, leaving the ankle joint a mush of broken bones. Coworkers gurneyed him to his car and carefully folded him in. Someone was appointed to drive him.

The nearest hospital was Our Lady of the Lake Sanitarium, built in 1923 on the bank of what was then called the LSU Lake. The university had long since moved and in its place, on the other side of the lake, stood the "new" State Capitol building, erected by Huey Long in the early 1930s. The hospital was owned and run by a Franciscan order of nuns. They could be seen floating up and down the hallways in floor-length black habits, nodding to the doctors and nurses they passed. Postulants, in white habits, kept the hospital spotless, scrubbing the floors and walls by hand with buckets and towels until they were shining.

Medical attendants helped Harvey Sr. onto a gurney and rushed him through the halls to an emergency examining room. A nun waited with Virgie, her two boys, and the man from the plant. Billy and Harvey Jr. said nothing, not daring to look at one another for fear of discovering in the other his own feelings of helplessness and terror.

When the doctors finally emerged, they assured Virgie that her husband's injuries were not life-threatening but were nonetheless serious. His major injury was complicated: x-rays showed multiple fractures in the ankle. An operation would be required to reset the bones, the incision would be stitched, and the lower leg wrapped in a plaster cast to hold it together. Recovery would be long, perhaps months, and the outcome was uncertain. Overwhelmed with anguish and relief, Virgie wept.

What relief there was gave way slowly, week by week, to profound anxiety and concern. Billy began this new chapter in his life by assuming the best, that his father would steadily improve, that the shattered bones would mend until the cast could be removed, that after a period of rehabilitation, Harvey Sr. would once more be walking and working. But almost from the beginning, there were troubling signs. The surgical wound became infected and continued to bleed, spotting the cast with strange designs. Harvey returned periodically to the hospital for new dressings and new casts, but after several months of little improvement, the doctors decided on a second operation to stimulate blood flow for a normal healing.

Charity

The accident transformed life at home. It was the same house, same school, same family car—a black 1939 Ford two-door coupe—but none of these things seemed the same after the accident. The most obvious difference was income. "We went from being modestly well off to being stone broke," Billy remembered. Without Harvey Sr.'s paycheck, Virgie had to scrutinize every purchase; only essentials could be considered. Harvey Sr. belonged to two unions—a plant union and a carpenter union—but neither offered benefits to injured workers. Billy remembered his father receiving a workman's compensation check from Solvay Processing, Harvey Sr.'s employer, but it was far from adequate to meet the family's minimum needs. The boys' own after-school income, once used for socializing and treats, now went for groceries, but even that made little difference. The reality was the Cannons couldn't survive on what was coming in.

For Billy, much more difficult than the lack of money was the absence of the father he had known. In Billy's eyes, Harvey Sr. was the greatest man alive—strong, if stern, commanding, unconquerable, but also funny, affectionate, loving. To Billy, he was a force of nature.

"He taught us sports, he fished with us, he was involved in the life of our school," Billy recalled. "Now he could barely get out of bed, and he wasn't going to get any better soon."

Like his father, like thousands of American males of that era, Billy didn't express his feelings. He could hardly identify them. Disbelief, confusion, anger, sadness, betrayal, injustice were all tangled together. Even if he could have articulated some of these feelings, he wouldn't. Speaking openly of his father's injury would acknowledge that it was real. When asked by his friends about the accident, Billy usually said little. Apparently, Harvey Jr. felt the same way. Close as they were, the two boys never spoke to one another of their father's accident or condition, not even into adulthood, never.

Harvey Sr.'s long hospital stays were the worst. Billy would lie awake at night and think of his dad across town, also sleepless, staring at the ceiling of his hospital room, probably thinking of him and his brother. When Harvey Sr. came home from the hospital, he was often depressed and irritable. Billy and Harvey Jr. would do as little as possible to disturb him, moving quietly from room to room, but as the months passed during the years of 1949 and 1950, they began spending as much time as they could away from home.

Even after the second operation, Harvey Sr.'s wound was not healing properly. He left the house only to go to the hospital and back. One bloody cast followed another. He was on crutches, off crutches, on crutches again. The first time Billy saw the raw wound itself was when the nurses were changing bandages. It looked like a large, ugly boil. Harvey Sr. was taking sulfa drugs to stem infection, but the medicines were not working. Over time, boils began to creep from the wound up his leg.

Harvey Sr.'s one hope—it got him up and onto his crutches every morning—was to get well and return to work. He considered himself, as did many of the men of his time, primarily as a provider for his family. Regardless of the state of his leg, he would not be "healed" until he was earning a paycheck.

Periodically, men from the plant, three or four at a time, came to visit. They sat with Harvey Sr. on the front porch, laughing, telling stories, catching up on the latest goings-on at the plant. Sometimes, when the banter subsided, Harvey Sr. would quietly ask: "They're not going to take me back, are they?" The men assured him that his job—

or another one, less strenuous—would be waiting for him when he finally got better. Before they left, the men would discreetly leave on a front porch table an envelope of money—sixty or seventy dollars—collected from coworkers around the plant. Harvey Sr. wouldn't even look at it until the men were gone. Virgie would pick up the envelope, count the money, and put it in her purse.

When church members visited, Virgie joined them on the porch. After a short prayer, there was light-hearted talk. Carefully tucked into the conversation, one church member mentioned a radio show of the time, *Queen for Today* (later *Queen for a Day* on television), in which one of three needy contestants won prizes. "Harvey," he said, "looks like you've won 'Meal for the Day.'" One of the group went to his car and brought back a couple of cardboard boxes filled with canned and dry goods. Virgie and Harvey Sr. expressed their thanks—the thanks were genuine. These items, like the collections from the men at work, were desperately needed to keep the family going. Members of the church, not always the same, came with boxes of food three or four times a year, staying long enough for prayer and conversation.

Looking back, Billy remembered how humbled and grateful his parents were to receive such help. "We all dreaded being so poor, but they appreciated the help of friends and coworkers and church. It was much, much appreciated."

But Billy was puzzled by his own very different reactions to the charity his family was receiving. He would sit with his father when the men from work and the members of the church came to visit. He recalled that, "when the men from the plants would bring money, I thought that was good and proper, and I was happy they did it. Daddy was always happy to see them. But when the people would come from the church, I didn't like that. Why I didn't like that I can't tell you to this day. They were as good as God's green grass to do it. Surely some psychiatrist somewhere could tell you why, but I can't. I knew them, I saw them every Sunday, I went to school with their kids. How in the hell do you say, 'Much needed but not appreciated.'"

The Toolbox

It had been well over a year since Harvey Sr.'s accident, and his lower leg was worse than ever. "You could see the boils getting higher up his leg," Billy remembered. "They'd do surgery to remove the infection then come back and do more surgery a little higher the next time. But the infection was deeper than they could cut. It was the first time I heard the word *osteomyelitis*." The infection was in the bone.

"Finally," Billy recalled, "they told us they were going to have to cut his leg off. It didn't take a genius or an orthopedic surgeon to know if they didn't take his leg off, he'd lose his life. When they brought him home, I thought I wanted to see where they cut it off—that is, until I saw it. It was hard to look at." The amputation was six inches below the knee—far enough away from where the infection had been but low enough for his knee to fully accommodate a prosthesis.

After the amputation, some sense of normalcy began to return to the Cannon household, even as Harvey Sr. began his awkward and painful rehabilitation. He would walk again, after all. "I felt like a weight had been lifted," Billy remembered, "and we could all breathe again."

Early in his rehabilitation, men from work paid Harvey Sr. another visit. His successful operation and the new leg brought congratulations all around, but something in the tenor of the conversation was different. Harvey Sr. had understood for a long time that he wouldn't be able to return to the kind of physical labor he once enjoyed, but he had set store on promises that "the company will find you something." His worst fears were confirmed when a visitor from work, without a word, put Harvey's toolbox down on the front porch. In those days, workers owned their own tools, and Harvey Sr. had collected a wide assortment from his years doing many different kinds of labor. From the day of his accident until this day, his toolbox had been at the plant, like a visible and palpable promise that he would one day return to work. Now it sat next to his chair, no one acknowledging it. The men finally stood up, shook hands, and said goodbye. It would be their last visit. After they'd left, Billy came out onto the porch. His dad leaned over and, with some difficulty, opened the toolbox. "Damn bastards stole half of it," he said. He closed the box, and it was never opened again.

The oldest pictures of the Cannon family show Virgie Cannon animated and smiling. No such demeanor or expression is seen in photos taken of her after the accident. She treasured her role as mother and homemaker, even when her homes were small, cramped, rented places in faraway cities. She loved being a part of her sons' school lives, not just overseeing their studies but sewing uniforms and handling the books for the Istrouma High Band Club. The accident changed all this too. What Billy would later call the "dark years," endless months of uncertainty, poverty, and struggle after Harvey Sr.'s fall, left their mark on Virgie.

That Virgie would have to go to work was as inescapable as the loss of Harvey Sr.'s leg. Even with help from friends and coworkers, even with Billy and Harvey Jr. pitching in, the Cannons couldn't make it without a regular income. A friend from church, W. C. Windham, helped Virgie find a job as a secretary in one of the departments of state government.

Now, Virgie went to work every day, and Harvey Sr. remained at home. As he mastered his crutches and then his new leg, he began to do the cooking and cleaning. He made a garden in the backyard—its vegetables helped with the family budget, and working outdoors got him out of the house, gave him some fresh air. For the time being, he was safe. Safe but subdued, confined, depressed.

Rebel without a Cause

Cannon family life was now chaotic, especially in the early months after the fall. Billy felt isolated, trapped, and helpless. He and his mother and brother took turns tending to Harvey Sr., even as they struggled to meet the everyday demands of home and school. Billy was in the eighth grade. In the mornings, he left for school as usual, and faithfully brought his books home at night, but it was hard to focus; worries about his dad and the family's future rarely left him. Nothing could induce him to discuss it with friends. He began looking for a way to escape from the turmoil.

As he returned to school, Billy began hanging out with a classmate named Youngblood. In Billy's eyes, Youngblood was cool and carefree. He was older than Billy and owned a Harley-Davidson. Every day, Billy looked forward to leaving with Youngblood for an hour or two after school started, to wander the streets or stop at the pool hall before returning for sports practice, if he returned at all. On the back of Youngblood's Harley, Billy felt free—free from the worries and burdens of school and home.

One afternoon, Billy and Youngblood rode by the lake between Our Lady of the Lake Hospital and the Capitol. Several police cars were parked as close to the lake as possible, and men in hip waders were draining the lake and pulling nets across the bottom. Billy and Youngblood stopped to look. They learned that a girl had been missing for days, and police suspected she had drowned. Billy and Youngblood watched until the policemen found the body and pulled it out. The excitement of skipping school had disappeared; Billy's sadness was beyond words.

As the weeks passed, Virgie was too preoccupied to stay on top of her sons' schoolwork. In spite of the accident, Harvey Jr. was doing well in school and played on two back-to-back state-championship football teams. Virgie didn't often ask Billy about his schoolwork, and if she did, he was evasive, or he lied. He knew that his grades at the end of the school year would bring its revelation about skipping school and his downfall, but he would deal with that then.

In the meantime, there were sports to be played. Billy's junior high school fielded an eighth-grade football team, and Billy was a member. Uniforms were hand-me-downs from the high school. His feet were too small for the smallest available pair of cleats, so he had to watch practice from the sideline until his coach, Jim Smiley, found a pair that fit him. The helmets were used leather tank helmets, World War II surplus.

Billy was still small, but faster than the others. Even so, the season was "a bench story," as Billy remembered it later. He had a few good runs in a scrimmage, although he didn't get to play in a game. But Billy was determined to stay with football, or as he put it later, "I was not bad enough to put the fire out."

Basketball brought a bit more success. Again, he didn't start, but he did get to play in a few games. Coach Hornsby was an excellent coach, Billy recalled, in an era when players were still shooting underhand free throws, and Billy's skills, under his coach's tutelage, continued to improve.

Track was the sport in which Billy seemed to have the greatest promise. He could outrun anyone his age at school and a lot of older boys as well. But eighth-grade track consisted of little more than races during PE class.

When Billy brought home his eighth-grade report card at the end of the school year, Virgie and Harvey Sr. were disappointed—and exhausted; after their year of trials, disappointment was the most they could muster. He had failed almost all of his classes. His best grade, physical education, was a C. For Billy, his parents' disappointment, especially in light of how hard they had worked to lift the family into the middle class, was worse than the anger he would have preferred. All year, he had considered his "don't-give-a-damn" attitude to be cool, but now, his year of Harleys and rebellion seemed stupid and wasted. He would have to repeat the eighth grade, and a nice dose of shame would go along with it. Perhaps worse was that, once school started, he would have to wait six weeks—the beginning of the football season—to requalify for sports, the penalty for anyone who had to repeat a grade. Why couldn't he take his punishment now and get it over with? He almost wished his father had been angry—and healthy—enough to take him to the shed for a whipping.

Billy Cannon always wondered about his eighth-grade year. Was his rebellion related to the sadness he felt watching his father, the once-proud working man, reduced to shelling peas at the kitchen table or donning an apron, stirring the red beans? Was his willingness to break the rules related to the humiliation of accepting charity? Billy never thought of his truancy as a symptom of his family's trials, but he did see it as the first in a cycle of recurring misadventures, "stupid, criminal," as he would later call some of them, ever more serious, that would land him in trouble and that he would come to regret.

The Comeback

Billy Cannon started his second eighth-grade term with embarrassment and uncertainty—how would the other kids and teachers treat him?—but he didn't let it show. Something of a "bad boy" reputation now clung to him, and this slight air of disrepute was a useful protection from his shame and regret. In each new class, he sat in the back, stretched out his legs, and played it cool. But behind the facade, Billy was determined not to fail again, to succeed in school as well as on the playing ball field.

Billy's teachers surprised him. He assumed they would be wary, at best, and might even go out of their way to make his school year difficult. But two in particular offered extra help, encouraged Billy, and made him feel welcome. One was Nelson Clothier, a first-year teacher who impressed Billy with his energy and organization. As a former boxer for LSU, he recognized Billy's drive to succeed in sports and used this connection to push him forward in academics. As a result, he gained Billy's immediate respect, and Billy made As in his class.

Mrs. Tanner, whose science class Billy had failed the year before, was especially welcoming. On the first day of school, Mrs. Tanner greeted him warmly, "Billy, it's so good to teach you again." In response, Billy committed the uncool: he smiled. "She marked me," he remembered. "She got me. All through the semester, she did things to put me at ease and to help me succeed." Once again, Billy made As.

Another first-year teacher, Charles Chaudoir, was mild-mannered with a soft, precise speaking voice. From the outset, Billy and a fellow student, Jimmy Poirier, cut up and misbehaved as Mr. Chaudoir lectured. The teacher appeared not to notice, saying nothing about it until the end of the class when he asked the two boys to stay. Mr. Chaudoir took a paddle out of his desk and whipped them both. For the third time, Billy made As.

Return to the Playing Field

Even during Billy's six-week probation from the eighth-grade football team, he showed up for practice every afternoon, memorizing the plays and calls, sizing up every player, and weighing his own chances to get off the bench and onto the playing field. When his wait was finally over, he got his uniform—complete with helmet, no longer a leather tank helmet, but a shiny hard-shell helmet like the "real" players wore. By now he weighed 125 pounds and still had his speed. His coaches knew they could use him. At first, they tried him on defense at safety, a position in which speed is a particular asset. Later he was also moved to halfback and wingback. Again, he didn't start for the team, but he began to get into some games and even made several pass completions.

This time around, in his second eighth-grade year, Billy got to play a lot of basketball. His coach chose to "spot play" Billy, utilizing his quickness, speed, and growing skill with the ball by moving him into and out of the action. His playing time increased as the season went on, but his play was far from flawless. Once, in a game against Bernard Terrace, Billy dropped the ball he was supposed to be passing in, and an opposing player named Don Norwood scooped it up and scored. (Norwood would later play football and basketball for Baton Rouge High School, a bitter foe across the line of scrimmage, but would become Billy's teammate on the LSU Tigers championship team.)

Overall, Billy's basketball season was a good one, and the team ended the year by winning the city championship. To his great joy, Billy Cannon was awarded the tournament's Most Valuable Player trophy. It still holds an honored place among the many he would win in succeeding years.

The final sport of the school year was track, the one at which Billy had always excelled. By now, Istrouma eighth-graders were able to compete in two dual meets. Billy participated in the pole vault and was able to test his speed against athletes from other schools. Although he didn't win any sprints, he came in third, adding points to the team score.

During these troubled years of middle school, the "dark years" as he called them, Billy managed both to fail spectacularly and, when given a second chance, to succeed. He ended his second eighth-grade term with all As in his school work, a most-valuable-player trophy, playing time in three sports, and the pride of his parents. Like his father, Billy Cannon had recovered his balance.

5

HIGH-SCHOOL CHAMPIONS

Second Stringer

In over twenty years as a high-school football coach, James "Big Fuzz" Brown saw hundreds of boys transformed. As freshmen, players are all but lost in their helmets and shoulder pads, awkward arms and legs extruding, chasing after passes that they then drop and runners that elude their grasp. These same boys take the field as seniors like a herd of bison, their voices thick in their throats as they bark out calls or shout encouragement from the sidelines, pumping their fists in the air. If a coach has done his job, these same players, after four years, can read a defense and adjust at the line of scrimmage, keep linemen off their quarterback, or slip past a linebacker or safety to catch a pass. On defense, they can predict the next play by the movement of an opponent's head or foot and quickly plug the line or intercept the pass.

But not even Big Fuzz and the other Istrouma coaches anticipated the coming changes in Billy Cannon. Even with the extra year of growth afforded by his repeated eighth-grade year, he was skinny and light for a freshman player. His determination to play, learn, and improve had always impressed his coaches, and his speed and quickness earned him increasing time in the game. But he was still a second stringer, and unless he got much bigger, he might well stay that way.

As always, Billy was of two minds, happy and grateful to be on the team but ever looking for an opportunity to prove himself and rise in the ranks. There were more kids than ever out for football, many of them good athletes, and with sophomores as well as freshmen contending for coveted junior varsity positions, the competition was harder than ever. The best Billy could do as a freshman was to hold down a position as a second-string running back and third-string linebacker. In the half-dozen games of the JV schedule, he saw little playing time.

What hopes Billy had of a better basketball season were soon deterred by an onset of back pain. He tried to play through it, but the pain kept him from making the moves that had earned him recognition as MVP in the championship game the year before. It took him nearly an hour to hobble home in the evenings after practice. The trainer put heat on his back, but the pain only got worse. Fred Bankston, head JV coach, began to give playing time to other teammates Billy had fought so hard to beat out. Billy couldn't even catch his eye. The nightmarish days of his father's accident and slow recovery haunted him, and Billy began to wonder if he would have to give up athletics altogether.

Harvey Sr., driving once again, took Billy to a chiropractor, who discovered that Billy's right leg was slightly shorter than his left, causing a counter-curvature in the spine and, it was believed, simultaneously causing the back pain. The solution was simple—a series of spinal adjustments and a 3/16-inch lift for Billy's right shoe. Three weeks later, Billy was practicing basketball again without pain, once again making steady progress. He had missed much of the season, but the junior varsity was doing well, having held its first three opponents scoreless. Billy continued to wear the lift throughout his high-school, college, and professional careers.

First Game, First Tackle

On August 2 of every year, Billy's birthday, Virgie measured his height on the back of the kitchen door. Between his freshman and sophomore years, Billy Cannon grew five inches. He had put on weight too, but his newly lengthened arms and legs made it hard to tell. With summer football practice starting soon, Billy assessed his chances for the coming year. "I was just trying to hang on," he remembered. "Sitting on the bench didn't bother me at the time. The starters were better than I was. Hopefully, if I worked hard enough, my day would come."

So it was that Billy surprised even himself when, on the first day of his sophomore year of practice, he trotted right past the field where the junior varsity was gathering and onto the varsity practice field. In one sense, there was little risk. If he didn't make it with the older boys, he could retreat to the JV, where his chances of coming off the bench were good. The real risk would come if he made the varsity: at what position would they play him and would he get any game time at all? As he passed his old teammates on his way to varsity practice, JV coach Tommy McCoin called out to him, "I'll see you later," suggesting Billy would likely not make the cut and would have to retreat to competing against the players his age. Boldly, he waved and kept on going.

Billy's goal was to make the "traveling squad," the true varsity, the thirty-four or so players who rode the bus to away games. Daily practice was the proving ground, and Billy worked hard to stand out from the others. Practicing with the kickoff return team, Billy was assigned to block a starter at defensive end. "I hit him with everything I had, and we both just stopped. He was trying to get around me, and I was scrambling to stay in front of him. Finally he broke loose, but he didn't make the tackle. I glanced up, and Coach Lindsey was writing on a pad. It was a good feeling."

Every afternoon, walking home from practice, Billy did the math. "My mind was running through the roster over and over: 'He's going to make it, he's going to make it, he's not going to make it.'" Billy laughed as he remembered his calculations. "Sometimes I had to cut seniors for me to be in the thirty-four." Billy knew he was green, but he had a vision of what he could be. In his mind, he saw himself running the ball the way Odie Posey, the Southern University great, had run it, shifty, agile, and fast, threading through defenders for a touchdown every time he touched the ball.

When the traveling-team roster was finally posted, Billy was on it. "I looked up, and my name, unbelievably, was on the list. I wasn't the bottom—I was next to the bottom—but I felt like I was ruling the roost."

Billy's hard work earned him a spot on special teams, and his first playing time came against Lake Charles High School. Istrouma High was filming games before other schools had started the practice, and the Indians had watched the film of the previous year's game against Lake Charles. Since Billy was now on the kickoff team, he paid spe-

cial attention to a runner named "Boo" Mason who would be returning punts and kickoffs.

The Indians got off a good kick to start the game. Boo Mason
caught the ball and, just as he had done in the film, started coming
down the right side of the field. Billy was playing on that side and got
out ahead of everyone else. "I hit him hard on the twenty-yard line,"
Billy remembered, "and brought him down. I was so excited, I jumped
up and wanted to keep on jumping, but I didn't because Coach Brown
didn't like that kind of stuff." Billy came off the field after one play, but
it had been a good one.

It wasn't until the middle of the second quarter that the Indians
scored a touchdown, and Billy was once again called off the bench and
into the game. Another good kick, and again Mason caught the ball
and was coming down the right side of the field. Again, Billy got to
him first and brought him down. Teammates and coaches gave Billy
pats on the back and helmet as he came off the field. "I was thinking
about watching this film on Monday at practice," Billy said. "I was
going to be in the movies!"

A third kickoff in the second half didn't go as well. Mason received
it and repeated his familiar pattern. "I was going to bust him," Billy
recalled. "I was flying down the field. My eyes were on him and nowhere else. The next thing I know I'm hit by a blue pickup truck." (The
Lake Charles Wildcats wore blue.) "Somebody else got to Mason, and
I was out of the picture. There were no pats on the helmet this time."
Nevertheless, Billy and the varsity team were off to a good start. Istrouma ended the game with a 12–6 victory.

Billy began to return a few punts and kickoffs in games, and he caught
some passes, but in the game against Catholic High, he dropped a big
one, as he remembered all too well. The game was played in Memorial Stadium, a 21,500-seat arena built to accommodate schools like
Catholic and Istrouma that didn't have their own game fields. The
lights were on. Both sides of the stadium were packed. "Coach sent
me in with the play—a pass to me off the wing. I went down, made my
inside move, made my outside move, and then I broke off to the post.
I left my defender behind and was all by myself. All I had to do was
catch the ball. The pass couldn't have been thrown any better. I just
missed it. I wanted to keep on running—out of the stadium and back

home—but I had to turn back around and jog to the huddle. Everyone had been cheering when I broke into the open, but after I dropped the ball, it was so quiet you could hear a cricket walking. That is, except for Big Fuzz screaming at me: 'Cannon, catch the ball!'" In spite of Billy's drop, Istrouma beat Catholic 28–6.

Another disappointment in Billy's sophomore year was a loss to rival Baton Rouge High School. The Istrouma game against Baton Rouge High was a city favorite, regularly drawing up to 15,000 fans. Memorial Stadium was once again under the lights. Marching bands, pep squads, and cheerleaders traded fight songs and cheers. "Win or lose, both teams always gave it everything they had," Billy remembered. "Players who might be mediocre on any other night would make amazing plays."

On the other side of the field from Billy was Jimmy Taylor, the Baton Rouge High star running back who would win All-State honors that year and move on to LSU and an outstanding professional career with the Green Bay Packers. Taylor was two years older than Billy and known for his relentless play. "I was in and out of the game as a spot player," Billy recalled. "Jimmy was having a great night, so as the game progressed, we kept adjusting our defense to try to stop him. I was on the field with a special team defense—maybe a kickoff or punt—when Jimmy came storming down the sidelines. Paul Stevens, one of our best linemen, got to him before I did. You can hear it when a running back gets tackled really hard—the crack of the pads and air going out of the balloon. Paul's aim was perfect, a nose tackle right under the ribs. Jimmy knew he'd been hit. They might have gotten the better of us that night, but Paul got in a great lick." Jimmy and Billy would become good friends and play together one year on the LSU Tigers.

By trying out for the varsity as a sophomore, Billy had taken a risk, and it had paid off. The varsity ended the season with a record of nine wins, two losses, and a tie, the last loss coming in the state semifinal match against St. Aloysius. Billy had been able to practice—and occasionally play—with a fine group of experienced players under head coach Big Fuzz Brown. Even though the JV team, which he had so nonchalantly passed by, won the district championship, with only a single loss for the season, he was glad he had tried out for the varsity.

Had he stayed with the JV, he certainly would have had more playing time and probably would have excelled. But for once, his adventurous spirit had taken him in the right direction. It had been a difficult year, but Billy had proved himself in a challenging arena. He played only on special teams, not once running the ball, but he demonstrated his promise in a few outstanding plays. He would have plenty of chances next year to carry the football.

Cannon on the Track and the Field

As a sophomore, Billy was fast enough to be the backup on the sprint relays, and he could feel himself improving. "I was coming in second or third behind certain runners," he remembered, "trailing at a distance, but week by week I kept closing the gap." His race times kept descending until, by the end of the season, he had qualified to run in the Louisiana State Track and Field Meet in Natchitoches, a two-day competition for AAA-ranked schools. It was the first sporting event at which Billy would spend the night away from home.

Head coach Marvin Geller considered Billy for a spot on a sprint relay team, but eventually entered him only in the 220-yard dash. The favorite to win that race was Dominic "Mickey" LaNasa, a star football tailback and four-sport letterman for Jesuit High of New Orleans. (After graduation from Jesuit, LaNasa attended Loyola for one year and then was signed by the Baltimore Orioles to play baseball.) He had already won the state meet's 100-yard dash with a time of 9.9 seconds. By placing in his preliminary heat, Billy qualified to run in the final against LaNasa.

Billy was by nature cocky and brash; getting to the finals boosted his confidence even more and brought out all his bravado. Shortly before his final race, Billy, spindly arms and legs sticking out of his team shorts and shirt, approached LaNasa as he stretched on the infield of the track. LaNasa was everything Billy wanted to be—an all-around athlete of the highest caliber. His speed and power were apparent, even under a full Jesuit sweat suit. Billy admired LaNasa's cool and easy demeanor, the way he wore a towel around his neck with the ends tucked, like an ascot, into his zippered sweat jacket. Mickey La-Nasa carried himself like a winner. Billy didn't bother to introduce himself. He told LaNasa simply, "I'm going to win it." LaNasa smiled

at Billy. "I'll show you where the finish line is, kid, Just follow me."
LaNasa won. Billy followed.

On the long ride back to Baton Rouge, Billy pictured himself breaking the tape at next year's state meet and then putting on a full Istrouma sweat suit with a towel around the neck.

Summer of a Million Nos

Billy approached his summer with all the ardor of a new season of
sports. Baseball was no longer important to him, so he decided it was
time to get a steady job. Starting in his own neighborhood and moving outward, Billy spent his first couple of weeks looking for summer
work. Up and down Scenic Highway and then Plank Road, he stopped
at every store and business, politely informing owners and managers
that he could—and would—do anything. Days of searching turned up
nothing. One business after another told him it needed no extra help
or were already covered for the summer. He remembered the experience as "the summer of a million nos."

Billy finally got a yes from Manda Brothers Provision Company, a
local meat distributor. He joined older workers unloading semitrail-
ers of frozen chicken, turkey, sausage, and beef and reloading them
onto Manda trucks for distribution to grocery stores across the city.
The work was physically demanding. It took three men to move a bull
hindquarter, wrapped in gauze and weighing six hundred pounds.
The Manda Company would then cut and repackage the meat under
its own brand. Even more exhausting were the chicken fryers, as
Billy discovered early on. When the eighteen-wheeler backed up to
the loading dock, Billy noticed that his fellow workers had disappeared. The chickens came packed in ice in wooden crates, about
fifty pounds each. Billy was strong enough to handle one crate himself, taking it from truck to cooler, but the semi was loaded front to
back, floor to ceiling. It took him two hours to unload the truck. That
night, as he pedaled home in the early hours of the morning, he made
a note to himself not to be around when the next truckload of chickens arrived.

Billy relished the camaraderie of his fellow workers, proud to be
holding his own with grown men, and they enjoyed ribbing the skinny

high-school kid about his steadfast claim that he would one day play running back for the LSU Tigers.

With newly made money in his pocket, Billy was able to socialize. He didn't have a car, but some of his friends did, and there was usually a party or a dance at a recreational club or someone's house on any given night. Occasionally they crossed the bridge to Port Allen and drank a beer at a nightclub, but mostly, the kids danced to a jukebox, a car radio, or 45-rpm disks in somebody's living room.

Billy fell into a summer routine. He rose from bed around noon, showered and ate, then headed for the pool hall to play billiards, dominos, and listen to music and gossip. "It was a small town within a bigger town," Billy remembered Istrouma that summer. "Everybody knew everybody's business. You could hear anything but meat frying and money rattling." At around four or five in the afternoon, he would head for Hoppers, a drive-in restaurant where curbside waitresses delivered trays of hamburgers, fries, and malts. Packs of boys and girls would drive in circles around the lot or talk in clusters, leaning up against someone's car. The ritual was being reenacted by teenagers across the country and would later become the staple of nostalgia movies such as *American Graffiti*. By ten or so at night, Billy was back at Manda's, heaving boxes of sausage and chicken, then home by seven or seven-thirty in the morning.

At the end of the summer, the Manda brothers offered Billy the chance to work during the school year on Saturdays and holidays, and Billy agreed.

1954: A Winning Season

As strenuous as it was, Billy's work at the Manda Company didn't prepare him for fall practice. Nothing ever did. A couple of weeks before the start of school, Billy and his teammates began the dreaded "two-a-days," calisthenics and drills in the mornings and again in the afternoons. Billy described them as "miserable, whether you were in or out of shape." Now a junior, he weighed in at 180 pounds, finally big enough to be a running back—and he was faster that he had ever been.

In the opening game of the season against the always tough Lake Charles High School, Billy, still on special teams but now also at fullback, made what a Baton Rouge *Advocate* reporter called "the slickest play of the night," As Billy received a fourth-down punt on his own 38-yard line, he was able to elude several Wildcat defenders by running laterally until he could toss the ball to fellow running back Johnny Yaun, who then sprinted 62 yards for the game's first touchdown.

Unlike many high-school coaches of the era, Fuzzy Brown employed a lot of passing as well as running in his offense, and his two quarterbacks, B. L. Fairchild and Ronald Suire, regularly connected with downfield receivers. The mixed offense kept the Indians in the lead until the last twelve seconds, when Lake Charles scored a final touchdown to tie the game 27–27.

In newspaper accounts of the following ten games of the 1954 Istrouma season, Billy Cannon emerged from just another running back into a headline player. To the sportswriters, it seemed like he came out of nowhere. Ted Castillo, who covered high-school sports for the *Advocate,* called him exceptional: "He was an amazing athlete. You wanted him to get the ball, and when he got the ball, you held your breath for what was going to happen next." In the course of a single season, Billy Cannon became a high-school star.

In Istrouma's next game, against Humes High School of Memphis, Tennessee, fellow running back Johnny Yaun scored three of the Indians' four touchdowns, but the first touchdown of the game—and his first ever—belonged to Billy Cannon. At the end of the game, Billy had compiled the most yards rushing for either side, 123 yards in ten tries, 12.3 yards per carry, in Istrouma's 27–6 victory. Fans, sportswriters, and teams around the state began to take notice of this new name, Billy Cannon.

Before a crowd of 12,000 fans in Memorial Stadium in Baton Rouge, Billy Cannon scored four touchdowns in Istrouma's 32–20 victory against the Warren Easton Eagles of New Orleans. One of those touchdowns was a spectacular 83-yard punt return. This time, instead of giving the ball to Yaun, Billy faked a handoff to him and raced down the sideline from his 17-yard line for the score.

Billy continued to make plays and touchdowns in every game. In one of his two touchdowns against the Jesuit High School Jays of

New Orleans, he sailed 43 yards into the end zone. His average for the night was 13.9 yards per carry. He was returning punts, catching passes, breaking through the line for long yardage. Fans began to understand that every time Billy touched the ball was the promise of a big play.

Against Sulphur High School, Billy made what a sportswriter called the game's "fanciest exhibition" as he "stepped and spun . . . crashed through left tackle, dodged three tacklers, picked up a pair of blocks and scooted 74 yards for Istrouma's second TD of the game." Billy's average per carry for the night was 16.3 yards. The Indians beat the Golden Tornados 25–6.

Game after game, Cannon and a winning Istrouma team accrued more victories, more headlines, and more fans. Billy scored two touchdowns against Catholic High School of Baton Rouge, three against Bogalusa High School, and four against Terrebonne High School of Houma.

A Bitter Loss to Baton Rouge High

Istrouma's first game of the season, a tie against Lake Charles, and a mid-season loss to Holy Cross of New Orleans were the worst it had to show for the season until its last match against Baton Rouge High School on November 19, 1954. The Bulldogs were long-standing crosstown rivals, the games always hard-fought and well attended. In the long-running series, Istrouma and Baton Rouge High had each won ten games, with only one tie between them. This year's winner would take the city title and the District 3-AAA trophy. In the plants and across the city, Istrouma was the favorite in the lively betting on the Baton Rouge game of the year.

Coming into the Istrouma game, Baton Rouge High had won eight of its nine games. The Bulldog offense featured a single-wing formation opponents had a hard time stopping. Quarterback Warren Rabb was an outstanding runner and passer. Like Billy, he had also made headlines and, like Billy, he was seen as one of the most promising athletes in the state. Rabb and two of his favorite receivers, Don Norwood and Gus Kinchen, would later play with Billy at LSU. A record-breaking 23,000 fans poured into LSU's Tiger Stadium—more fans than attended some LSU games—to see the two teams slug it out.

It was not the game Istrouma fans had hoped for. Rabb threw two touchdown passes—one to Norwood and one to Wayne Stabiler—and he ran for a third TD. For the Indians, it was a night of fumbles and missed opportunities. Their offense, dominant all season, was held to 116 yards rushing and 22 yards passing. In spite of 16- and 35-yard runs, Billy averaged only 5.4 yards per carry. The one Istrouma touchdown was made on an interception by Bobby Kopsco.

This last game of the year was a devastating 18–7 defeat at the hands of a bitter adversary. For Billy, the game was another unpleasant first—the first time opposing fans had turned on him personally. He had never experienced cramps in a game, but during the play with Baton Rouge High, he had fallen to the ground twice with leg pains so severe he had to be helped off the field. By now, he had become well accustomed to the cheers—when he or the team scored or pulled off a particularly good play. But the opposing team's fans were cheering this night because he was hurt. He understood, of course, that fans will applaud whatever helps their team, but on top of the loss itself, the experience left a nasty taste. He was angry, angry at himself for his vulnerability and his mistakes, angry at the mistakes of teammates. He told himself—as he told the other players on the bus ride back to school—that next year, Istrouma would beat the Bulldogs.

The loss made it hard for Billy to enjoy the accomplishments and honors of his junior year—first-team All-City and All-District and second-team All-State. In ten games, he had run the ball 700 yards, more than any other running back on the team, for an average of 9.4 yards per carry. But it wasn't simply his statistics; it was his dazzling style of play—defensively as well as on the offense—that made him a favorite in the city and increasingly known throughout the state.

Weights

The Monday after New Year's Day, 1955, a Saia Freight eighteen-wheel tractor-trailer parked in front of Istrouma High School. Coaches from across the school rounded up their athletes and ordered them to begin unloading it. When the stacks of wooden boxes were dollied off the truck and opened, students and coaches alike began pulling out heavy steel bars and round black weights of various sizes and carrying them into to the gym, one piece at a time.

Until this moment, no American high school, college, or professional team utilized weightlifting programs to complement its team athletics. It was popular wisdom among coaches that weights were good for bodybuilding but a detriment for other sports, that the muscles produced by weightlifting rendered an athlete slower and more awkward. Some even thought lifting dangerous.

One man had been trying to change this perception, and Istrouma High School was going to be his testing ground. Alvin Roy had played football and basketball at Istrouma High until his graduation in 1938. After playing basketball briefly as a walk-on for LSU, he left for the U.S. Army and World War II, where he won four battle stars and a bronze star for his service in Europe. While still in the service, Roy had organized athletic events and competitions for the troops. After the war, he began to work with the U.S. Weightlifting Team and its head coach, Bob Hoffman, where he saw firsthand that weights, contrary to popular belief, could increase an athlete's speed and athleticism.

Roy returned to Baton Rouge to open up his own weightlifting gym and to continue his efforts to convince coaches of the efficacy of weight training as a crucial part of any team sport. He knew if he could get one team to seriously adopt his methods, he could prove his theories, and programs across the country would take him seriously.

After Istrouma's crushing defeat by Baton Rouge High School in the fall of 1954, Coach Fuzzy Brown was finally willing to give the weights a try. Brown's athletes began their weight program the day they unloaded the Saia truck and set up the weights in a newly designated area of the gym. The regimen was simple but carefully calculated and tested by Roy. Three days per week, athletes went through a series of eight lifts—the military press, bench press, clean and jerk, and others. Each lift was performed with precise form, three sets of three repetitions for each, utilizing the maximum weight an athlete could manage. When an athlete successfully performed the required sets and reps of a lift at a given weight, he moved up to a slightly higher weight.

The Istrouma players, motivated by their loss to the Bulldogs of Baton Rouge High, took to the weights with enthusiasm. "Everyone sensed it was a way to give us an edge," Billy recalled, but it turned out to be much more than that. Noticeable results appeared in weeks and months as athletes picked up strength and weight. "You could feel it happening," Billy remembered. "It was even improving our quickness, our explosiveness. We were all excited, all doing it, all improving."

Alvin Roy handpicked a number of the best Istrouma athletes for special treatment. With his natural strength and speed, and a highly successful football season behind him, Billy Cannon was at the top of the list. Others included Billy Castilaw, Luther Fortenberry, and Oscar Lofton. These players began working out at Alvin Roy's gym on Oklahoma Street near LSU, as well as at school. In his own gym, Roy could personally oversee their training and carefully measure the results. Roy had something to prove to the sports world; Billy and the other boys would become his best evidence. The boys worked out every Monday, Wednesday, and Friday throughout the summer. "We stopped two weeks ahead of fall practice," Billy recalled, "so we could start running and get our wind back. We had all gained weight and picked up strength. Our defining lift became the bench press, and I got up to about 320 pounds, far beyond anybody's expectations, including mine. We were all stronger and, as it turned out, as quick or quicker."

The Other Sports

When basketball season arrived, Billy walked onto the court bigger, stronger, faster, more confident, and with a proven reputation for hustle, hard play, and success. Under Coach Bobby Meador, the Indians won seven of their eight regular-season games, placed second in district and third in the state playoffs. Bobby Wicker, a senior forward, was the pacesetter for the Indians, consistently scoring the most points game after game but, for the first time, Billy's contributions to the total scoring were second or third. He usually scored in the double digits—he put up 19 in the game against Bogalusa—and his aggressive defensive play often helped keep opposing team scores as low as 20 points below their own.

Track followed basketball, and here too, Alvin Roy's weight training was starting to pay off. Billy consistently led in three events throughout the season. He ran a 9.7-second 100-yard dash in the district meet in Houma, tying a state record that had been set in 1941, ran the 220-yard-dash as fast as 21.5 seconds, and was putting the shot up to 52 feet. At the Meet of Champions, held in Martin Berman Stadium in New Orleans, Billy walked away from the awards table holding four first-place trophies (he also ran the anchor-leg in the winning 440-yard relay). When the entire stadium stood and cheered, Billy was caught by surprise and moved. "It was spontaneous," he said, "and I wasn't expecting it. It felt good."

Billy ended his junior year as a star. A dominant running back in football, he had also proven himself on the basketball court, and was the state's premier track-and-field athlete. He was featured in sports-page headlines and talked about in offices and bars all over the city. His fame was spreading to other parts of the state as well. A student at Albany High in neighboring Livingston Parish, Bobby Olah, remembered when he first heard the name Billy Cannon. He was working weekends in Andy's Café, his family's restaurant, a favorite stop for fishermen on their way down and back up from fishing the Tickfaw, Amite, or Natalbany rivers. "Baton Rouge plant workers would come in talking football," Olah recalled. "I started hearing the same name over and over again—Billy Cannon this and Billy Cannon that. Sometimes they'd get so tanked up on beer that they'd move tables around and start running the plays from the night before. 'He's on the thirty, the twenty, the ten, he's over the line. Billy Cannon scores another touchdown!' I don't know how many points 'Billy' scored in our restaurant, but it was a lot!" Bobby Olah would eventually become close friends with Billy. He would also, within a year, collide with him on the basketball court.

School Life

With all the demands of multiple sports, Billy stayed on top of his grades, taking every honors course his high school made available, and consistently earning As and Bs. As a varsity football coach at Istrouma, Clyde Lindsey knew very well Billy's prowess on the playing field, but he had also been Billy's honors math teacher, and remembered him as an excellent student as well. He got no special treatment from faculty, nor did he need it. In a piece for the Baton Rouge *Advocate*, a classmate, Smiley Anders, remembered, "In Janie Bankston's American history class, I sat behind Billy Cannon. Janie cut the future LSU football star no slack at all, and, as far as I could tell, didn't even know he was a top athlete. But Billy was a bright kid and needed no favors to make his grades."

But teachers and classmates also knew the darker side of Billy—his impulsiveness and his restless attraction to trouble. For one thing, Billy never completely gave up skipping classes. At Istrouma, students who had missed school reported to Ellis "Little Fuzz" Brown for an absentee form to get into class. During Billy's freshman and sophomore years, Little Fuzz, brother of the head football coach, was assistant principal and was, as such, the administration's front-line disciplinarian. On his desk, Brown kept a pad of student absentee forms. Like a precocious undercover agent, Billy discovered that a combination of liquids he found at a stationery store would remove the red letters, turning Mr. Brown's form into an excused absence.

Billy was usually paddled for infractions, but such punishment was hardly a deterrent. Coaches eventually discovered a more effective technique: forcing him to sit out a game. Once, when a cafeteria worker refused him seconds, Billy slammed his tray on the serving line, spraying the worker and others with spaghetti and meat sauce. As punishment, Billy had to watch his football teammates board a bus without him for a game against St. Aloysius in New Orleans. Being on a team, having a chance to contribute, a chance to excel; all these were the reasons he'd loved sports since grade school. Regardless of his punishment, Billy did not intend to miss a game, even if he couldn't play in it. Without another thought, Billy hitchhiked the ninety miles to New Orleans to cheer on his teammates. Midway through the first half, Billy surprised his coaches and teammates by walking onto the sidelines and taking his place on the bench; they nudged one another but said nothing. At the end of a victorious game, amid the celebration, Lindsey told Billy he could ride back with the others. Billy humbly thanked his coach and boarded the bus without another word.

James Dean in a Slow Car

With the good looks of a Hollywood star, humor, and charm, Billy never had trouble getting dates. He was, after all, a football hero, and his reputation as a rebel added something to his allure. "I had lots of girlfriends," Billy remembered. "I couldn't understand guys that were afraid to ask someone out. I had no fear of rejection. Somebody turned you down, you just asked the next one. A breakup wasn't that big a deal either. You went with somebody for a couple of months and then you started dating someone else—and sometimes I was the one who got told to hit the road. But there wasn't much drama. You stayed friends. These were all nice girls, sweet girls. We were all having fun. We were just kids finding our way in the world. We grew up and we got married. Lots of us are friends today."

But one rejection Billy did remember well. On a fall evening of his senior year, he went to pick up a date to go to someone's birthday party. When she got into the car, Billy could see she was upset. She told him, "Daddy wants to talk to you." As he followed her inside the house, he knew what was coming. Only a couple of months before, the newspaper had published the story of his arrest for theft—Billy had assaulted and robbed a man, and he and his friends had tried to sell the valuables on the street. Many, but not all, were willing to forgive Billy. "When her father asked me about it, all I could say was, 'I messed up,'" Billy recalled. "He told me I was welcome to come to the house, but I couldn't take her out. I understood, and he was nice about it, but that pretty much ended things. She and I talked for a couple of hours that night, and I think I went back once, but basically it faded away."

One girl Billy found special was Dorothy Dupuy, known as Dot. Because many of the girls Billy dated were friends with Dot, they were often together at the same dances and parties. It didn't hurt that Dot was herself a star athlete—All-State in basketball her junior and senior years. It also didn't hurt that she was pretty, outgoing, and a terrific dancer. Like Billy, Dot had grown up in the Istrouma neighborhood; her father, like so many Istrouma fathers, worked for the Standard refinery. Like Billy, Dot was funny and strong-willed, something of a maverick. And like Billy, Dot was an entrepreneur, making money booking the fan buses for out-of-town athletic events. Dot even helped Billy get through a class he dreaded—typing—and he was grateful; a bad grade would have marred his academic average.

Year of Champions

Istrouma's 1955 lineup was formidable. Senior quarterback B. L. Fairchild had proved himself the previous season as both as a passer and a leader (classmates elected him senior class president). George

Guidry, second only to Cannon in scoring, would be joining Billy in the backfield. Linemen included center Duane Leopard, guard Billy Bueto; at tackle Billy's close friend Luther Fortenberry, and Oscar Lofton at offensive end. A transfer from Catholic High, Pete Gremillion, joined A. J. Millet as a defensive end, bookend defenders that would render offensive sweeps all but impossible. Again, Billy would start as fullback on offense and safety on defense.

Motivated by their defeat the year before at the hands of rival Baton Rouge High, players had been working steadily during the spring and summer months lifting weights, Istrouma's secret weapon. "We knew we were strong," Billy remembered. "We'd seen ourselves progress, individually and as a group. Everybody participated. That was the great thing. Weightlifting for football—the first time in organized sports. Not for bodybuilding, for strength."

The power and speed of the Indians were apparent from their first game as they beat Humes High School of Memphis by a score of 55–20. Billy Cannon and George Guidry were deemed that night "twin terrors" by a local sportswriter, each scoring three touchdowns. Guidry's average per carry was 16 yards, and Billy's was 14. B. L. Fairchild connected with Oscar Lofton for two more touchdowns as Istrouma totaled 399 yards rushing and 86 yards passing.

Billy Cannon and the Istrouma Indians thrilled their fans with a 31–13 victory against a traditionally tough Lake Charles High School before a crowd of 10,000 in Baton Rouge Memorial Stadium. Billy ran an 84-yard sprint for one touchdown and 25 yards for another. Not only was he scoring multiple touchdowns every game, Billy was kicking the extra points, field goals, and punts.

Prominent among Istrouma's opponents was Central High of Little Rock, Arkansas, one of the biggest prep schools in the nation. It was an out-of-state trip and a night in a hotel, a rare event for the boys from the industrial neighborhoods of north Baton Rouge. The Central High stadium was set on a wide, beautiful campus, unlike anything else the boys had experienced at a high school. More notably, it was a chance to compete against a top-flight school. Istrouma had managed, from time to time, to beat Little Rock Central when the game was played in Baton Rouge, but they had never been able to beat them in their home stadium. Almost no team had. Billy put it simply: "We were going to find out in Little Rock just how good we were."

Billy and his teammates were warming up when the Central High Tigers took the field. "They kept coming and coming," Billy recalled. "We couldn't believe how many. When they formed up for warm-ups, it was easy to count their numbers—they had five lines of twenty players each—but I still had trouble believing it. My dad confirmed it for me later—'Yep, there were one hundred players'—and we were on the other side with our thirty-three. I gathered everybody and told them, 'Gang, we can win this game, but we can't win a brawl. Don't anybody start a fight!'"

Coach Brown and his players had studied the films of other Central games and knew the team's defense was stout. "One Central player was huge," Billy remembered, "a man-child. He shifted from tackle to end, and he was almost always there to greet you when you crossed the line." A successful play for the Indians the previous year had been a running option, a precursor to the "read option" popular in today's game. Most of the time, quarterback B. L. Fairchild took the snap, faked it to halfback George Guidry, who dove up the center of the line and then handed off to Billy, at fullback, for a run off tackle. "We kept running it that way, and I got to know that big player very well that night," Billy remembered. But in one version of the play, Fairchild exercised his other option, faked it to Billy and gave the ball to Guidry. "I'd been tackled without the ball, and I was looking up from the ground for George. They hit him with an arm-tackle, but an arm-tackle wasn't going to stop George. After that, he was nothing but 'assholes and elbows' for the next 87 yards and a touchdown. Nobody else was close."

Guidry's average for the night was over 7 yards per carry, Billy's over 5 on twenty-five carries, mostly banging through the line but with one streaking 21-yard end-around. Guidry punched in two touchdowns, Billy scored one and kicked an extra point. The Indians left for home with a confidence-soaring 19–7 victory over Little Rock Central.

By early October, Billy had accumulated sixty points, leading a tight race for total points in the state. Up to that point, he had scored nine touchdowns, but it was his ability to kick extra points—six at this stage in the season—which gave him the edge. His crosstown rival, quarterback Warren Rabb of Baton Rouge High School, was third in the standings with eight touchdowns and four extra points, and teammate George Guidry was fourth with seven touchdowns and forty-two points.

Istrouma's toughest game of the year was against Sulphur High's Golden Tornados, a defensive slugfest that ended in a 7–7 tie. The Tors held Billy to a 6-yard average and George Guidry to 4.3. But Billy scored the only touchdown, kicked the extra point, and made two game-saving tackles. One of those saves Billy described as "one of the best plays I ever made as a safety." A Tornado running back broke free of the line with nothing between him and the goal line. "To catch him cross-field, I had to fly. I caught him on about the eight or nine yard line and knocked him out of bounds into the band which was lining up for halftime. A step or two later, he'd have scored and we might have lost the ball game."

The Istrouma Indians continued their dominant season unabated. They beat Jesuit High School of New Orleans 40–0, Holy Cross of New Orleans 33–0, Catholic High School of Baton Rouge 26–0, and Bogalusa High 42–0. Billy was keeping the fans on their feet with long runs, scoring multiple touchdowns per game, and displaying dizzying athleticism on defense, often picking off at least one pass a game. During the game against Catholic High, he reached 1,000 total yards for the season and 122 total points scored.

But for Billy and his teammates, the most important game had yet to be played. Their long-standing rival, Baton Rouge High, had beaten them badly the year before, and much of the energy and drive of the succeeding months had been fed by the thought of a rematch. In particular, Billy remembered rival fans cheering when he'd cramped up and had to be taken from the field. Like Istrouma, the Bulldogs had kept many key players from the previous winning season—including Warren Rabb, Don Norwood, and Gus Kinchen—and were having a fine season as well. This, more than any other game of the season, was the one Billy wanted to win.

"I wanted to win so badly, I guess I was thinking I was going to do it single-handedly," Billy recalled, "but Coach Brown helped me refocus fast. The week before the game, we were practicing plays against the defense, semi-contact. One of the guys who played behind me at fullback was Don 'Catfish' Smith. When coach kept letting Catfish run, I got frustrated and finally yelled out something I shouldn't. Coach asked me what my problem was, and I complained that Catfish was getting the ball, and I wasn't. 'So what?' he asked me. That's all he said. I didn't have a good answer. He was the coach. I was the player. I got it."

Istrouma and Baton Rouge High met in Memorial Stadium on a rainy night before an estimated 18,000 fans. During his pregame speech, Coach Brown wrote a list of objectives on the blackboard. "I don't remember all of them, but it was a sizable list," Billy recalled. "We needed to recover one fumble, intercept one pass, make so many points, commit no errors—no offsides, or turnovers. When we got back for the half-time talk, I walked up to the board—something players never did—and I checked off every one of those things he'd written. I said, 'What else, coach?' He just grinned."

By the end of the game, Billy Cannon had scored 32 of Istrouma's points in its 38–26 victory. Among Billy's five touchdowns were three on the ground, along with 106 yards rushing, a 77-yard interception return of a Warren Rabb pass, and a 55-yard fumble return.

Billy's night also included many fine defensive plays. One in particular was remarkable in that he stopped two offensive players at the same time. "I was playing safety on the right side. They had a little pass where they would snap to Rabb, he'd fake to the fullback and then hit Don Norwood with a little toss as he came off the tight end. The tailback, Wendell Harris, would circle behind him, and when the safety came up to tackle Norwood, he'd lateral to Harris. It had been very effective. I'd seen it live, we'd watched it in films, and we'd chalk-boarded it. I timed it just right. I got there just as Norwood was starting to lateral and I jammed both of them up at the same time and brought them both down." In the next morning's Baton Rouge *Advocate,* sportswriter Ted Castillo crowned Billy Cannon "king of Louisiana prep football."

The win over Baton Rouge High qualified Istrouma to meet Terrebonne High School of Houma in the playoffs. The Indians won easily, 32–0, and featured what fans had come to expect: dominant running, kicking, tackling, and multiple touchdowns by Billy Cannon. But for Billy, the game was notable not so much for the play or the victory but for an unusual feature of Istrouma's all-white school and team— a black cheering section: "Baton Rouge was segregated back then— the whole South was—but many who worked at the plants followed Istrouma High football, including a lot of African-Americans. They sat together near the south end zone at Memorial, and they could really make it rough on the other side." One of the best players for Terrebonne was Carroll Bergeron, a big lineman who would play in subsequent years with Billy at LSU. "Carroll told me the story later," Billy remembered. "While their team was warming up, the black fans kept needling him: 'Hey, white boy. You better get ready. Billy Cannon going to get you. Billy Cannon coming to get you. That's right, white boy, I'm talking to you. Billy Cannon going to get you.' Bergeron said they didn't let up."

The second round of the playoffs—which amounted to a semifinal game—was at Tiger Stadium in Baton Rouge against St. Aloysius High School of New Orleans, another large-margin victory for Istrouma with a final score of 33–7. *Morning Advocate* sportswriter Jim Falkner reported that Billy's 14 points in the game pushed him to 207 points for the season, a new all-time state scoring record, even though, as Falkner noted, his coaches often kept him out of the second half to keep from running up the score. Billy and halfback George Guidry each scored two touchdowns, and Billy kicked two extra points.

That year, the north Louisiana state finalist, Fair Park High School of Shreveport, hosted the state championship game. "We were somewhat concerned," Billy remembered, "since they were quite a bit bigger than we were. But it didn't take us long to figure out that our speed was going to more than make up for the difference." Billy scored three touchdowns and four extra points. The final TD, a beautifully placed pass by B. L. Fairchild from behind Istrouma's 17-yard line, connected with Billy at the 40, and he broke away, sprinting the final 60 yards for his final touchdown of the night. He called it "icing on the cake." The final score was 40–6, and Billy ended the game and the season with a record-setting 229 points for the year.

The victory celebration that night was all the sweeter for Billy because it was also the night of his first date with Dot Dupuy, his longtime friend, fellow athlete, entrepreneur, and very pretty typing mentor. He'd finally asked her out, and the occasion could have hardly been better. "The team was ecstatic. We were surrounded by our teammates, friends, family, and fans. College coaches from all over had come to see us play, and were celebrating with us. We had played a great game, and it was a great game for me personally. We had really accomplished something."

Early in the season, the team had hung a handmade sign in the locker room they'd passed every day on their way to the practice field: "You have gotta want it." In one yearbook photo, teammates Oscar Lofton and Luther Fortenberry are pointing to the sign. In the next photo over, Billy and George Guidry are holding the state championship trophy. The caption: "Gets it."

The Rest of the School Year

Billy's drive to excel in sports didn't flag even though he'd just experienced an undefeated football season and a personal set of record-breaking performances. He enjoyed the moments of glory—he always would—but his aim, as ever, had shifted to what was ahead of him. Not surprisingly, he was selected to All-City, All-District, All-State, and All-America teams, and won a local honor known as the "Star of Stars" (for which LSU coach Paul Dietzel, among others, cast a ballot), but waiting for him were a season of basketball and a season of track as well as the all-important decision about which college program to choose. Just like that, Billy quickly refocused his priorities and got back to the weight room.

In basketball, the Indians had a winning but far from perfect season. "We were good, respectable, but we weren't great," Billy remembered. "We won a lot of games, had a lot of fun. Coach Bobby Meador had taken over from Tommy McCoin the year before, and we were still learning his style. Meador had played at LSU and was outstanding as a coach. He brought in some good things with him. We felt like we had a new beginning."

For Billy, the most memorable game of the season was against a small team from neighboring Livingston Parish, Albany High School. Istrouma met them at the annual Wedge Kyes Tournament towards the end of the season. Named after one of its former coaches, the tournament was hosted by Baton Rouge High for schools in the city and at least one other outstanding team from the outlying area. The other school that year was Albany.

"A couple of weeks before the tournament, Coach Meador took a few of us out to see them play," Billy recalled. "Albany High wasn't big enough to have a football team so they played basketball year-round. We played maybe twenty-eight games the whole season, but they had probably already played forty games. They were good. And of course it would have been the crowning day of their season if they could knock off Istrouma. We had the bulls-eye on our chest since we'd just won the state championship in football."

Albany's best player was named Bobby Olah. He was small but quick, agile, a slick shooter and ball handler. "As you watched them, it didn't take you long to figure out it was all Bobby Olah," Billy recalled. "The others fed to him. He made the play happen, penetrated, kicked out, and scored a bunch of points. I think he was averaging thirty, thirty-five points a game."

Billy was a strong shooter himself, usually second in points only to Billy Castilaw, but he was particularly effective on defense. Because of his aggressive style of play, Billy was always assigned to guard an opponent's top scorer, and as Billy watched Olah play, he analyzed how he should defend him. "He was so finessed and quick, nobody ever roughed him, nobody ever body-checked him. If I'm going to keep him off the scoreboard, I'm going to have to keep him from shooting," Billy decided. "That's what I needed to do for the team to be successful."

When Istrouma met Albany the next week in the tournament, Billy followed through on his plan. "I totally roughed him. After he'd shoot, I'd hit him. After he'd pass, I'd bump into him with a shoulder. When he'd drive, I'd cut him off physically. I did as much as I thought I could get away with, and sometimes I'd get caught. Baton Rouge High was playing after us that same night, and all their players were in the stands. The football team was out there too, and they hadn't forgotten about our game against them, so they were pulling for Albany and booing me." Bulldogs receiver Gus Kinchen was on crutches, leading the group. "He'd had an operation for a football injury right after the season, and he was shaking his crutches, and of course everybody was hollering at me. Every time I hit Olah, they'd scream at the ref to call a foul. Sometimes he did."

"We jumped out to an early lead," Billy remembers, "but towards the end of the game, Coach Meador went into four-corners play to slow the game. But the slowdown didn't work. It killed our momentum, and they started to cut into our lead. Right before the end of the game, I fouled out—the Baton Rouge High fans erupted when I had to leave—and Albany continued to peck away at our lead until they passed us and won the game 45–43."

Bobby Olah, the star of the night (and later good friends with Billy) remembered the game from a different perspective: "I distinctly recall looking up at him from my back on the floor. He was standing over me, grinning."

To no one's surprise, Billy was the featured athlete at every track meet Istrouma entered. Crowds gathered two or three deep near the starting and finishing lines of the 100- and 220-yard races and near the shot put ring when Billy was putting. And he disappointed no one, winning in every event and anchoring the sprint relays, at least early in the season. He continued to run the 100-yard-dash in 9.7 (at a Holy Cross High School meet, he ran a wind-assisted 9.65) and the 220 under 22 seconds. Early in the season, he broke the state shot put record with a heave of 56'-6 1/4" and then later broke his own record twice, once with a put of 56'-8 1/2" at the Ed Young Relays and again at the state meet with a throw of 57'-4". But Billy could run no faster that season. He sustained a hamstring injury at the Ed Young Relays in late April, an injury that never fully healed that season, so that he pulled up on the anchor leg of the 440-yard relay in the district meet and again in the state meet as he tried to run the 100. He would run eventually again, he knew, but he would have to wait until college.

A Coach and Two Cannons

From the stage at high-school graduation, Billy looked out at his classmates and remembered the previous four years with a deep sense of satisfaction and gratitude. He had entered Istrouma as a troubled freshman, one year behind because truancy and failing grades had forced him to repeat the eighth grade, but during the next four years, he had earned nearly all As and Bs. Two years of consistent improvement in practice and a steady commitment to weight training had combined with his natural athleticism to transform him into a multi-sport star and the best-known prep football player and sprinter in the state. His family had successfully weathered his father's awful accident and his mother's having to go to work. He had found in Dot Dupuy a girl he was serious about. Even the trouble he had gotten into, the worst of which was an arrest for theft, seemed mitigated by his achievements. And after much deliberation, he had decided where he wanted to go to college.

Billy's commitment to LSU was officially signed on April 29, a Sunday afternoon, in the office of Ralph Moran, a car dealer, an LSU supporter, and a friend of the family. Moran and Billy were joined by Billy's father, Harvey Cannon Sr., and Coach Paul Dietzel. But the scene was reenacted the following day for reporters and photographers on the LSU campus. Described in the *Morning Advocate* as "one of the most sought-after football and track stars in the annals of Louisiana prep history," Billy was the forty-second member of Dietzel's recruiting class and the seventh from the Baton Rouge area. Many of the others in the freshman class were either teammates or opponents of Billy's. In one of the pictures, above the cutline: "Coach and Two Cannons," a smiling Billy and Paul Dietzel stand in front of one of the polished brass ROTC cannons that were symbols of "the Ole War Skule." (Billy was accustomed to plays on his name: Cannonball and Cannonball Express were common tags for him among sportswriters; his friend and fellow running back, Jimmy Taylor, laughingly called him "Pop Gun.") Dietzel was lauded by local sportswriters for having made the catch. In his column, "Random Shots," *Advocate* reporter Bud Montet concluded, "The announcement of the signing of Billy Cannon, sensational young athlete of Istrouma, just about concludes the recruiting efforts of the LSU Bengals for this year and climaxes one of the best jobs done . . . in recent years."

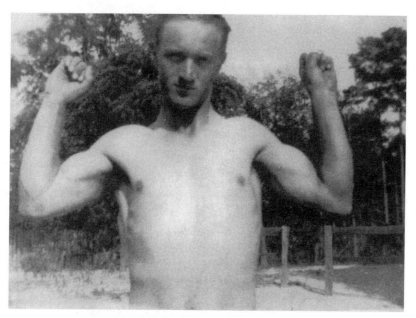

Harvey Cannon Sr. grew up in Neshoba County, Mississippi, playing baseball, basketball, and Native American stickball. (Courtesy of Cannon family.)

Harvey Cannon Sr. and his basketball team, around 1921. *Sitting:* Johnny Breeland; *kneeling, left to right:* Bankston Cannon, Howard Breeland; *standing, left to right:* unknown, Harvey Cannon Sr., Carroll Clark. (Courtesy of Cannon family.)

Harvey Cannon Jr., born in 1933, plays in front of the Neshoba County, Mississippi, homestead. Billy would be born in this house in 1937. (Courtesy of Cannon family.)

Billy with his mother, Virgie, in Memphis, where Billy's father worked on the riverfront in 1940. (Courtesy of Cannon family.)

Harvey Jr., *left*, and Billy with their father in front of Churchill Downs in Louisville, Kentucky, May 1941. Harvey Sr. was working in a coal mine across the Ohio River in New Albany, Indiana. (Courtesy of Cannon family.)

Billy, *left,* Harvey Sr., and Harvey Jr. in front of their first Baton Rouge home, a converted store on Scenic Highway in the Istrouma neighborhood. (Courtesy of Cannon family.)

Harvey Jr., *front*, and Billy. The Cannons attended Istrouma Baptist Church in Baton Rouge. (Courtesy of Cannon family.)

Billy Cannon in front of the Osceola Street house, around 1955. (Courtesy of Cannon family.)

Billy with Virgie and Harvey Sr. during his high school years. (Courtesy of Cannon family.)

Istrouma High School varsity basketball team, 1955. Billy, a junior, and some team-mates have middle fingers extended, "shooting the bird." *Sitting, left to right:* C. J. Payne, Sonny Hill, Billy Cannon, Howard Pritchard, Earl Turner, Malcom Meliet; *standing, left to right:* Coach Bobby Meador, Carl Coghlan, Jimmy Henson, Hulon Walters, Billy Castilaw, Oscar Lofton, Bobby Wicker, Ray Davis. (From 1955 Istrouma High School yearbook, *Pow Wow.*)

Istrouma High School backfield, 1955: *left to right:* George Guidry, halfback; B. L. Fairchild, quarterback; Billy Cannon, fullback; and James Teague, halfback. (Courtesy of Cannon family.)

Billy Cannon, Istrouma High School's All-American running back, 1955. (Courtesy of Cannon family.)

Istrouma Indians, 1955 Louisiana AAA State Champions. Billy is number 42, *second row from top, third from left*. (Courtesy of Cannon family.)

Billy Cannon was named Most Valuable Player in the East-West Prep High School All-American game in Memphis, 1956. (Courtesy of Cannon family.)

Billy Cannon and LSU head coach Paul Dietzel. (Courtesy of LSU Sports Information.)

LSU's star halfback, Billy Cannon. (Courtesy of LSU Sports Information.)

Coach Paul Dietzel, Billy Cannon, Johnny Robinson, and Warren Rabb. (Courtesy of LSU Sports Information.)

Billy Cannon: the face of LSU football. (Courtesy of LSU Sports Information.)

LSU Tigers: 1958 National Champions. (Autographed copy courtesy of George O'Neal.)

Billy Cannon and Dot Dupuy's wedding, November 23, 1956. *Left to right:* Oscar Lofton, Luther Fortenberry, Billy Cannon, Dot Dupuy Cannon, Kahne Dipola, and Billy Castilaw. (Courtesy of Cannon family.)

Coach Dietzel has a meal with the Cannons, 1957. *Left to right:* Harvey Cannon Sr., Virgie Cannon, Paul Dietzel, and Dot Cannon (pregnant with Terri). (Courtesy of Cannon family.)

Billy strains as he winds up to let go in the shot put event during the Southwestern Relays in Lafayette, Louisiana, April 11, 1959. (AP Photo/Richard Tolbert.)

Billy breaks the tape to win the 100-yard dash during the Southwestern Relays, April 11, 1959. His time was 9.5 seconds, 0.2 of a second off the world's record. Dave Styron, *right*, of Northeast Louisiana State College, was second, and Dee Givens, *third from right*, of Oklahoma University, was third. (AP Photo.)

Billy slips by tacklers at the start of his famous 89-yard punt return for a touchdown to help the Tigers beat third-ranked Mississippi 7–3 on October 31, 1959. (AP Photo.)

Billy poses with his Heisman Trophy in New York on December 8, 1959. (AP Photo/Jacob Harris.)

As a halfback for the Houston Oilers, Billy runs upfield against the Dallas Texans in a 20–17 overtime loss in the 1962 AFL Championship Game on December 23, 1962, at Jeppesen Stadium in Houston. (AP Photo/NFL Photos.)

Playing tight end for the Oakland Raiders, Billy catches a touchdown pass in Oakland on November 19, 1967. Billy caught six passes for 99 yards, three of which were touchdowns in his team's 31–17 win over the Miami Dolphins. He was AFL player of the week. (AP Photo.)

Oakland Raiders teammates in the locker room after a win: *left to right,* Billy Cannon, Tom Flores, and Hewritt Dixon. (Photo by Ron Riesterer/PhotoShelter.)

Cannon children in 1969, *left to right:* Terri, holding Bunnie, Gina, Dara, and Billy Jr. (Courtesy of Cannon family.)

Dr. Billy A. Cannon, DDS, examines an x-ray in his Baton Rouge office in 1972. (Courtesy of LSU Sports Information.)

Billy relaxes poolside in 1983, the summer of his arrest. (Courtesy of Cannon family.)

Billy, *left*, leaves courthouse with Secret Service agent Michael James, July 9, 1983, the day of his arrest for counterfeiting. (*Sunday Advocate*, July 10, 1983, Capital City Press/Georges Media Group, Baton Rouge, LA.)

Burl Cain, warden of Louisiana State Penitentiary at Angola. (Courtesy of Louisiana State Penitentiary.)

Warden Burl Cain, *left,* and Dr. Billy Cannon confer in Cain's office at Angola in 2015. (Photo by Charles N. deGravelles.)

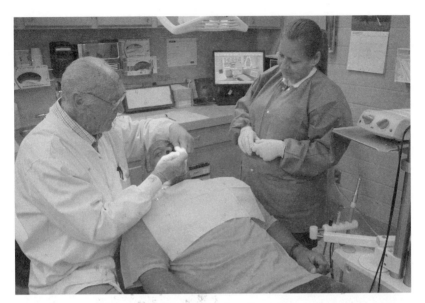

Dr. Cannon and Master Sgt. Tonia Rabalais, dental assistant, work on inmate Johnny Jones. (Photo by Charles N. deGravelles.)

Angola dental staff, *left to right:* Dr. Billy A. Cannon, Dr. Donald Kozan, Master Sgt. Tonia Rabalais, Dr. Charles Hebert, Master Sgt. Jessica Dupuy, Dr. Carl Anderson, Sgt. Katelyn Ducote, Dr. William Hill, Sgt. Ashley Lamana, Sgt. Brittany Shoemake, Master Sgt. Don Fountain. *Not pictured:* Dr. Ernie Beier and Emily Barton. (Photo by Charles N. deGravelles.)

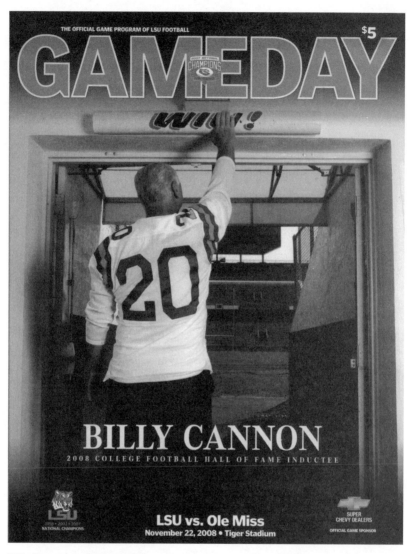

Billy Cannon on the cover of Game Day program for LSU–Ole Miss game, November 22, 2008. Cannon is coming out of the Tiger tunnel, touching the "Win!" bar. (Courtesy of LSU Sports Information.)

Billy is inducted into the LSU Alumni Association Hall of Distinction, 2010. (Courtesy of Cannon family.)

LSU's 1958–59 White Team backs reminisce for a gathering at the Andonie Museum before the homecoming game against Western Kentucky, 2014. *Seated, left to right:* Billy Cannon and Johnny Robinson; *standing, left to right:* Warren Rabb and Jim Engster of *Tiger Rag* magazine. (Photo by Charles N. deGravelles.)

Tiger teammates, *left to right,* Johnny Robinson, Warren Rabb, and Billy Cannon pose next to a statue of LSU defensive end Abner Wimberly in 2014. (Photo by Charles N. deGravelles.)

The Cannons in 2003: *back, left to right:* Bunnie, Terri, Gina, Dara; *front, left to right:* Dot, Billy, Billy Jr. (Courtesy of Cannon family.)

Billy with his thoroughbred racehorse, Ms. Charles, and her new filly in March 2015. (Photo by Charles N. deGravelles.)

Former LSU running back and Heisman trophy winner Billy Cannon watches his famous run on the scoreboard screens at the end of the first quarter of the LSU-Tulane NCAA college football game in Baton Rouge, Saturday, October 31, 2009. This was the fiftieth anniversary of Cannon's 89-yard run against Mississippi. (AP Photo/Bill Haber.)

Author Charles N. deGravelles poses with Billy Cannon under the oaks on the LSU parade ground. (© 2015 by Marie Constantin Photography.)

6

GO, TIGERS!

LSU Meets Billy Cannon

Even for an old-school sportswriter, given to colorful language and hyperbole, it was a grand and sweeping statement: "In the 44 years that this writer has gone up to LSU to observe and write about athletic doings at the Ole War Skule, this past Saturday [September 8, 1956] furnished the most impressive afternoon he ever sat in judgment on." What had so impressed New Orleans *Times Picayune* reporter Bill Keefe was, surprisingly, not an athletic contest but a pep rally, designed with care by head football coach Paul Dietzel and his boss, athletic director Jim Corbett.

Hired at virtually the same time, both Dietzel and Corbett were young, energetic and dedicated to turning LSU's losing program around, and both men understood the essential chicken-and-egg relationship between a winning team and a large and enthusiastic fan base. Together, the pair traveled across the state, visiting high schools, service clubs, anyone who would have them, to raise awareness, expectations, and support for the future of Tiger football. Their work was paid off in part by the talented recruiting class of 1956, which included Billy Cannon. These young talents, Dietzel was convinced, would save Tiger football.

The pep rally about which journalist Bill Keefe wrote was for freshmen only, and, according to Keeth, the entire class turned out, cheering from the west stands of Tiger Stadium. It was a smart move. Upper-class fans would have been more skeptical since they had endured not only one losing season under Dietzel but several lackluster seasons before that under head coach Gaynell "Gus" Tinsley. Even though the varsity team, which included many fine players, was introduced first, it was the freshmen recruits Dietzel really wanted to showcase, and that the freshmen wanted to see. This was another reason only freshmen had been invited. Most of the recruits had been stars in their own high schools in Shreveport, Houma, New Iberia, Lake Charles, Bogalusa, Baton Rouge, and elsewhere. The freshmen fans knew of (and in many cases had been classmates of) this accomplished squad and were anxious to see them all play together at what was now their university.

Dietzel instructed the excited crowd to hold their applause until all players and coaches were introduced, but, as Keefe noted, that wasn't easy. "It was with difficulty that the high-spirited frosh kept their silence" as quarterback Win Turner, star fullback Jimmy Taylor, and other varsity standouts ran onto the field. But, as Dietzel anticipated, the freshmen had come above all to see the stars from their own high schools make their first appearance in Tiger Stadium, especially the already famous running back from Istrouma High. Keefe wrote that, "when tall, high-stepping Billy Cannon ... trotted out" onto the field, the fans "had to use lots of will power to suppress themselves."

It would take time, Dietzel knew, but he was convinced that soon all of the student body, all Tiger fans, and all of Baton Rouge and beyond would join in the freshman fans' excitement about Billy Cannon and his talented fellows in the recruiting class of 1956.

Shooting Buzzards and Free Gas

One recruiting tool that Coach Paul Dietzel used to good effect was to help his players find summer work, a policy that had made a big difference for Billy Cannon. Billy had known real poverty and had held down some kind of job most of his life. Knowing that a good job would come with taking the LSU scholarship had clinched his decision to be a Tiger. And so it was that, after high school graduation, Billy reported to work at the Gulf Refining Company (later Gulf Oil Corporation) petroleum cycling plant south of the little town of Krotz Springs, Louisiana.

Krotz Springs, forty-five miles due west of Baton Rouge, was a one-time logging town embedded in the northern end of the Atchafalaya Basin. Hundreds of thousands of acres of cypress-tupelo forest, lakes, rivers, and bayous, flowing southward from Simmesport to Morgan City, the Atchafalaya is the largest swamp in the United States. By the time Billy went to work in the area, the low-lying basin had long been an overflow spillway to safely divert Mississippi River flood waters away from Baton Rouge and New Orleans to the Gulf of Mexico.

Billy knew well the area around Krotz Springs since his father had taken him and his brother fishing there many times. The swampland was rich in wildlife, and it was also rich in petroleum. Gulf had found oil and gas south of the town in 1912, one of the earliest finds in Louisiana (the state's first producing field was discovered in 1901 near Jennings). The company built a natural gas cycling plant near its wells, a fortress in the swamp, to extract the liquids from the natural gas for transport via tanker trucks and railcars. Here at the Gulf plant, Billy would spend his summer working and waiting for the start of football season.

The Initiation

Billy was essentially an intern, working under close supervision to perform the more menial tasks around the plant and relieving workers when they took summer leave. The work wasn't difficult, but it could be dangerous—within that network of pressurized pipes and vessels bubbled exotic gasses at extreme pressure. Billy admired and appreciated the men he worked with. "I guess they were pretty much like workers anywhere," he recalled, "but in a plant like this, where safety is critical, they were very cautious, careful in their work. They knew I had a football career, and I was only working there for three months, but they took the time to teach me, to test me. They made sure I knew what I was doing." They taught Billy to gauge, periodically checking meter readings and tank levels along the operation's complex route and making appropriate adjustments to insure the process was running correctly. He recorded his measurements in a logbook along the way. It was mundane work, but concentration and precision were necessary, as he learned one morning when a high-pitched roar ripped through the plant. "In an instant, it sounded like we were inside a train whistle," Billy remembered. "I took off running away from the sound and toward the gate until I saw the others running toward it, so I circled back to join them." A night-shift worker had misread the gauge, and a tank of liquefied gas had overfilled and triggered the shrieking relief valve. "When I went to pick up my check that Saturday, the head engineer told me, 'You were running the wrong way, Billy.' 'No, I wasn't,' I told him, 'because I wouldn't have known what to do when I got there.'"

For a while, Billy filled in for the man who loaded the liquefied gas into tanker trucks and rail tankers from a terminal dock, connected to the plant by a pipeline. Billy would pump the gas through pressurized hoses coming off the pipeline, keeping careful records in his logbook and phoning them in to the plant. "It was near the highway," Billy remembered, "almost to Krotz Springs, but you were out there by yourself. You never knew when you showed up in the morning how many trucks or tankers you'd have to fill. You might be busy most of the day or you might be twiddling your thumbs."

The loading process included pumping a small amount of the additive mercaptan from fifty-five-gallon drums into the mix to give a smell to the gas. The mercaptan was colorless, but it had a distinctive putrid smell that made an otherwise odorless natural gas leak easy to detect. Once, when the mercaptan pump was broken, Billy had to add it by hand, using a coffee can, and he soon noticed that the rancid smell drew in buzzards. On a particularly slow day, he left a can of the mercaptan out to evaporate, and sat in a chair outside the shack with a rifle in his lap. When the buzzards began circling, he started picking them off, starting with the highest and working his way down. It wasn't long before the phone was ringing in the shack. When his boss asked him how things were going, Billy reported a slow day. "The reason I ask," the boss said, "is that the sheriff called wanting to know about some shooting coming from your area." "Oh, that," Billy said. "Yeah, I heard those shots too. Must be some crazy fool out here somewhere shooting buzzards."

Billy felt at home among the other men at the Krotz Springs plant. They could have been his father or any of his father's friends who made their livings at one plant or another in the Standard Oil complex back in Baton Rouge. These were working-class wage-earners, pulling a weekly check, not unlike the men with whom Billy had wrestled crates of frozen chickens at Manda Fine Meats. He admired the pride these men took in their jobs, their hard work, their toughness, their rough camaraderie and easy humor.

But the men were not so at home around Billy. He was young and educated, a college boy bound for a professional career, and these differences were barriers that kept the men at a distance. Billy was sure he could eventually break through the barriers as he'd done at Manda's, but he wondered if he would work at the plant long enough to gain their trust.

"It was a slow process," Billy recalled,

but after awhile, you could feel things change a little. They'd ask me how the Tigers were going to do next season, and I'd always tell them we were going to win them all. They'd look at me like I was crazy and laugh. They were good guys. This one raised a few cows. This one liked to hunt. Finally, one night when I was there between shifts, one of them said, "you want to take your car down to the line and fill it up?" He took me to a storage tank that held condensate, the liquids filtered out of the natural gas. We pulled in behind a line of other workers who were filling their cars with this stuff. "Be sure to leave a little room in your tank," he told me, "and when you get to the gas station in town, put in some premium gas with the anti-knock compound." When I left, the car was running okay, but the engine was clattering like hell. Once I put in a little of the good gas, though, I sailed on home.

Now Billy was on the inside. He had become one of the boys.

By accident, Billy was also able to find acceptance in the village. On his way to work, he picked up a man whose truck had broken down. It was a fisherman with a sack full of fish he'd already caught that morning, and he needed to get them to the ice house before they spoiled. "Was he glad for the lift!" Billy said. "He and his family ran a little restaurant out of their house where I ate at night. They had always been polite, but after I gave him that ride, he—and everybody in Krotz Springs—treated me like family." Billy loved it.

The worst thing about working out of town was that he missed Dot. He kept a picture of her on the window of his room at the boarding house. They were dating on the weekends and calling one another and trading letters during the week, but he knew she was popular, and there were always social events he couldn't attend. "We really liked each other, but it was hard," Billy remembered. "We had our ups and downs. It was on again–off again throughout the summer. We had a friend named Tom Nolan. He'd played football at Catholic High and was going on to play at Tulane. He called Dot for a date. He asked Dot, 'Are you and Billy on or off?' 'Looks like we're on right now,' she told him, 'and I'm hoping he's going to ask me to marry him.' 'Good,' Tom told her, 'then I'm not going to ask you out.'"

Towards the end of the summer, it looked as if their relationship was going to be permanently off. Dot wrote Billy telling him she wanted to break up, and he wrote back saying he understood. "I didn't call her, didn't write anymore. Just as the summer was ending I got another letter. She said she was wrong and hoped I'd forgive her."

By the time he got home, Billy and Dot had both decided to keep the relationship permanently on. Once school started, they set a date to get married, November 23, the day after the final game of the freshman football season.

LSU Recruits

Many of the highly touted incoming LSU freshmen players knew and respected each other as former opponents. Istrouma High stars Billy Cannon and Duane Leopard had spent four years battling their Baton Rouge High counterparts Warren Rabb, Don Norwood, and Gus Kinchen, often for the district championship. And all of the Baton Rouge players knew hard-hitting linemen Carroll Bergeron of Terrebonne High and Emile Fournet from Bogalusa High since both schools were a regular part of their district roster. Billy had competed both with and against Ferriday High School center and defensive back Max Fugler in post-season all-star games. Billy knew Fugler's physical prowess, furious competitiveness, and uncanny ability to read an offense; among his new teammates, it was Fugler whom Billy most admired.

Many recruits knew each other only by reputation. Running back Johnny Robinson, familiar to local sports fans, came from University High of Baton Rouge, too small a school to have contended with Istrouma and Baton Rouge High. Don Purvis was one of the top high-school running backs in the country the previous year. He had played for Crystal Springs High School in Mississippi. "I remember the first time I heard the name Billy Cannon," Purvis remembered. "It was in the latter part of my senior season. We were undefeated and untied, and I'd scored somewhere around 175 points at that stage. My coach, Wendell Webb, told me I had a chance to be among the top four or five scorers in the country, and that's when he told me this boy from Baton Rouge, Billy Cannon, was probably going to win it all. When he said that name, Billy Cannon, it just stuck with me. It just rings of a football player."

In spite of his small size—155 pounds—Purvis was a fine running back, so agile and quick that he was later nicknamed "Scooter." Both Mississippi State and Ole Miss tried to get him, and his hometown community expected him to stay in state.

But Paul Dietzel also wanted him. He invited Purvis and a star lineman from Crystal Springs High, Royce Whittington, to come to Baton Rouge for the Ole Miss game. "We were impressed," Purvis recalled. "For one thing, it was a night football game which nobody else then was playing in the SEC. And when I saw Tiger Stadium, I was just floored. It wasn't as big back then as it is now, but it was bigger than anything I'd ever seen. And then I met Coach Dietzel. My goodness, he was just a fantastic individual." Both Purvis and Whittington signed with LSU later that year.

Purvis remembered the first freshman practice, under the watchful eye of freshman coach Clarence "Pop" Strange. Everyone was sizing each other up, gauging where he stood in a very steep pecking order. "It was a team of players who were stars in their own schools," Purvis recalled. "Every runner wanted to run the ball, every receiver wanted to catch, and there was Coach Strange, having to make choices and meld us into a team with one common purpose. This was going to be an adjustment. We all knew it wasn't going to be easy for anyone.

"They split us up by positions," Purvis said. "Suddenly I was standing in a line of seven left halfbacks. We didn't have seven in the whole backfield back at Crystal Springs. I looked up ahead of me, and there stood this big guy, and I was thinking to myself, wait a minute, he's in the wrong line. He's not a back. He's a lineman. That was the first time I saw Billy Cannon." As the practice progressed, Purvis was impressed by more than Cannon's size. "What a physical specimen.

When I saw him run, moving that much weight that fast, I was fasci- nated. I'd seen fast players—and I had speed myself—but to be that big a man moving that fast!"

Purvis studied Cannon's style of running and compared it to his own. "He was not like me. Because I was small, I had to be to be able to cut ninety degrees sideways and then come back forty-five degrees the other, just to be able to get by people. I couldn't just lower my head and knock somebody into the stands like Jimmy Taylor could. Tay- lor was like a bowling ball. He ran low so you couldn't get your arms around him. Billy wasn't like that. He ran with his torso up so he could move side to side—which he did as well as anybody I'd seen— and when he got that opportunity to turn on that burst of speed, when he hit a seam, he was gone."

Johnny Robinson also looked forward to playing alongside Billy Cannon. Son of LSU's tennis coach, W. T. "Dub" Robinson, Johnny had been a high-school standout in football, basketball, and baseball. Like Cannon, Robinson had been small in early high school, strug- gling—and eventually succeeding—to put on enough weight to play football; using his own dietary regimen, he went from 120 to 150 pounds between his freshman and sophomore years.

Before playing with them for LSU, Robinson had joined Billy, War- ren Rabb, and other high-school luminaries in the Louisiana All-Star game. "I had heard of these guys, of course, and I was just happy to be playing with them," Robinson remembered. "They took me in. They really treated me great." The three backs—Robinson, Rabb, and Can- non—became the heart of perhaps the most successful team in LSU history. All three would earn All-SEC honors along the way (Cannon would earn a great deal more), and each would move on to a success- ful career in the pros.

According to Robinson, even among these exceptional athletes, there was no question who was the leading player. "Even if we hadn't known Billy, we knew of him. He was above everybody else. He was the star. He could do everything." Scooter Purvis agreed. "There wasn't anything he couldn't do—run, kick, pass, block, tackle—and he did all of them well." Another freshman teammate, Hart Bourque of Gonzales, described it this way: "Anything he tried, he was the best at. It was part of who he was."

Billy Cannon was tough but not invincible. Purvis laughed as he told the story of a nasty hit from a teammate that Billy took during his last season at LSU. "We had a sweep play where one of us would take the handoff and the rest of the backfield would lead the blocking for the ball carrier. Dietzel had recruited this guy from north Louisiana named Fred David Miller to play defensive tackle. He went on to play with the Baltimore Colts forever. He was a solid country boy built with tremendous strength. He was a man. As we practiced this play, Billy came around to block and ran into Fred David. He hit Billy with his forearm so hard it broke his face mask. They had to change out his helmet right there. When Billy came back to the huddle, he told Rabb. 'Hey, don't call that play anymore. I'm not going to block that guy.'"

For his part, Billy was thrilled to be playing with the talent that Dietzel had assembled, and he was looking forward, as always, to proving himself at an ever higher level. "Of course there was some jealousy, some animosity, especially among the older guys, but that's human nature," Purvis said. "In that kind of environment, you have to earn your spurs—nobody just reads a newspaper story and takes your word for it—and it didn't take Billy long to earn his." In spite of his fame, Billy always stressed that he was part of a team. "He had such great respect for the other players," Bourque remembered. "From the beginning," Purvis said, "Billy was highly supportive of his teammates—to the point where he was projecting attention on them and away from himself."

Feuding with Dietzel

Pop Strange and other assistant coaches practiced the freshmen daily, teaching and running plays over and over—and then once more—until they were executed with precision. Because Billy was shoulder to shoulder with the best young football players in the state, he quickly became bored and frustrated with the dull repetition of drills and plays. He longed for a scrimmage, longed for contact, to run and block and tackle in full pads at full speed and full strength. Never one to hold back his feelings, Billy complained to Coach Strange, "We're not doing anything out here, Coach, but pissing in the wind. It's all busy work. We're accomplishing nothing."

"Let me tell you something, Cannon," Strange responded. "This is the best team in the school's history. There is more talent out here than has ever been assembled. We're not going to get hurt in practice. We're not going to scrimmage the varsity. We're going to play our three games, and we're going to win them. In the spring, when this team joins the varsity, no one will be injured. You kids will be ready to take your place, and some of you will start." As Billy remembered, "I thought about it, it made sense to me, and I shut up."

But practice was not Billy's only frustration. Head coach Paul Dietzel rubbed Billy the wrong way. With Dietzel's military background and deep Christian faith came a strong sense of order and decorum. "It is best not to have a volume of rules," Dietzel said of his philosophy of coaching in his memoir, *Call Me Coach,* "but the ones you have must be consistently and fairly enforced."

For many of the players, especially the young ones, Dietzel's coaching style was that of a strong but protecting and guiding hand. "Other than my own father, he was the best thing that ever happened in my life," Purvis remembered. "He was a first-class individual. He had so much to teach us—not just football but his organizational skills and his religious convictions. He motivated us. He was constantly trying to convince us of the importance of our spirituality. Everything he did, everywhere he went, he left people better because of it. He never professed to be a great technical expert in football, but he was a great coach." Purvis and other key players under Paul Dietzel's LSU teams—Warren Rabb, Lynn LeBlanc, Jerry Stovall, and others—continued to meet with their old coach long after his retirement, having breakfast together once a month at Le Madeleine restaurant in Baton Rouge.

Dietzel's close oversight of his players, which felt protective and comforting to some, was stifling to Billy. From the time he was a boy, sleeping on the porch rather than in a room of the Osceola Street house, Billy relished his independence and autonomy. If he occasionally misused that independence, he was willing to take the consequences. He was constantly testing his parents, teachers, coaches—and himself—but as often as his misbehavior drew punishment, Billy would own up to his mistakes and take what he had coming. But punishment did little to tame him. Because of his talents and achievements—academic as well as athletic—his work ethic, and his charm, Billy was also accustomed to getting a pass when he was caught. The star player and the strict young coach were bound for conflict.

Coach Dietzel closely monitored the movements and activities of his players, as he put it, to keep them out of trouble, but Billy, just back from his first stint of independent living in Krotz Springs, wanted the freedom to make his own decisions, to come and go as he pleased. With the start of fall practice, Dietzel insisted his players park their automobiles in a lot under the stadium and turn their car keys over to a member of the staff. Billy simply refused, keeping his keys and driving his car where and when he liked. He was never punished for the infraction. In *Call Me Coach*, Dietzel alludes to the difficulty of enforcing this rule, but doesn't mention Billy by name.

Dietzel's rules extended to the players' dorm rooms. Billy roomed with star linebacker Max Fugler in Broussard Hall, the athletic dorm, where players were expected to keep their beds made and rooms tidy for a daily inspection. It was an era when ROTC was compulsory for every male student; as Scooter Purvis put it, room inspections were "military all the way." Dietzel personally made the review once per week and occasionally left players notes when a cleanup left something to be desired. After one inspection, Dietzel left a note in shaving cream on the mirror above their sink: "Clean this." It was another irritation for Billy. "Max was able to blow it off," Billy remembered, "but this kind of stuff irked me. It stuck with me."

Star halfback and coach finally collided over a pair of shoes. "I went to the equipment room to get my stuff," Billy recalled, "and the guy at the window hands me this beat-up second-hand pair of shoes. I was furious. Poor guy. I slammed the shoes down so hard, they bounced off the counter and hit him in the chest. Now he was mad. I wasn't surprised when I got a call later that Coach Dietzel wanted to see me." Billy laughed.

When I walked into his office, he didn't chew my ass out—he chewed around it, and let it fall out. When he was done, he asked me if I had anything to say. I reminded him of the promises he'd made to my mom and dad back at my mother's table when he came to recruit me. He'd told us this was going to be a first-class operation all the way, and we believed him. I told him, "Coach, I've been poor all my life, and I've never worn anybody else's shoes, and I'm not going to start now." I went to the trunk of my car and got my old pair from Istrouma. The next day, the equipment manager reluctantly gave me a brand new pair of shoes, and two weeks later, the whole freshman team had them. It was only later, when I saw the sophomores dressed out for practice, that I knew what happened to the old shoes. We got new ones, and they got the old ones, and they weren't too happy about it!

Three in a Row

The Tiger freshmen didn't see their first action until mid-October in a home game against the freshmen of Ole Miss. By this time, the varsity had lost every game—to Texas A&M, to Rice, and to Georgia Tech. Dietzel and the other coaches rushed back from the Atlanta defeat—only the night before—anxious for a freshman victory that might appease the fans.

The freshmen did not disappoint. Baton Rouge *Morning Advocate* reporter Jim Falkner crowed, "Warren Rabb and Billy Cannon, a couple of Baton Rouge products, painted a beautiful picture of things to come" with a "thumping 44–20 victory over the Ole Miss Rebel freshmen team." In spite of the score, Billy remembered it as a "knock-down drag-out game" against a tough and talented team. The victory was a balm for fans who were enduring yet another losing varsity season. "The powerful Cannon turned in a brilliant exhibition of running, scoring three touchdowns," Falkner wrote, "once on a 37-yard interception, once on a 44-yard pass from Rabb, and again on a three-yard run around right end just as the game ended." Falkner concluded, "undoubtedly the fastest footballer ever to appear at LSU, Cannon makes a perfect running mate for Mr. Rabb . . . a cinch to make Tiger football fans forget Y. A. Tittle." From safety, Billy played excellent defense as well, recovering a fumble, making an interception and multiple tackles. Among other Tigers playing well were Johnny Robinson, Scooter Purvis, and Max Fugler.

"We were elated," Billy recalled. "There was such great camaraderie We all went out with our girlfriends, meeting up at different places in town to dance and celebrate."

The following Monday, Billy noticed something different at practice: the varsity coaches came out. "The varsity hadn't played well against Georgia Tech. Coach Dietzel warmed them up, ran them through a few plays, and then sent them in. And then all the varsity coaches descended on us. Student coaches were pushed to the side.

Suddenly, the shine was on us, and they couldn't wait to get their hands on us. We were getting all the attention now."

The varsity backfield coach was Carl Maddox. Along with Coach Abner Wimberly, Maddox had gone to Istrouma High School earlier in the year on a mission to recruit Billy Cannon. Known as a perfectionist, he began to work with Robinson, Rabb, Purvis, and the other freshmen. As Purvis remembered, "He taught us that successful ball handling depends on a whole sequence of events that have to be repeated exactly the same way every time. He'd go out with chalk and put dots on the field exactly where he wanted you to go. 'I want this foot here and this foot there.' And he'd draw a little trail with the chalk. 'And I want you to run exactly this way to that point. One step to the right, then cross over with your left foot and plant it where that other dot is. . . .'" One player remembered that Maddox wanted the running backs to all wear their socks at exactly the same height.

Hart Bourque, a freshman from Gonzales, recalled how quickly the backfield coach became exasperated with Billy Cannon. "Maddox would tell you how you were supposed to run and exactly where and how far to go. Billy really enjoyed messing with him. Every play you were supposed to run your assignment out to the end, but Billy would run just past the line of scrimmage and stop and come back to the huddle. Poor Maddox. It would burn him up, and he was such a nice guy. But Billy was the king of the show. He did whatever he wanted to do."

"Knowing Billy the way I do now," Purvis said, "I can understand why Billy drove Maddox crazy—and why Maddox drove Billy crazy!"

Maddox finally decided to just steer clear of Billy. In the coaches' dressing room, Maddox asked Coach Pop Strange to correct Billy's stance. "He wanted me in a three-point stance before the ball was snapped," Billy remembered, "but I preferred to lean, with my forearms on my knees, the way I always had. Coach Strange assured him he would talk to me, but he never did. (I only heard about all this later from Pop's son, Bo.) When Maddox again asked about it, Pop told him, 'Billy said that's his speed stance.' Coach Maddox wandered off, shaking his head and muttering, 'his speed stance . . . his speed stance. . . .'"

Billy and Coach Maddox eventually became great friends. Many years later, with a grin, Billy asked him: "Coach, you worked with [Durel] Matherne, Purvis, Rabb, and the others, but you never worked with me. How come?" Maddox smiled back. "'Billy,' he told me, 'we just left you alone.'"

As the 1956 Tiger varsity continued to lose, the younger Tiger team, known by now in headlines as the "Baby Bengals," continued to dazzle and excite the fans. Next, they defeated Mississippi State 28–13, and in their third and final game of the season, they crushed Tulane 47–0 on Thanksgiving Day. "It was not the kind of competition we'd had from Ole Miss or Mississippi State," Billy remembered. The Tigers piled up 487 yards rushing—159 of which were Cannon's—and 108 yards passing. "People were starting to echo what Pop Strange had already said—that we were the best team ever recruited." After Fugler, Cannon, Robinson, and Rabb each scored touchdowns, Coach Strange put in the second string, and they continued to add points.

After losing its first six games, the Tiger varsity was able to recover some dignity with three wins, mostly on the running prowess of Jimmy Taylor. Taylor missed the 1956 spring practice and spent the first half of the season learning Dietzel's plays. Once he found himself, he turned the Tigers around, leading the Southeastern Conference in rushing with 762 yards, and was the second-highest scorer in the nation with twelve touchdowns. According to sportswriter Peter Finney, he probably saved Paul Dietzel's coaching career.

But it was the freshmen who, in only three games, had captured the imagination and enthusiasm of the coaches, the reporters, and the fans. In his column, "Random Shots," *Morning Advocate* sports editor Bud Montet tallied the accomplishments of the "Baby Bengals." With twenty-seven carries, Billy Cannon led in rushing with 265 yards— an average of 9.8 yards per carry. Max Fugler, playing fullback on offense, was next with 168 yards in twenty-six carries, and "little Don Purvis" was third with 138 yards in twenty-one carries. Quarterback Warren Rabb completed 17 passes for 325 yards and no interceptions, and Cannon led in interceptions with 4, returning them for 158 yards at what Montet termed a "sensational" 39.5 yards per carry. Coach Maddox called Billy "the best defensive back I ever saw."

A New Home Front

On November 23, 1956, the day after the final game of the freshman season, Billy Cannon and Dot Dupuy were married. After their many break-ups and make-ups, Dot had finally made up her mind about Billy. This decision came in spite of her mother's objections (Dot was raised Catholic, and her mother didn't think she should marry a Baptist). The couple set a date. "Billy and I would have been happy without a formal service," Dot remembered, "but it was important to Billy's mom. It's really what Virgie wanted."

The *Advocate* society page carried the story: "Miss Dorothy Dupuy and Mr. Billy Cannon were married . . . in an 11 o'clock service at the Istrouma Baptist Church. The Rev. S. A. Rushing officiated. . . ."

In addition to shots of the wedding, the Cannon photo album shows family and friends gathered at a shower, rehearsal dinner, and reception. Harvey Sr., Virgie and Dot's parents, Mr. and Mrs. Paulin Dupuy (Mrs. Dupuy relented and gave Dot her blessing), stand proudly with the newlyweds.

In the last photo of the set, Billy, with Dot at his side, grins from behind the wheel of their car, ready to leave on their honeymoon to the Gulf Hills Dude Ranch in Ocean Springs, Mississippi. When they returned, Billy was able to move off campus with its many restrictions and military-style inspections. The newlyweds rented a garage apartment in the old Fairfields subdivision of north Baton Rouge, an equal distance between their two families' homes, and began their married life together. A small cash stipend replaced the value of campus room and board, but Billy and Dot would need more than that to make it.

More Tickets

Selling football tickets had been a source of income for Billy since he was a boy. Able to buy them early from Peabody's Service Station at a reduced price, Billy would sell them for their face value at the gate for a profit. By the time he was in high school, it was his business, and he saw no reason why he shouldn't continue at the college level. Each of the freshmen players got several free tickets to the LSU varsity games. To supplement his own, Billy would buy at a discount any tickets his teammates were willing to sell, and before each kickoff, Billy stood in front of Tiger Stadium, waving them in the air, hawking them to fans.

So it came as a surprise when Broussard Hall's dormitory manager, "Brother Ike" Mayeaux, mentioned to Billy that athletic director Jim Corbett was looking for him. As he often responded to such moments, Billy wondered, "What have I done now?"

"When I got to the AD's office," Billy remembered, "I was brought right in. Corbett invited the head basketball coach, Harry Rabenhorst, to join us. Corbett was very proper, and I guess he wanted someone else in the room with us as a witness. He asked me if I'd been selling tickets. 'Yes, for about six years now,' I told him. He asked me if I was scalping them, and I told him no, that I was selling my own and those I could get at a discount from other players. 'Well, you can't do that here while you're on a scholarship,' he told me. 'I didn't read that anywhere,' I said. All the while, I'm thinking to myself, 'I'm here three weeks, and already I'm going to get kicked out!' 'It's an unwritten rule,' he said. 'Don't do it anymore.' I told him I'd quit selling tickets in front of the stadium, and that was that; I kept my word." But Billy's ticket-selling days were far from over, and he'd be back to talk to Corbett about it again before very long.

Hitting the Books

Almost all of Billy's classes in the four-year pre-dental curriculum were required; there were few electives. The early years required English, history, and other humanities courses along with the math and science in which he excelled. Many of the early classes were taught in large auditoriums packed with students.

As soon as Billy began attending classes, he discovered just how well Istrouma High School had prepared him for college. "I learned it was easy for me to make a B in anything but English and Spanish, but to make an A, I had to go to class and spend time with the books and my notes."

But Billy did not excel in English, and he had to work just to get by. His freshman year he took a composition class in which students learned and practiced various types of writing. The first assignment was given in class—a thousand-word theme in any style or form.

> I wrote mine out in a bright blue ink on white paper, and I thought it really looked good. When we finished, the professor collected the papers and handed them back out randomly and asked students to read them out loud. A friend, Butchy Saia, raised his hand. It was my paper. I'd written a short story—a kind of science fiction—about

how football had progressed beyond human participation and was played by robots. LSU was playing Tulane. A robot from LSU broke off on a run, but about the 30-yard line, his fuse burned out, and he collapsed, and Tulane won the game. Everybody knew I was a ball-player, and we all had a good laugh. But really, I was proud of it, and I was looking forward to getting my A or B. When I got it back the next class and opened it up, there was so much red in there with the white and the blue that it looked like an American flag! So much off for this spelling error, so much off for this grammar error. At the bottom was my grade: an F. Welcome to college! I showed it to Butchy, and he said, "If I'd have known it was that bad, I wouldn't have read it." I did a little better with my next ones, and I finished decently. I worked hard at it and earned a solid C.

Speed and Power on Track and Field

Every one of Billy's many scholarship offers came with the under-standing that he wanted to—and would—run track. They also all came with the stipulation that, during his first year, he would partici-pate in spring football practice before moving on to track. As much as he looked forward to competing on the cinders, Billy understood the reasons he had to wait. Spring practice was critical for freshmen players who, until that time, had not worked with the varsity. It was the same across the SEC: freshmen had their own practices and play-ing schedule. For players and coaches alike, this was the first time to test a new crop of players in the context of the larger team. And Billy was also looking forward to playing with (and competing for prized slots against) veteran running backs like J. W. "Red" Brodnax and Jimmy Taylor, the lionized fullback who was LSU's leading rusher in 1956 and the SEC leader in touchdowns. It was tough competition. Taylor would earn All-America status the next season, move on to a sensational career with the Green Bay Packers, and be voted into the Pro Football Hall of Fame.

The Race of the Season

By the time spring football ended, 1957 track practices were well under way. Billy joined an accomplished team whose varsity standouts included hurdler Harry Carpenter, co-holder of the SEC low-hurdles record and top point scorer in the 1956 conference meet; Ernest Wall of Kentwood, a sophomore who ran the fastest half-mile (1:53.2) of any collegiate freshman the year before; and Tommy Dukes, who set a new SEC freshman broad jump record of 23.1 feet. Among the promising crop of fifteen freshmen was a sprinter from Memphis, Tennessee, named John West who had equaled Billy's best official 100-yard-dash time of 9.7 seconds.

Because his brother, Harvey Jr., had run sprints and thrown the discuss for the Tigers, Billy knew and admired head track coach Al Moreau. A farm boy from Marksville, Louisiana, Moreau ran hurdles as a Tiger in the early 1930s, setting an SEC record of 14.56. After he graduated, touring Europe with the United States track team, Moreau equaled the world record of 14.2 seconds. On the same tour, he became the first man to break 14 seconds. His 13.9 time was so mind-boggling to meet officials, they refused to certify it.

For teammates as well as fans, the race of the season was not between LSU and another collegiate power but between the Tigers' two fastest sprinters, freshmen Billy Cannon and John West. Created by Moreau at the insistence of fans and touted by sportswriters as the "century special," the head-on-head contest came at the end of a triangular meet with McNeese State of Lake Charles and Loyola of New Orleans. Some 2,500 fans and athletes overflowed the bleachers onto both sides of the track. "It was the first time I'd seen the track stands that full," Billy remembered. "Usually, you had only a couple of officials timing the race. This time, there were at least ten, and one of them was Coach Dietzel." The two sprinters crouched into the blocks, the starting gun was raised and fired. Billy, always a fast starter, burst to the lead, but West was quickly closing the margin as they approached the finish. In a *Morning Advocate* photo, both runners grimace as they lean forward. Billy is reaching the tape first, only inches ahead of West. "Although I did well that season in the sprints, relays and shot, it seems like my whole season revolved around that race." Billy shook his head. "I don't think John ever forgave me. At the end of the year, he transferred to Memphis State. If he'd have stayed, we'd have set records in the 440-yard relay. They would still be talking about us."

Edward Grady Partin, Jimmy Taylor, and the Teamsters

Before the spring semester was finished, Billy got an offer to work for the summer with the International Brotherhood of Teamsters, better known simply as the Teamsters, an American and Canadian union formed in 1903 to represent truckers. Baton Rouge Teamsters business manager Edward Grady Partin sent word by a contractor that he'd like to see Billy. The union hall was on Plank Road, not far from Billy and Dot's apartment. "I stopped in and we talked," Billy recalled. "He offered me a summer job, and I was happy to take it. We had a good conversation. That was the beginning of a warm relationship with Ed Partin that lasted until his death."

The Teamsters hired other LSU players for summer work. Billy, finishing his freshman year, and fellow running back Jimmy Taylor, finishing his junior year, got office jobs and the promise that they would be given plenty of time to pursue summer training. "It was ideal," Billy said. "I didn't have to live out of town as I had in Krotz Springs the summer before. I was close to my family. I could work out at Alvin Roy's. And I was glad to work with Jimmy."

The 1950s and 1960s were an era of strong but often corrupt unions—and legal troubles for their leaders. In 1957, the year Billy, Jimmy Taylor, and other LSU athletes went to work for Teamsters Local No. 5, the U.S. Senate created a bipartisan, special Select Committee on Improper Activities in the Labor or Management Field. Senator John McClellan was committee chairman, and its chief council was Robert F. Kennedy. The committee's first target was national Teamsters president David Beck who was accused of misusing Teamster funds. When he appeared to testify before the committee, Beck invoked his Fifth Amendment right against self-incrimination 117 times. Beck was eventually prosecuted and served time for falsifying income tax returns.

That same year, James Hoffa succeeded Beck as Teamsters president, despite pending federal trials for perjury and wiretapping, new charges from the McClellan committee, and a suit in federal court for improper selection of convention delegates. And that same year, the AFL-CIO, America's largest confederation of unions, expelled the Teamsters from its membership for corrupt leadership. As attorney general under his brother's presidency, Robert F. Kennedy continued to pursue union corruption and Jimmy Hoffa, who was eventually convicted in 1964 of jury tampering, attempted bribery, and fraud, and sentenced to thirteen years in prison. He mysteriously disappeared in 1975, a case that has remained unsolved.

Billy Cannon and Jimmy Taylor paid little heed to committee hearings in Washington and federal trials in New York or Chicago. They were drawing a good income, had little real work to do, and as much time as they wanted to work out. "Plus we believed in the unions," Billy said. "We both came from blue-collar families so we empathized with the working man. Jimmy's dad had been a watchman and his mother had done alterations for a laundry—and somehow put three kids through college. My dad had worked in the plants. Unions could be a very good thing. If the unions had been stronger when my dad had his accident, he'd have been better taken of."

Billy surmised that hiring LSU athletes was more than good public relations for the Teamsters. "I think they saw it as a chance to introduce the union's point of view to young leaders in the community, kids who would graduate and play important roles wherever they went."

Billy and Jimmy worked five days a week. Often they were asked to check on Teamsters work sites. "We drove around together a lot," Billy remembers, "which gave us the chance to get to know each other. We had so much in common. We both grew up poor, both of us had paper routes, we were both married, and both of us were competitive at everything we did. He was every bit as competitive as I was."

Sometimes their inspections led them to sites where Tiger teammates were working. "Jimmy and I loved to razz them. They'd be cleaning out a boxcar or unloading lumber in the summer heat, sweating up a storm, and we'd drive up in our air-conditioned car, get out long enough to give them a hard time, then get back in our air-conditioned car and drive off."

Billy and Jimmy worked out every day. Mondays, Wednesdays, and Fridays they lifted weights at Alvin Roy's Gym. "Jimmy hadn't done much lifting," Billy recalled. "He was just extremely strong and extremely determined." On Tuesday and Thursdays they would play handball. "It really created a bond," Billy said. "Jimmy and I don't see each other very often any more, but we will always be great friends."

Ed Partin, the union boss and his employer, took a special interest in Billy and, throughout the summer, gave him rare glimpses into the inner workings of a union. "He would take me to negotiations with business owners and explain to me what was happening," Billy remembered. "Ed knew his stuff. It was a real education."

On May 15, 1957, the Teamsters No. 5 and another union went on strike and set up picket lines at a local company, Dolese Concrete Company, over a contract dispute. Partin invited Billy to attend some of the lengthy negotiations that began at the end of May and continued into June. "It was an important contract for the drivers," Billy recalled, "because it would mean more per hour for them, but it was also important for the industry, because if Dolese had to go up on its wages, the other concrete companies in the area would have to meet the raise." The strike was settled with a new three-year contract signed on June 9, 1957.

Years later, Billy was able to use his union education to do something for the man who had given him a summer job. At Partin's request, Billy helped him organize and lead a union of city-parish public workers.

As the summer wore on, Billy was called in once again to see athletic director Jim Corbett. "We exchanged pleasantries," Billy said, "and then Corbett told me he'd had some complaints about me being on the picket line. I told him, 'That's what happens when negotiations break down. I haven't been on a picket line where there was a fight or anything bad happened. And the picket lines I've been on have been settled. And on top of that, I've gotten to sit in on the negotiations.'

"'We just can't have that,' Corbett said. 'You can't be going out picketing supporters of the university. I don't want you to go on any more picket lines.' It was all very nice, very cordial. 'We'll see what we can do,' I told him. I never said anything to Ed about that conversation."

Billy continued his friendship with Edward Grady Partin, who, for many years to come, was in one form of trouble after another. In 1962 alone, he accumulated three significant charges: one for embezzling union funds and falsifying records, another for first-degree manslaughter for driving his car off the road and leaving two passengers injured and one killed at the scene of the accident, and a third for aggravated kidnapping by assisting a father to take his own children during a custody dispute. Pending his trials, all charges were dropped when Partin became the surprise star witness against national Teamsters president Jimmy Hoffa. On March 12, 1964, with Partin's help, Hoffa was convicted of jury tampering and sentenced to eight years in prison.

Partin served his own jail time when, in June 1980, he was imprisoned for extortion. During his imprisonment, he pleaded *nolo contendere* to charges of conspiracy, racketeering, and the embezzlement of some $450,000 in union funds stemming from a 1973 indictment. U.S. District Judge John Parker subsequently reduced Partin's sentence, and he was released to a halfway house in 1986.

When Edward Grady Partin died in 1990, one of his pallbearers was Billy Cannon. In spite of his obvious faults, Billy called him a friend. "In his own way, he was a good man," Billy remembered, "a good guy who cared about his men."

The 1957 Tigers

It was the Tiger backfield, and the prospect of Billy Cannon joining forces with Jimmy Taylor, that gave fans hope for the coming year. In his book *The Fighting Tigers II: LSU Football, 1893–1980*, Peter Finney wrote, "As the 1957 season approached, the prospect of Cannon and Taylor in the same backfield had LSU fans starry eyed." One headline in the September 17, 1957, issue of *The Morning Advocate* read, "Tigers Loaded with Soph Backs," and a photograph featured Billy's teammates, quarterbacks Durel Matherne and Warren Rabb, and running backs Max Fugler and Scooter Purvis. A second headline read, "Billy Cannon on First Team for Rice Battle; Squad in Sharp Workout." A national magazine, *The Saturday Evening Post,* drew on the hype, advertising an upcoming fall issue: "Will sensational sophomore ball mover Billy Cannon give state the needed winning punch? Can the '57 squads' all-round scoring speed even bring home the Conference title?"

There would be no titles for the Tigers in 1957, but Billy Cannon and his celebrated sophomore teammates would join with Taylor, Red Brodnax, and other veterans to give the Tigers its first non-losing season in three years. In the season opener against Rice in Tiger Stadium, his debut performance as a varsity player, Billy got a 42-

yard run from scrimmage and ended the night as the team's leading rusher with 71 yards in six tries, an average of 11.2 per carry. But with half the team down with the flu, the Tigers couldn't hold onto a first-half lead and lost the game 14–20.

By the following week, with the team recovered, Billy was once again able to show his stuff on a varsity playing field. Finney wrote, "For the conference opener with Alabama . . . only 32,000 showed in Tiger Stadium, and they went away spreading the word on Cannon. He was for real. Billy showed the home folks his dazzling speed . . . as a varsity player. He zipped around end and simply outran his pursuers on a 53-yard gallop. A few minutes later, Billy faked a punt on fourth down and again outran every defender on a 73-yard scoring touchdown run." As Billy recalled, "I went into the end zone virtually untouched." The Tigers finished with an encouraging 28–0 win.

Things were also going well for Billy at home. Dot and Billy's first child, a girl they named Terri Lynn Cannon, was born on September 10. Harvey Sr. and Virgie Cannon relished having a new grandchild and were there to help Dot while Billy was at school or away at games.

LSU's next win was 19–14 against Texas Tech in Lubbock. "It was a great game for me personally," Billy remembered. "Poor Jimmy [Taylor] took the brunt of the beating from the defense, while I sailed along and had a fun time." Billy made two spectacular touchdowns. His first was a pass reception in the flat and a 59-yard sprint down the sideline, hurdling a defender en route to the end zone. His second score was a 97-yard all-out kickoff return. The officials had stopped the clock at the previous touchdown, started it again at the kickoff and stopped it again at the end of Billy's run. Ten seconds had elapsed. Billy described it as "a 10-flat 100-yard dash in full pads through an opposing team." Finney concluded, "There was no question that Billy had LSU fans in orbit."

By the time of their fourth game against Georgia Tech, defensive coaches were beginning to switch their attention away from the celebrated Taylor, who led the conference in touchdowns the year before, and onto Billy and his yard-burning outside sweeps. "I wasn't so happy about all the attention I was getting," Billy laughed. The Tigers responded accordingly: when Georgia Tech defenders ganged up on Billy, they gave the ball to the fullback, and Taylor won the game with three successive touchdown runs straight up the middle. The final score was 20–13. The two backs shared the glory in the following week's 21–0 victory against Kentucky in Baton Rouge, with Billy scoring twice and Taylor once.

It was halfway through the season. The Tigers had a 4–1 record, 3–0 in the SEC, and the prospects for the remainder of the year looked good. But the high hopes began to dissipate one game at a time as the Tigers dropped the next four, owing, according to one sportswriter, to a lack of depth on the line.

Florida was the hardest-fought loss, with defenders ganging up on Billy Cannon as well as Taylor. "I fielded a punt and handed off to Red Brodnax," Billy recalled. Referring to a rough part of New Orleans, Billy described what happened next: "Three Gators jumped me like a Julia Street–Camp Street mugging. When I could finally get up and see, there goes Brodnax fifty, fifty-five yards, and goes in untouched for a touchdown." In spite of that score, the Tigers lost 14–22.

After nine games, the Tigers were one game away from a losing season. It was against longtime rival Tulane University who'd had a dismal season of two wins and seven losses. Playing a poor team may have seemed a good thing, but Dietzel told a friend, "If I don't win this game, I'm through as a football coach." It was Jimmy Taylor who saved Dietzel and the day. In the 25–6 victory over Tulane, Taylor scored touchdown runs of 48 and 32 yards, ending the night with a total of 171 yards on seventeen carries.

In some ways, 1957 was a disappointing season. "We ended with five and five," Billy reflected, "when it could easily have been seven and three and a shot for a bowl game." But it had been a strong year for Billy personally—as a freshman, he ended the season as the team's leader in yards per carry (5.6, ahead of Taylor and Brodnax), and he was voted to the All-SEC second team. More importantly, he left Tiger fans with the memories of many dazzling plays and the promise of many more to come.

Football and Track

After football was over, Billy went to Coach Dietzel with a proposal. The terms of his scholarship required that Billy attend only the first spring football practice, after which he would be free to run track in the spring of his final three years. This had been an important part of his negotiations with each of the schools that wanted him, but after the successes of the previous football season, track seemed less important. As Billy remembered, "I told Dietzel I believed we had a chance to be a very good team next year. I knew how good those players were who were in my class, and Red Brodnax would be back. (We didn't know it at the time, but they would move Brodnax to fullback and let Robinson play the other halfback.) I told Dietzel I'd like to go out for spring practice if I could run track when we weren't practicing. He was very happy that I would do that. I was at practice every day that spring; all I missed were the Saturday scrimmages because I was running in the meets. It worked out good for everybody. I felt good about it."

With John West gone, there was no special intramural race to worry about. Billy continued to improve, even with his attention divided between football and track. Because he wasn't practicing with the track team, head track coach Al Moreau limited Billy's role in meets mainly to the shot put and the 100-yard dash.

Billy loved his track coach. "Coach Al Moreau was such a great guy," Billy said, "a delightful guy. He was this old Cajun from south Louisiana who had been a great runner himself, and he knew what he was doing. He worked us hard, but he was so easy to work with. What a gentleman. When we got off the bus for the Florida Relays, he had his wife with him, and he began to introduce her around to all the coaches. When he'd finished his last introduction, he just looked at her and beamed. 'Isn't she pretty,' he said." One of Moreau's many children, Doug, would go on to be a Tiger football star in his own right—an All-American split end at LSU and later a tight end for the Miami Dolphins.

The 1958 SEC track-and-field meet was held at Legion Field in Birmingham, Alabama. Billy was entered in the discuss, shot, and 100-yard dash. When it came time for his race, he encountered an unexpected problem. "Back then," he recalled, "the track was on the inside of the stadium. The cinder track was ancient and in terrible shape. I had put my blocks in place and was warming up for the race when I discovered a large chunk of cinder sticking up in my lane. It was about a foot long and eight inches wide. I took it out and threw it to the side. I was just starting to scrape over the hole with my cleats to cover it up when they called the runners to the mark. When the starter fired the gun, I was running as fast as I could, all the while looking for that hole so I didn't trip and bust my ass or step in somebody else's lane. I can safely say, that was the worst track I ever ran on." Billy finished first in the meet with a 9.9.

Billy's best time in the 100 was a wind-assisted 9.4, run in 1959 at a dual meet in Baton Rouge. "The officials were very particular about that," he remembered. "I got some wind behind me the last twenty yards and that was enough to make it unofficial. I did run a 9.5 in a number of meets that year." For the second year in a row, the Tigers won the SEC meet and would win it every year after until 1961.

The Summer of Sachse and the Wing-T

Billy assured athletic director Jim Corbett he wouldn't be returning to the Teamsters for summer work. He had received a better—and less controversial—offer to work for Sachse Electric, Inc., a Baton Rouge subcontractor for electrical work and supplies. Billy drove to the company's headquarters on Greenwell Springs Road and interviewed with the company's general manager, Frank Tickie Saia. As with the Teamsters the summer before, the work was nominal and would allow Billy lots of time to train for the coming season, and it paid twice as much. After a brief visit, Tickie took Billy in to meet his summer boss, Anthony "Dap" Giganti, the purchasing agent. Tickie and Dap had been friends since boyhood, playing basketball and baseball on some of the same teams. Tickie Saia had played ball at different times for both Catholic High and Baton Rouge High and had gone out for the basketball team at LSU until, it was decided, he was too short. Giganti had been a fine baseball catcher, coming up through the ranks until he was, by all accounts, worthy of the pros— had it not been for bad eyes. He wore heavy, thick-lensed glasses.

Billy's new job was less than strenuous, and he quickly established a comfortable routine. He arrived at work between seven and eight, after which he and Dap would read through the newspaper together, paying special attention to the sports section. If there was some work for Billy to do—unpacking and shelving incoming purchases, for instance, or delivering supplies to a work site—Billy would do it. "But mostly," Billy remembered, "I hung out with Dap."

Dap's office was next to the estimators' office, where bid propos-
als were carefully calculated to be low enough to get the job and high
enough to make an acceptable profit. An estimator nicknamed "Peg
Leg" Braud once asked Billy to ride with him to check on a job. After
Peg Leg had reviewed a long list of items and made some calculations,
they got back in his truck. "How'd we do?" Billy asked him of his calculations. "We did fine," Braud answered. "We got out of that room!"

Some afternoons, Billy joined some of the guys for a beer at Big
Phil's Lounge on North Thirteenth Street. Big Phil was Tickie Saia's
brother-in-law, and the bar was frequented by supervisors and workers for Sachse Electric, many of whom had grown up in that neighborhood. "Nobody had over a couple or three beers," Billy recalled,
"and by six or six-thirty, everybody'd gone home to supper, but if you
wanted to talk sports and get the latest office gossip, that was the
place to go after work. It was a great bunch of guys, and I got to know
them all. They worked hard, but they knew how to kid and laugh and
have a good time."

But for Billy, the summer was truly about preparing for what would
perhaps be the greatest season in the history of LSU football. Few
foresaw what was coming. Jimmy Taylor was gone, along with seasoned starters on the offensive line. New Orleans *Times-Picayune*
sportswriter Bill Keefe called the Tigers "overbacked and under-
lined." With Cannon, Rabb, Robinson, Brodnax, Purvis, and many
others, Keefe suggested Dietzel "put up a 'No Vacancy' sign on the
backfield wing of LSU's athletic dormitory." On the other hand, Keefe
wrote, "Lack of good line prospects . . . caused nearly all of the pre-
season dopesters to rate the Tigers low down on the conference totem
pole and entirely out of sight in national ratings." Dietzel was happy
to go unnoticed since he knew very well the potential of his team.

Throughout the summer, Billy continued to lift weights at Alvin
Roy's Gym. "It was a good summer for me health-wise," Billy remem-
bered. "That was the first summer that I bench pressed 400 pounds.
The next summer I military pressed 405. We were ahead of our time."

That same summer, Coach Dietzel began to work out there as well.
"He could see the difference in body size and strength between those
of us who lifted and the others. The team had gone five and five the
last season, and he was looking for an edge. I'm sure Alvin and Fuzzy
Brown were telling him how much it had helped Istrouma. Coach

Dietzel was very faithful in his workouts—three days per week. He did the same eight lifts we did for strength and explosiveness. At the end of the summer, Coach Dietzel could see in himself his own progress."

Billy's preparations for the 1958 season got an unexpected boost with a telephone call from the offensive line coach, Bill Peterson. "He gave me a call at the house," Billy remembered, "and asked me to stop by the next day about four-thirty or five o'clock. Rabb, Robinson, and Brodnax (the other designated backs for the coming season) would meet us." What Peterson unveiled the next day to Billy and the other first-team backs was brand new to them: an offense called the Wing-T. "Peterson was ecstatic about it," Billy said.

Bud Johnson had just joined LSU in February as sports information director and was able to witness the inception of the Wing-T. "Dietzel installed a whole new offense during spring practice. In preparation for the change, Dietzel invited Iowa coach Forrest Evashevski to speak at the LSU Clinic for high school coaches in the spring of '58. Evy also spent hours with the LSU staff explaining the Wing-T he used in Iowa City and loaned films of Hawkeye games. Dietzel liked the system because it took advantage of the Tigers' speed at every backfield position. Basically a T-formation with single wing principles, the Wing-T set one halfback next to the fullback behind the quarterback but often stationed the other halfback just outside one end where he could come inside for crossbucks and reverses or sprint out for passes. No team in the Southeast had played against the formation."

Teams in the SEC—and most teams in the country—were running a more straight-ahead offense in which linemen opened holes for halfbacks or fullbacks to run through, or else fellow backs led interference for the runner on sweeps. Billy called it "smash-mouth football." Pass plays were relatively rare. The Wing-T often placed a halfback in the "wing" slot just outside the tight end, and a split end on the weak side, putting all three running backs in prime locations for pass routes, counters, fakes, and other misdirection plays. Billy would play at the left wing position, Johnny Robinson on the right. One would run, the other would block. "The key block was on the defensive end," Billy said. "With help from the blocking wingback, you could get him out of the way. You could seal him off and allow the runner to get outside. There were so many variations, but that was the core: if I blocked well, Johnny ran well, if Johnny blocked well, I ran well. Red Brodnax, who had been a great running halfback the year before, was now at fullback and mostly blocked. He was selfless that year, a tremendous blocker, and a good ball carrier when he got the chance."

The system also gave a good quarterback—such as Warren Rabb—more options to run or throw, and was designed to create many problems for the defense. The Wing-T was not a passing offense, but there were more opportunities for the quarterback, and sometimes even a talented halfback, to throw the ball. Johnny Robinson made one such pass to Billy Cannon later in the year. Cannon made the game-winning pass to Mickey Mangham against Clemson in the Sugar Bowl 7–0 victory at the end of the 1958 season. Billy described what the Wing-T could do for the quarterback: "Rabb could be faking handoffs, distracting linemen, and giving receivers time to run their routes. He could pass or run himself. You could put a back in motion, which we hadn't done before. There were so many opportunities that hadn't been there before. We were like a kid with a new toy. We kept playing with it. It was new and exciting."

The four backs met every afternoon to run through some of the many variations of plays now open to them. Peterson and Maddox would check in on a regular basis to see how they were doing. Dietzel came out to watch one afternoon. "Whether he was impressed or not, I couldn't tell," Billy said, "but when he was watching us, there was extra spark in our step."

Maddox talked to the boys about what stance they wanted to use. "God bless him," Billy said, "he had already been through the 'speed stance' thing with me. Under the new formation, the backs were going to be moving laterally more than forward. Instead of telling us what he wanted, he asked us what we thought. Johnny and I both wanted to be in a stand-up stance so we could move to the side more easily than if we'd started in a three-point stance. So Coach Maddox took our suggestion."

Even though his backfield had practiced it so hard, it was not a foregone conclusion that the Tigers would use the Wing-T in the fall. "One night, I got a call at home about eight o'clock," Billy remembered.

It was Coach Peterson. You could tell he was excited. "Tomorrow is the day," he told me. This was about midway through the summer and getting on towards fall practice. We'd run pass patterns, reverses, counters. Against the dummies, we had the Wing-T perfected. I had no idea what he was talking about.

I said, "Good, Coach, what's happening tomorrow?"

"Tomorrow," Peterson said, "Coach Dietzel and I are driving to Lake Charles. He's going to make a speech there, and on the way back I'm going to get a commitment from him to use the Wing-T in the fall." The following morning after the trip, he got back with me. I suppose he'd had to brow-beat Dietzel all the way there and back. He was practically singing: "Dietzel made the commitment!"

Billy envisioned what the new offense would look like in a game. "We could hardly wait to share what we were doing with the rest of the team. It was a great, great summer," Billy said. "Needless to say, we were eager for the season to start."

Billy's summer was great for other reasons. Dot was pregnant with their second child. Billy's parents and in-laws were thrilled at the prospect of a new grandbaby. Harvey Sr. and Virgie were both in good health, both working. Not only was Billy doing well in sports and studies, he was making more money than he ever had, money that would provide him the chance to invest in tickets for Tiger football.

I Believed!

Billy remembered well how he felt as the 1958 football season approached. "You weren't reading about it in the paper, but there was enthusiasm that we would have a better team—better than the five and five we'd had the year before. Of course, nobody—including me—had any idea we'd win a national championship or go to a major bowl game. Believe it or not, I didn't know they were ranking the teams. I thought the big reward for a great season was to go to a bowl. I wanted to go to the Rose Bowl." He laughed. "I didn't know the Rose Bowl was tied down between the West Coast and the Big Ten. But I personally felt it was going to be a great, great year, and I was so glad to be a part of it. We had a great new offense, and I knew what we were capable of on defense. We had more speed and more talent. The recruiting they'd done was finally going to pay off."

Billy had an idea of how to combine his optimism for the coming season with his entrepreneurship, and he scheduled an appointment to see athletic director Jim Corbett. "So far, I'd had three meetings with Corbett," Billy said, "once when he was recruiting me, once when I was a freshman and he told me to quit selling varsity tickets outside the stadium, and once to tell me to quit working for the Teamsters. I know he must have wondered what I was up to now." The meeting was cordial. "We exchanged pleasantries for a while," Billy said, "but he finally asked me why I had come." Billy put on Corbett's desk a list of the home games in the fall schedule and beside each game, the number of tickets he wanted to buy. "They were all in Section 32 in the north end of the stadium, end-zone tickets selling for $2.50 each. I listed the different number of tickets I wanted for each game. I put down a couple of hundred tickets for Ole Miss and maybe another couple of hundred for the Tulane game." Attached to the list was Billy's personal check for the full amount needed to purchase them.

Corbett hesitated as he tried to understand what his star athlete was up to. "Uh, Billy, I don't think I can do this."

"Why not," Billy insisted. "It's my money, and I'm paying the full price." To pay for the tickets, Billy had put together almost his entire savings; only one hundred dollars and the final paycheck he had coming from Sachse Electric were not tied up in the ticket purchase. "I'm putting up everything I own, and I'm hoping to make some money off this. I believe I'll turn a profit." Billy reminded Corbett that he was married with one child and that another was due in September. This was an investment he needed to make to provide for his family.

Again, Corbett hesitated. "I think I'm going to need to talk to someone about this." As he had for a previous meeting with Billy, Corbett brought in Coach Harry Rabenhorst. Billy remembered what happened next. "I admired Coach Rabenhorst. He'd been with LSU a long time—as a basketball and baseball coach. There was no phoniness about him. He was straight as a string. Corbett explained to Coach Harry exactly what I wanted to do, went through the schedule and number of tickets, and showed him my check for the full amount.

"Rabenhorst asked him, 'Jim, you got anybody else to sell them to?'

"Corbett said, 'No.'

"'Well,' Rabenhorst said, 'then sell them to him.'"

At Corbett's request, Billy agreed to purchase the tickets in some-one else's name. Billy's summer boss Dap Giganti reluctantly agreed to be Billy's agent. Billy remembered, "Dap looked at me through those big thick glasses and finally said, 'Okay, if you're that crazy, I'll do it. I'll help you.' He thought I was throwing my money away, that I'd never resell the tickets. I gave him a check, and he wrote one out in the same amount to the Tiger Athletic Department and mailed it in.

"'One other thing,' I said. 'You can't tell anybody.'

"Dap said, 'Don't worry. I'm not going to tell them you're crazy ... or that I'm crazy to help you!'

"A lot of people thought I'd lost my mind," Billy reflected, "and when I finally got the tickets, it was a bundle! Dot and I had just bought a new bedroom suite, and there were so many tickets I couldn't get them all into one dresser drawer. It was a sobering moment. I thought, 'Is Dap right? Am I crazy?' Now I had to sell all these things." Billy's doubts disappeared. He had always been a risk taker, he knew he needed the money, and he knew what the team could do. "I was that enthused about the team and our prospects. Truth is, I would have bought more tickets if I'd have had more money. I knew what we could do. I believed!"

White, Gold, and Bandits

The first day of fall practice, the full team was there. "They ran us through our physicals," Billy remembered. "A physical exam back then was pretty much a 'how-de-do' and a handshake. They listened to your heart and took your blood pressure. Of course, Marty Brous-sard [the team trainer] knew us from daylight to dark."

At the first team meeting, the coaches explained the basic Wing-T formation. Billy remembered the excitement. "This was the first time that the whole team really understood what we were going to do. You could just feel the electricity in the air, especially from the running backs. I looked over at Scooter Purvis, and I knew he was thinking, 'I can run this! This is not power football. This is deception football with power mixed in.' They would show it on a blackboard. Then Rabb, Robinson, Brodnax and I would run it. Then the coaches made the other backs walk through it, but they didn't want to; they wanted to run it. They were as excited as we were. Finally they brought in the line, and we started working it together against live players on defense. It just blossomed. The excitement was contagious and infectious!"

It was at this time that Paul Dietzel devised another brilliant strategy: a system of three separate units that he could put into and take out of the game. According to halfback Scooter Purvis, a new NCAA rule had triggered the idea. The new college rule was designed to discourage teams from playing one offensive team and another team on defense. "Somebody thought it would be more interesting if everybody had to play both ways," Purvis said. The rule stipulated that a player could enter a game only twice in one quarter. If he started the quarter and came out for any reason, he could go back in during that quarter only one other time. If he came out one more time, he was considered "dead." An official had to track the comings and goings of players each quarter.

The new rule may have discouraged two-unit football, but it ended up encouraging three.

Dietzel named his three platoons: the White Team, the Gold (later called Go) Team, and the Chinese Bandits. The White Team was comprised of top players who would play both offense and defense. It included Billy and his summer practice pals, Rabb, Robinson, and Brodnax. The Gold Team was designated as offense only and featured Durel Matherne at quarterback, Scooter Purvis and Donnie Daye as halfbacks, and Tommy Davis at fullback. The Chinese Bandits were an exclusively defensive squad which included Billy's high-school teammate Duane Leopard at tackle, former Baton Rouge High rival Gus Kinchen at end, and Billy's new friend Hart Bourque at cornerback.

Bud Johnson remembered Dietzel's dilemma. "As much talent as he had, he didn't have the kind of depth that would allow him to field two complete offensive-defensive teams. He was looking for a two-squad solution and he came up with three instead." Johnson called it a "manufactured depth."

The three-platoon system provided a brilliant way to continue using full units. Dietzel would send his White Team—the offensive-defensive squad—on the first play of every quarter. Mid-quarter, the Gold Team or the Bandits would go in, depending on who had the ball. Dietzel could switch them out twice in the remaining part of the quarter as circumstances dictated, and could always send the White Team back in if he had to. According to Dietzel, "Our scheme worked perfectly. During the 1958 season, the White Team averaged thirty-five minutes per game, while the Go Team and the Chinese Bandits split the other twenty-five minutes almost exactly between them."

Dietzel's system circumvented the limitations of the new rule by swapping out squads that could play either way rather than offensive and defensive units, thus keeping substitutions to a minimum. And the three-platoon system had many other advantages for the Tigers. It utilized LSU's remarkable breadth of talent and kept fresh players in the game, wearing down bigger opponents. Dietzel's 1956 prize recruiting year had netted over forty top players, and they were joined by experienced seniors such as Red Brodnax and Billy Hendrix, and talented sophomores such as Bo Strange and Mickey Mangham. (The Wing-T offense, with its multiple fakes and counters, was an extra plus for a smaller, faster team.)

Another advantage to three units was that everyone got to play. Each player on the three platoons was guaranteed playing time in every game. "It was a great morale booster," Billy remembered, "that made a tremendous difference. Every practice, every team meeting, every player was participating, giving it his best, because he knew he had a personal stake in the next game."

A final, and unexpected, advantage was that each platoon had its own pride and spirit. Dietzel began to notice that, at meals and in meetings, members of the same squads were sitting together. Each unit had its own identity. No one felt like a second-stringer.

Surprisingly, this was especially true of the Chinese Bandits. Over and over, the pride of this defensive unit allowed it to exceed the limit of the individual players' abilities. And their unusual name caught the imagination of the fans. Dietzel had grabbed the name from a cartoon strip, "Terry and the Pirates," in which Chinese bandits were the epitome of ferocity and fearlessness. Thousands of fans began to show up at games and pep rallies in "coolie" hats. A newly written fight song became a rallying cry on defense (and remains so to this day—the Tiger band plays it when LSU gets a turnover or a defensive stop).

Billy looked back at the many factors that contributed to LSU's extraordinary season: "All these things snowballed into peak performances for everyone. It added up to a full effort by every player every game."

Eleven Games, Eleven Victories

The Tigers flew into Houston for their first game against Rice University and took a bus to the Shamrock Hotel, where they would spend the night. Dot, who loved watching Billy play, would not be going to this game. On September 1, she had given birth to their second little girl, Gina Leigh Cannon. As they had with the first grandchild, Dot's mother and Billy's parents were there to help with the new granddaughter.

Because it was raining in Houston, the coaches decided against their normal Friday-night light practice and called the team together for a meeting. The meeting would change the way the Tigers handled pregame days for the rest of the season and the next. There was much to cover at the meeting. It was the first game of the season and against an opponent who had beaten them the year before. The Wing-T offense and the three-platoon system were both new and complex. Because all thirty-five members of the traveling squad would be on the field, each player needed to be on top of the scouting report, the team strategy, and his particular assignments. The practice would have been light, but the team meeting was not. The coaches began a rapid-fire drilling of the players. Billy was impressed. "Every player down to the last man knew the answers to every question. Responses were crisp, quick, and right on target. This was a new way to get us ready for a game, and it worked. Our play on the field the next day reflected our readiness. We never went back to the old Friday night field practices."

Billy roomed with cornerback Hart Bourque. Bourque had been an excellent running back for Gonzales High School. Because he, like Billy, was married and lived in north Baton Rouge, he had begun riding to school and back with Billy and another student. He was light-hearted and funny, and he and Billy became lifelong friends. When Bourque graduated from LSU he would return to Gonzales and, before long, be elected as the Ascension Parish Clerk of Court, a post he held for over fifty years.

Saturday morning, it was still raining. As Billy and Hart Bourque got dressed in the slacks and blazers that were their off-field uniforms, they watched TV. *American Bandstand* was on, and host Dick Clark kept plugging the featured artist, the Big Bopper (J. P. Richardson), who would be on live later in the program. Richardson was a master of the rock-and-roll music that was such a part of the young players' high-school years. Billy wanted to see him perform. "We knew we were late," Billy remembered, "a big no-no with Coach Dietzel, but we really wanted to see the Big Bopper. Naturally, he was the last thing on the program." When they finally got to the bus, everybody else had boarded, and the ever punctual Dietzel was tapping his foot. "He was not happy," Billy said. "I think the Big Bopper sang 'Chantilly Lace.'"

On hand to scout the game was Alabama's new coach, Bear Bryant. Having had great success at Kentucky and then Texas A&M, he was starting his first season as head coach at his alma mater. His reign at Alabama would become one of the best coaching careers in college football history. And having had Paul Dietzel as an assistant at Kentucky, Bryant knew the young coach's determination and talent, and wasn't about to take LSU for granted; he wanted to see for himself what the Crimson Tide would be facing the following week.

Some feared that on the soggy field the Tigers might lose the advantage of their speed, but in fact Rice did little to stop them. Not only the backfield but the line showed quickness and skill. Bryant's assessment: "I don't know if I've ever seen a team with more overall speed." The 26–6 victory included a Tiger touchdown in each quarter. Billy's night included a 30-yard punt return for a TD, and a punt of his own which landed dead on the Rice one-foot line.

Billy's one disappointment was that Dietzel chose not to fully unveil their Wing-T offense. They ran a few plays from the new repertoire—one was a halfback pass from Robinson to Cannon—but the Tigers mostly relied on plays from the previous season. "I couldn't understand why we'd worked so hard to develop this great new offense and weren't using it," Billy said. Dietzel later wrote that he was focusing on his platoon system in the first game, and he was pleased with what he saw, especially "the way the second and third teams performed." Another reason Dietzel held back on the new plays was that Bear Bryant was in the stands, something Billy didn't know but his coach surely did. "We didn't show everything," Dietzel said, "and saved a few surprises for our next game, which was very special for me." It was so important to Dietzel to beat Bear Bryant, the man he once worked for, he even made a special appeal to his players to win the game "as a personal favor."

Billy would understand better why Dietzel kept the Wing-T under wraps when LSU met Alabama in Mobile the following Saturday—at least he would in the second half of the game. Bryant was taking a losing team, as he had at A&M (and as Dietzel had when he'd come to Baton Rouge) and, true to form, turning it into a winner. Over time, he would turn the Crimson Tide into a dynasty. This was Dietzel's first game against his old boss, and he was determined to win. He knew from experience that rules didn't always limit Bryant (he'd personally witnessed Bryant's less-than-orthodox recruiting tactics), so he expected some surprises. But then he was prepared with some surprises of his own.

"The Crimson Tide came out fired up," Billy remembered. "Coach Bryant had them so jacked up, they were flying. We could tell that their last year's record wasn't going to matter much. We were going to have a fight on our hands."

Mobile's Ladd Memorial Stadium was sold out. A special set of stands had been erected near the end zone to accommodate overflow crowds, and it was filled too. "The people in the stands were as pumped up as the players," Billy remembered. As the game progressed, the Tigers were going nowhere, and Billy kept asking himself, "Why aren't we using the Wing-T?"

Despite a Bryant gimmick—switching his players' jersey numbers to confuse the Tiger defense—the first half ended with Alabama up by only 3–0. But switched jerseys wasn't the only distraction of the game. "As I went back to receive the first kickoff of the second half, all hell broke loose," Billy remembered. "I turned around. There had been so many people in that extra set of stands, they had collapsed. I could hear people groaning. Refs were all blowing their whistles. People were trying to get out. There were broken bones, concussions. People were screaming, crying for help. It was mayhem."

It was a long time before people were evacuated and order was restored. Eventually, the referees signaled they were ready. Billy got back into position to receive, he took the kick, and the game resumed. It was the perfect moment to unleash the Wing-T. As the Tigers began to pull from their stockpile of deception plays, Billy kept an eye on the Alabama bench. "You could see Bryant trying to figure out what was going on. He started screaming: 'What the hell are they doing out there? Somebody better tell me quick!' You could see the assistants running for cover. They were hiding behind the players!

"Once we started using our new plays, I knew it was going to be all right," Billy remembered. The platoon system was doing its job too. "It was still a work in progress, but it was already working for us." Billy picked up 86 yards in twelve carries, one of which was a 12-yard touchdown run right up the gut of the defense. The game ended with all three platoons having shared the field and a scoreboard that read: LSU-13, Alabama-3.

"It was a come-from-behind victory," Billy recalled, "a real booster. It showed us how effective the new system could be against a totally aggressive defense—just as effective as we thought it would be."

The next week's match, against Hardin-Simmons of Abilene, Texas, the Tigers' first home game, was supposed to be a "gimme game," as Billy put it, but he was not surprised when it wasn't. He knew the head coach, Sammy Baugh. A two-time All-American from Texas Christian University, Baugh had been a star quarterback for the Washington Redskins and a Pro Football Hall of Fame inductee. Billy had met him when Baugh coached Billy and Max Fugler in the East-West Prep All America game. "People wondered why someone of that caliber would be coaching at a little west Texas school, but I knew Hardin-Simmons was close to his ranch in Rotan.

"Baugh was the first coach I know who brought pro-style offense to college," Billy said. This meant audibles—the quarterback calling plays and giving vocal instructions—from the line of scrimmage, the use of wide receivers, and lots of passing; the only touchdown scored by the Cowboys came on a series of pass plays in the second quarter. But the Tigers were well prepared. "Coach George Terry had done a great job scouting," Billy recalled. "He passed out a game plan with a separate report on each player. It was a picture-perfect description of their defense." Quarterbacks Warren Rabb of the White Team, and Durel Matherne of the Gold Team, each led a successful scoring drive in the first quarter. An 11-yard touchdown run by Billy in the second quarter gave the Tigers a 20–6 lead, which they maintained in an uneventful second half.

Tigerland Is Partyland

In the preface to his book, *The Perfect Season: LSU's Magic Year—1958,* Bud Johnson traces the confluence of events and developments that not only helped lift the LSU Tiger football team to prominence, but lifted the game itself and the season of football into the premier social and cultural event in Baton Rouge. Expanding media coverage was one such development. Beginning in the early 1950s, two 50,000-watt clear-channel radio stations, WWL of New Orleans and KWKH of Shreveport, began broadcasting Tiger football nearly nationwide. NBC's national game of the week, also begun in the early 1950s, brought the game to the country in the new and captivating medium of television. A 1954 enlargement of Tiger Stadium allowed for over 67,000 fans to attend games, and, of course, the 1958 winning Tiger season gave fans a reason to come.

Baton Rouge residents have long been accustomed to the way their city nearly shuts down on Saturdays during football season. Social, business, and political agenda-makers know better than to schedule anything for a game day. As a Saturday home game approaches, local fans and Tiger diehards from around the state and country begin to move onto campus in every imaginable vehicle, many bearing the team colors of purple and gold, and they commence to party—a mix of cooking, eating, drinking, and, hopefully, celebrating a Tiger victory. It is said that the city's mood is governed by how well the Tigers are doing in football.

What today may seem to fans a tradition that has always been a part of LSU football got its start with the national championship season of 1958. One of the earliest social pacesetters was Billy's former employer, Tickie Saia, general manager of Sachse Electric. "After every home game, Tickie would have a big company party at his house on Airline Highway," Billy recalled, "and he would invite me and the other players. There were always lots of prominent people from the community—[U.S. Senator] Russell Long or the governor [Earl Long] came—as well as electrical linemen for the company. It was a great mix of people. And somebody was always handing out a little money to the players, especially if we'd won."

Over a year later, after Billy Cannon had won the 1959 Heisman Trophy, he heard that Tickie Saia was in the hospital, recovering from an injury sustained in an automobile accident. Billy lugged the twenty-five-pound cast-bronze trophy to Tickie's room so his friend and former boss could get his picture taken with it and the star who won it.

The Press Takes Notice

Even with three consecutive wins, LSU had hardly created a stir among the pollsters. The Associated Press listed the Tigers as eleventh in the country and United Press International as fifteenth. Their next game would change that. The Tigers traveled to the Florida Orange Bowl stadium, where they dismantled the University of Miami Hurricanes 41–0. It was the worst beating Miami had suffered since 1944. Everyone but the Tigers seemed surprised. Puffing on a cigar after the game, Miami head coach Andy Gustafson was philosophical: "A year ago, Paul Dietzel told me he was building for 1959. It looks like they arrived a year early."

For the fourth straight game, the Tigers displayed dazzling offensive speed. They executed for the first time a crossover exchange on a kickoff with Johnny Robinson fielding the ball then feeding it to Cannon, who ran 47 yards before being stopped at midfield. Tommy Davis, Johnny Robinson, Scooter Purvis, and Billy all had a great night. "My vote for most valuable player was Scooter Purvis," Billy said. "He ran as I never saw him before or since." Purvis scored the opening touchdown with a 53-yard run. "Tremendous moves, great fakes," Billy said. "I would have broken both ankles."

The White Team and the Chinese Bandits held the Hurricanes scoreless. "Our defense kept getting better and better," Billy said. "Max Fugler had a particularly good night. He was always two steps ahead of me in reading the offense. He couldn't be fooled." Years later, when Billy met Fugler's high-school coach, he asked him, "What did you teach him?" "Nothing," the coach said. "I recognized what he had and left it alone."

The platoon system was evolving, but it was already working well.

A writer heard Dietzel talking after the game about his three units but mistook "Gold Team" for "Go Team." When the misnomer was printed, it got repeated until it stuck.

"We were ecstatic after the game," Billy remembered. "The coaches had brought their wives, and everybody went out on the town." Only the coaches came in at a reasonable hour. Billy and some of his teammates, joined for a time by a member of the LSU Board of Supervisors, Horace Wilkinson, went for an all-night ramble. When they got back to the hotel in the morning, they met the coaches at the elevator coming down for breakfast. Billy laughed. "Busted again!"

Billy called the victory in Miami a "national win. For the first time, the eastern press took notice of us, and we began to get national attention." Both the AP and UPI polls put the Tigers at number nine. "It was the first time I remember a large group of fans meeting us when we got home from an out-of-town game," Billy said.

The fans, 65,000 of them, showed up for the next game as well, against Kentucky at home. Another Billy Cannon gamble was paying off. He had invested almost his entire savings into LSU football tickets, banking that a successful season would allow him to sell them for slightly more than their face value and thereby turn a profit. "Everything we owned was in the top drawer of the dresser," Billy said, referring to where he and Dot kept the rolls of tickets, but his investment was beginning to pay dividends.

Coach Paul Dietzel, in his own understated way, agreed with Billy's assessment of the Tigers' future. In his memoir, *Call Me Coach,* he wrote that, after the Miami game, "I began to think that maybe we had a pretty darn good football team." The fans agreed. They were crazy about Billy Cannon. Bumper stickers began to be seen that read "Have Cannon, Will Travel." They were crazy about the Chinese Bandits too. Thousands of "coolie" hats suddenly appeared in the student section at games. "The tickets were selling like hot cakes," Billy said.

LSU scored at least one touchdown in each quarter and gave up only one the entire game. In the first half, the Tigers ran sweeps to the outside and, after halftime, as the Wildcats adjusted, Billy Cannon tore through the middle time and again. He scored two touchdowns, rushing 108 yards in nine carries. The final score was a 32–7 victory. Suddenly LSU was ranked fifth in the UPI ratings and third by AP, the highest an LSU football team had achieved since 1937.

The value of one particular player came into focus during LSU's next game against the University of Florida in Baton Rouge. Tommy Davis, whom many considered the best collegiate kicker in the country, had been performing all season, of course, picking up considerable yardage as a fullback for the Go Team as well as booting punts, extra points, and field goals. Against the Florida Gators, Davis would make the difference. It was the Tigers' toughest and tightest game to that point in the season. "They were a good team," Billy remembered, "and Coach [Bob] Woodruff had them ready to play." It was mainly a defensive battle. "The Gators did a better job of hemming in Billy Cannon than any other team," the Baton Rouge *Morning Advocate* reported, and the two teams traded possessions until the second quarter when a 32-yard punt return by Billy sparked a scoring drive. "Cannon scored LSU's touchdown on a superhuman plunge after the Gators had held three times inside the one." The Tigers protected their 7–0 lead until the Gators scored during a fourth-quarter series, and the game was tied. Billy produced a series of hard-earned runs up the middle that finally put the Tigers on the Florida 19-yard line, easily within Davis's field goal range.

What happened next surprised even Billy. "We were off on the far right hash mark," Billy remembered. "Coach Dietzel decided to let the play clock run out, and we were penalized five yards, but of course, it allowed for the ball to be replaced midfield, giving Tommy a better angle. I knew it was a good decision, but we'd fought so hard for every yard, I sure hated to give them up that easily." Thankfully, Davis's kick pushed the Tigers to a 10–7 victory.

Davis had surely saved the game, but much of Coach Paul Dietzel's postgame analysis was in praise of Billy's play. "If there's a better college football player in the United States than Billy Cannon, I'd like to see him. His blocking was vicious, and he saved a touchdown in the first quarter when he nailed a Florida runner after a run of thirty-one yards. This is definitely the finest team we've played so far."

Nervous? My Whole Section Sold Out!

The "so far" in Dietzel's reflection was an important caveat because LSU was set to face the University of Mississippi. Not only were they ranked sixth by both UPI and AP, not far below LSU's AP ranking of No. 1 and UPI's No. 5 ranking, but Ole Miss was unbeaten in six games, and, it went without saying, they were the Tigers' most hated and respected foe. "It's not a rivalry because somebody says it is," Billy mused, "or because you've been playing against a team for a long time. It's a rivalry when two good teams meet and either one could walk out the winner. This was a rivalry."

Baton Rouge, and the entire state of Louisiana, had caught Tiger fever. On campus, students were delirious, hanging the UPI in effigy for its less than No. 1 ranking. No less energized, Ole Miss fans returned the favor; during game week, a small plane dropped leaflets on the LSU campus which read, "Go to hell, LSU." Because Paul Dietzel had flown B-29s in the Second World War, rumors started that the coach had himself dropped the leaflets to rally his troops. He denied it, but said he was happy for the help. Billy summarized the delirium with a laugh: "There was a lot of warfare between the non-combatants."

Billy's heavy investment in tickets, never far from his mind, was no longer a source of worry; it was a cause for celebration. The Ole Miss game was the first sellout in the history of the stadium, and, because the sellout came early in the week (Billy's allotment was sold by the Monday before), ticket prices rocketed. According to writer Peter Finney, "Some people were willing to swap television sets for tickets. One fan in particular made an offer of $800 for 'eight good sideline seats.'"

When game day arrived, the Tigers, as always, were warming up on the field well in advance of kickoff time, the stadium was beginning to fill, and the atmosphere was already charged with excitement. Billy and Johnny Robinson were talking as they fielded punts. "How are you feeling," Johnny asked. "Are you nervous?" "Nervous?" Billy said. He pointed to the north end zone. "I'm feeling great. My whole section sold out!"

Billy's section wasn't the only one sold out. Stadium capacity at the time was 68,000. *Times-Picayune* sportswriter Bill Keefe estimated the crowd at 70,000, "jammed at every corner. Hundreds sat in aisles or stood up." Dan Hardesty of the *State Times* introduced his readers to the game this way: "The No. 1 team in the nation faces its No. 1 test here tonight in college football's No. 1 game of the year."

LSU played like a No. 1 team, especially on defense, keeping Ole

Miss scoreless. The White team held the Rebels on four consecutive plays at the one-yard line. "When you get shoulder-to-shoulder in an eight-man defense, you can't afford a mistake," Dietzel said of the goal-line stance. "We didn't make one." Max Fugler made the stops on two of the plays, Rabb made another and, on the other, Billy hit star running back Charlie Flowers at the line of scrimmage so hard, it knocked him back a yard.

Billy remembered the two scoring plays of the LSU 14–0 victory: "Ole Miss had an excellent defense, but we were making enough yardage each play to move up the field. When we got close, Rabb decided to run a bootleg. He faked to me, and the posse followed—just like they were supposed to—and Rabb ran it in for our first touchdown."

In the second half, it was the Go team that marched down the field to within scoring distance. Quarterback Durel "Matherne called the same play that got us our first TD," Billy said, "but this time, instead of sailing in, he was really struggling to get across the goal line. That's when this hefty Ole Miss tackle came in late and hit Matherne so hard he pushed him in. That was the game! We shut them out."

It was the seventh consecutive victory for the Tigers. There was jubilation in the stands and in the LSU locker room. Tom Gallery, NBC director of sports, joined Jim Corbett and Paul Dietzel to congratulate a weary squad. "I have the best three teams I've seen all year, tonight," he said, "and all three were wearing the uniforms of LSU." Dietzel gushed with his own praise. "It was the most wonderful victory I have ever been associated with. I'm proud of you."

Marty Broussard's Miracle

At Wednesday practice before the Saturday night game against Duke, Billy felt a sudden and severe pain in his right ankle. Tough and experienced, he immediately recognized this was an injury that would only get worse with play. Instead of doing post-practice sprints with the rest of the team, he walked off the field, through the chute, and into the stadium training room. "Doc, this is killing me," he told his friend and trainer, Marty Broussard. "I don't know what I did." As Broussard began probing, pinching, and rotating Billy's foot, Coach Dietzel walked in. "Billy, why didn't you run your sprints today?" Broussard answered for Billy, "Coach, we got a problem here," and he pointed to

Billy's tendon. Dietzel's expression turned from disapproval to worry. Whatever tension had developed between the player and the coach, Dietzel knew he couldn't afford to play without Cannon.

Dr. Noto, the team physician, injected Billy's ankle (with what, Billy was never sure), wrapped and taped the foot. "Go to class but stay off your foot otherwise." The following afternoon, Billy came back to Broussard for his first rehab treatment: immersing his injured foot in a hot whirlpool for fifteen minutes and then in a bucket of crushed ice for fifteen minutes. Three cycles of the alternating hot and cold took an hour and a half. "It was miserable," Billy recalled. "The cure was worse than the sickness." When he was done, Dr. Noto gave him another shot, wrapped and taped the foot. The entire treatment was repeated Friday afternoon and Saturday morning. Before the game, Broussard taped it so high and tight, it pulled Billy's foot back. He fitted Billy with a new pair of high-top cleats and patted him on the shoulder: "Okay, let's see if you're tough enough."

Duke was a major player in the Atlantic Coast Conference. Though it had lost four games in the 1958 season, each of those had been by only a slight margin—a touchdown in one and a field goal in the other three—against top teams such as Notre Dame and Georgia Tech. Dietzel called Duke "another Florida." Baton Rouge *State Times* sports editor Dan Hardesty reported that the Tigers would be "looking to their All-America candidate, Billy Cannon, to have a big night," but he worried that Billy might be getting a swell head from the "Saturday Hero" treatment of big national magazines such as *Sports Illustrated* which, he said, were "putting him up on a pedestal." Nobody in the press knew that Billy was nursing a bad foot.

"When we took the field," Billy said, "the first thing we noticed was how big they were." The first quarter of the game against Duke seemed to confirm the prognosticators' worst fears. Duke stopped an early Tiger advance and then promptly drove for a touchdown in ten plays. But it took only one more play, the first after LSU received the next kickoff, to completely turn the game around. "I decided to call the pass before we went back on the field for the kickoff," Rabb remembered. "They were playing their backs real close, and it wasn't much for Billy to run by them."

Billy also recalled the play. "I was running a pattern off the wing, I could tell I had my defender beat. Warren [Rabb] hit me perfectly on a dead run, and I took it sixty-three yards for a touchdown. The crowd ignited. The pass revitalized us. After that pass, it was a different team and a different game."

Billy hadn't noticed his injured foot on his dash across the gridiron. Nor did he notice it in the second half as the Tigers racked up more points against the Blue Devils to end the game with a dominating 50–18 victory. "I didn't think about my foot until it was time to unwrap my foot. It was hard to believe it had hurt me so badly three days before and that I hadn't felt a thing. And thanks to 'Doc' Broussard, I never felt it again."

As he did in the aftermath of each contest, Billy reflected critically on the Duke game. "In retrospect, we weren't as prepared defensively as we should have been. They weren't as good as Ole Miss or Florida, and yet they ran lots of yards and scored eighteen points on us when we'd held Florida to seven and Ole Miss to zero." And as he often did in the aftermath of each contest, Billy regretted that teammates hadn't gotten more recognition for their play. "In the papers, I got all the credit, but Warren [Rabb] and others deserved more. It was a tremendous team effort."

Billy's 63-yard scoring pass reception and run in the Duke game made him regret that the Tigers hadn't utilized their passing game as much as they might have during the rest of the season. "One of the great things about the game was that we threw the ball more, but for the rest of my career at LSU, we never used that play again. The Wing-T was a great passing offense, but we never threw deep again. It was sickening to me, stupid, but I never said a word about it." Billy would come to appreciate the style of play in the pros—where he proved himself an outstanding receiver—because there the passing game was stressed.

"All in all, a great night," Billy said. "We'd had a run of excellent games." He laughed. "By this time, we were full of ourselves."

A week later, the Tigers traveled to Jackson to meet Mississippi State in what would prove to be the closest game of the season. LSU was by this time ranked No. 1 in the nation in both major polls, but a strong Mississippi State team and miserable weather would play their own parts in the outcome of the game. It had been raining two straight days, leaving Hinds Memorial Field saturated. "We had to wait for the rain to stop to go out and warm up," Billy remembered, "and when it finally quit raining, things weren't much better. The stadium had terrible drainage. The rain ran down the steps in torrents and onto the field. They had these plank bridges over pools of water and slop to get you onto the field. I stepped off one of the boards, and the mud came over my low-top cleats. I had to go back in and get the high-tops I'd used the week before because of my bad foot."

Both teams played against the weather in the low-scoring game. Billy fumbled twice and lost the ball, but he was far from the only player to drop a handoff or a pass while trying to maintain control of the slick, sodden football. "The ref would dry off the ball with a towel between plays," Billy remembered, "and then stick it right back into the mud." It was a fumble by Donnie Daye, the Go Team's right halfback, recovered by the Maroons, that set up their only touchdown. They missed the extra point, and the half ended with Mississippi State up 6–0.

In spite of the weather conditions—and the turnovers they caused—the Tigers played impressively. Billy ran 57 yards on thirteen carries, caught a 25-yard screen pass, prevented a State TD by knocking down a pass in the end zone, and two of his punts rolled to a stop within the State five-yard line. LSU White Team fullback Red Brodnax recovered a State fumble, allowing for a Warren Rabb to Billy Hendrix touchdown pass. But the ultimate hero of the game was LSU's star kicker, Tommy Davis, who kicked the game-winning extra point, giving the Tigers a 7–6 win.

In his first tackle in a high-school varsity game, sophomore Billy Cannon stopped a Lake Charles High running back named Claude "Boo" Mason. Boo was still playing football, now as a running back for Tulane University, and it was Boo Mason's quote in the New Orleans *States-Item* that inspired the LSU Tigers for their last game of the season. Tulane hadn't beaten LSU since 1948, and Coach Dietzel feared his players would take a victory for granted. When Dietzel, a master motivator, read Mason's quote—"LSU will choke"—he cut it out, had it reproduced, and taped it all over the Tiger locker room.

Tulane was no pushover. Alabama coach Bear Bryant had called Tulane's defense the best he'd played all season, and Green Wave quarterback Richie Petibon would soon be selected All-SEC by UPI. But by the end of the season, the Tigers were at the top of their game, and LSU crushed them 62–0 in Tulane Stadium. *Times Picayune* sportswriter Billy Keefe (the same writer who had reported on Paul Dietzel's introduction of Billy Cannon at an LSU pep rally three years earlier) rhapsodized: "With engineer Warren Rabb at the throttle and firemen 'Cannonball' Cannon and 'Jackrabbit Johnny' Robinson shoveling the coals, a throng estimated at 85,000 sat in on a show of football power that exceeded even the hopes of the most ardent Tiger fans.... Using double reverses that found Cannon, Robinson, and Red Brodnax functioning as never before this season, the Tigers' offense in the last half would have beaten any team in America."

It was a day of glory for LSU, and everyone and everything on the 1958 Tiger team—including the Wing-T offense and the three-platoon system—had a share of the glory. Tulane's lack of depth and the Tigers' three rotating units were determining factors in the lopsided score, but everyone on the Tigers' bench was in top form. "Cannon played magnificently," Keefe wrote, "both on the offensive and on defense. When he wasn't carrying the ball, he was decoying or blocking; when he was carrying the ball, he ran roughshod over the Green Wave, especially in the final quarter, when he had so little resistance."

"The Tigers were running past a tired and beaten team in the final fifteen minutes," according to writer Bud Johnson. "Virtually every play they ran resulted in a long gain. Robinson averaged 9.1 yards per carry; Rabb, 9.0; Cannon, 7.8; and Purvis had 6.5 yards per carry." Billy remembered many exceptional plays. "Johnny [Robinson] made a great catch. Nobody else would have even attempted it. He was running a crossing pattern and had to overextend to reach the ball. He came down stumbling a few steps, but he had it. Then he recovered his balance and took it in for a score." Robinson would win national back of the week honors and Max Fugler would win national lineman of the week.

Another recovery play that stood out was a field goal by Tommy Davis. The snap was too high for the holder, and Tommy caught it. He didn't hesitate. He drop kicked the field goal. "I hadn't seen a drop kick since middle school," Billy said, "and of course he made it. It was Coach Carl Maddox's greatest head shake." Drop kicks remain legal in the NCAA and NFL but are rare.

LSU players and fans took no pity on Tulane. They reveled in demolishing their longtime in-state rival. It was now clear that the 1958

Tigers would go undefeated, guaranteeing LSU a berth in a top bowl game against a national adversary and the possibility of a national championship. But the scale of the one-sided victory was embarrassing for Coach Dietzel, and as the game came to a close, he wanted to mitigate the size of the win.

With the score 55–0 and Scooter Purvis sidelined with an injury, Dietzel sent in Billy with instructions to run out the clock, moving the ball only enough to keep possession. Durel Matherne was at quarterback. "Tell Durel to run it up the middle, keep it on the ground," Dietzel told Billy, "and let's get this thing over with." For Billy, it was an opportunity to defy Dietzel and to get in another run. He wasn't about to slow things down. When he entered into the huddle, he called another play. "We'd come up with this play the week before," Billy remembered, "where Robinson is flanked and I'm in the backfield and Rabb tosses it to me. I got up right on Matherene. 'Durel, Coach Dietzel said to run that toss play to me. Don't wait. Right now!' And like the true quarterback of that era, he called the play, I broke one tackle, and I scored." It was a 45-yard touchdown, Billy's longest of the season. He laughed to recount the consequences. "After the touchdown, Tulane's head coach, Andy Pilney, came out onto the field screaming at Dietzel, accusing him of running up the score and trying to get him fired. And Dietzel was making these hand motions and screaming, 'I didn't do it! I didn't do it!'"

Years later, at an event where Billy and Paul Dietzel were featured speakers, Billy told the audience the story of the last touchdown against Tulane. "Afterwards," Billy said, "Coach Dietzel came up and told me that a Tulane fan claimed to have watched through a pair of binoculars Dietzel calling that toss play. 'Well, Coach,' I said, 'next time you see him, tell him I did it. I've been accused of a lot of stuff, but that one I did!'"

The Tigers were invited to play in the Sugar Bowl in New Orleans on January 1, 1959. The game traditionally hosted the Southeastern Conference champion against a top-tier at-large opponent. In the twenty-four-year history of the bowl, LSU had played—and lost—four times. The Tigers were favored to win this year's matchup against Clemson, an 8–2 unranked team.

"They were good," Billy remembered, "better than we expected."

The game remained scoreless until the third quarter. Time and again, the LSU defense held, but, as Billy put it, "the Clemson defense was as good as any we'd played all season," and it fended off several Tiger advances. Quarterback Warren Rabb had hurt his throwing hand in the first half of the game (later it was found to have been broken), and, as Dietzel noted, "Clemson was putting a lot of pressure on our quarterbacks every time they went back to throw." Dietzel looked to Billy Cannon for help—but this time, not as a runner. The Clemson defense had held Billy to 51 yards on thirteen carries. The halfback run-pass option had worked before. Why not let Billy throw the ball?

"We were somewhere on the inside of their ten-yard line," Billy recalled.

> The version of the play we decided to run was a fake screen to the right. I was delighted because it would give me the chance to throw. If the defense read the play, I could still run it. The two ends— Mickey Mangham to the right and Scotty McClain to the left— fake blocked then ran their patterns into the end zone. As soon as I cleared the outside of the offensive tackle, I could see both receivers were totally uncovered. (That meant, of course, that they were rushing me!) But I got the throw off and it was a pretty good pass. Mickey Mangham caught it and we scored. Scotty McClain (the other end) stayed mad at me for forty years. He always tells me, "I was wide open and I could have been the star," and I tell him, "Yea, but if I'd have thrown it to you, would you have caught it?" We've kidded about it a lot over the years.

Billy later joked that "the game was won by a pass the Lord threw."

After the touchdown, Billy kicked the extra point, and the Sugar Bowl ended in a 7–0 Tiger victory. Billy called his Sugar Bowl Most Valuable Player trophy "one of the most meaningful outside of the Heisman."

Honors, Adulation, and Repaying a Debt of Friendship

Predictably, the LSU team, its players, and its head coach were showered with honors and awards. By a wide margin, both wire services voted LSU as the national collegiate championship football team, and Paul Dietzel was voted Coach of the Year by various organizations. For the first time in history three backs from one team (Cannon, Robinson, and Rabb) were named by the Associated Press to the All-SEC team. Billy and Max Fugler were selected for *Look* magazine's All-America team. Billy finished third in the Heisman Trophy balloting behind halfback Pete Dawkins from Army, the winner, and Randy Duncan, a quarterback at Iowa.

It is an irony that Dietzel's three-platoon system, so successful on the field, possibly hampered Billy's statistical standings. Each of the three units played roughly a third of each game. On another team where he might have played the entirety of each game, Billy's statistics almost certainly would have been much higher.

"In Baton Rouge," Billy remembered, "we were the toast of the town. You couldn't go anywhere without being surrounded by people who wanted to congratulate you and to talk about the games and the season. It was a smaller town back then. This place loved the Tigers. But even as the town has grown, the love for LSU football has grown with it."

A prized memento of their extraordinary season was an LSU championship ring. Billy described it has having various symbols of the university: the Campanile tower, Tiger Stadium, mascot Mike the Tiger. "My guess is that Coach Dietzel, artist that he was, designed it," Billy said. "It was unique and beautiful—the prettiest championship ring I've ever seen. I was driving home and passed Moran Motors and stopped in to see the man who had been there for me." It was Ralph Moran, owner of the dealership, who had convinced Billy to go to LSU by pledging his support if and when Billy ever needed it. "And I did need his help from time to time—especially in the early days before tickets were selling. My freshman year, we played only three games and my sophomore year, we hadn't won that many, but that wasn't the point. He was a backbone for me, a support."

After they shook hands, Billy took off his championship ring and gave it to Moran. "This was in the day when only players and coaches got a ring. He didn't want to take it; he said it was too precious." Billy wouldn't take it back. "You try it, Mr. Moran, see if it fits you, and if you don't like it, you can return it to me." Moran put on the ring. They laughed and talked about the upcoming season.

Billy looked back on the extraordinary year with a sense of appreciation for the many who made it what it was. "I never walked off the field thinking what if this or that. Every down of every play, I gave it everything I had, so that when I walked off the field, I had nothing left to leave. But the whole team was like that the whole year. It was a tremendous effort by every player, by the coaching staff. The strategies, the maneuvers, the play selections." When asked if he has ever had another season to match it, Billy paused before he answered. "No," he said, "but that's because every season is different."

Dietzel's Motivation

Whereas at the beginning of the previous season, the Tigers' future seemed uncertain, popular opinion in 1959 held that the Tigers would have an outstanding year, perhaps even win a second national championship. There was good reason to think so. Billy Cannon, of course, was coming back, along with his All-SEC teammates, Johnny Robinson and Warren Rabb. In fact, of the thirty-five players who constituted the famous three platoons, only three—Billy Hendrix, J. W. Brodnax, and Larry Kahlden—were seniors and would be graduating. The other significant loss was Tommy Davis, whose field goals, punts, and extra points had been critical contributions to the championship season. Davis, it turned out, had decided to give up his final year of collegiate eligibility to join the San Francisco 49ers. The practice was much less common than it is today. Because Davis was three years older than Billy (he had served a stint in the Army after graduating from high school), he wanted to take advantage of his remaining football years as a pro.

But there was an excellent group of rising sophomores joining the 1959 varsity to provide even more of the breadth than the Tigers had enjoyed in their championship year.

Coach Paul Dietzel must have been aware that among the most significant pitfalls his team would face in the coming year were overconfidence and complacency. The "magic" of 1958 which made the team's success seem inevitable had in fact been a fragile one. Many games could have gone either way, and what ended as an undefeated season could have easily been only a winning one. To keep his players sharp, he decided, he would need to keep them humble and self-aware.

Dietzel called Billy Cannon into his office before the beginning of fall practice, 1959. With Dietzel's knowledge and approval, Billy had missed spring practice to compete in track and field. "After we'd exchanged pleasantries, Dietzel told me Scooter Purvis had had an excellent spring practice," Billy recalled, "and that if I wanted to keep my starting position, I was going to have to give it my maximum effort. I was dumbfounded. Since I started playing this game, I had never given anything but my best. I found myself thinking, 'has this man lost his mind?' Of all the meetings we'd had, this was the worst. I had already considered leaving early—the way Tommy Davis had—for the pros. Only later did I find out that Dietzel had also called in Rabb and Robinson to tell them the same kind of thing."

Billy left the meeting fuming. "I never mentioned it to anybody, but it stayed with me. I couldn't quit thinking about it." A few weeks later, near the end of a fall practice, Dietzel called for a goal-line scrimmage with the White Team facing off against a defending Go Team. An off-tackle power play was called. "When Rabb handed off the football to me, a nice hole had opened up, and here came Scooter—trooper that he was—to fill it," Billy remembered. "We were going to hit, but I could have ricocheted off him. Instead, I hit him full force, helmet to helmet, and ran into the end zone. When I looked back, I knew he was hurt. He was on his back, his feet splayed out to the sides. I'd knocked him unconscious. Everything stopped until he came to and responded to questions. Like a lot of my life, I've regretted it ever since. I shouldn't have done it. Scooter didn't have anything to do with it. I was pissed off, and I took it out on him. Scooter is a dear friend and a good man. We weren't competing against each other. We were different kinds of runners who complemented each other. If I'd have tried to do his runs, I'd have broken both ankles." When asked about the incident, Scooter smiled and said he didn't remember it. "But then I wouldn't if I'd been knocked out, would I?"

A Great but Disappointing Season

As predicted, 1959 was a great year for LSU and for Billy Cannon. As they had done the previous season, the No. 1–ranked Tigers knocked off one opponent after the other: Rice, Texas Christian University, Baylor, Miami, Kentucky, and Florida. Their defense was especially strong. In the first six games, the Tigers amassed 103 points, holding their opponents to a total of 6. Billy Cannon was on top of both his offensive and defensive games, making long-yardage sprints, catches, interceptions, run-backs, and goal-line stops.

Much was the same as the year before. The platoon system was put back into service, though there were a few personnel adjustments among the positions. "Again, for every player, it wasn't if he was going to play," Billy said, "it was how many minutes he was going to play. It was good for morale, good for the team."

A big difference in 1959 was strategic. As defending champions, there was more to protect, and there were fewer reasons to take unnecessary chances. Only a year before, unnoticed by the polls, the Tigers had been willing to test a brand-new formation, the Wing-T. "Now we were playing more conservatively," Billy said. "We didn't take as many chances. We played a lot of the old-fashioned T so that we cut back on the reverses, counters, and around-end plays. If we got two touchdowns ahead, we'd shut it down." Even though the Tigers were winning games, Billy remembered that some of the excitement of the previous year was gone. "By our senior year, we knew what he was going to say and when," Billy said of Dietzel's pep talks, calling them "reruns of his Monday night radio shows."

There was no excitement missing at the Cannon household. Dara Layne Cannon, Dot and Billy's third child, was born on September 24, 1959, as the new Tiger season was getting started.

The Run

And there was plenty of excitement among LSU's fan base. Every successive victory produced a new wave of ardor in what had become an almost fanatical student body. By the seventh game—what sportswriters were calling "the game of the year"—the undefeated LSU Tigers against their undefeated archrival, the Ole Miss Rebels, Coach Dietzel wondered if they could be constrained. On October 30, the night before the home game, hundreds of raucous students had discovered and surrounded the practice field where the Rebels were running drills, taunting them with shouts of "Go to hell, Ole Miss! Go to hell!" At 2:00 a.m., Dietzel was called out to calm and disperse the crowd. "Save your voices for the game," he pleaded. "Besides, right now we are only a short block from Broussard Hall, where the team is in bed asleep, I hope. Do you think they can rest with all this noise and bedlam?"

The game lived up to the wildest expectations of its fans. So much has been written of the contest and its game-saving hero, Billy Cannon, that the night has since become the pinnacle of LSU football folklore. The same elements are always repeated: LSU was ranked No. 1, Ole Miss No. 3. It was Halloween, the night was warm and misty, and the stadium sold out. In fact, thousands more than the sellout crowd of 68,000 claim to have been at the game to witness Billy Cannon's remarkable run, and apparently they believe it. "I think people have seen the film of the run so many times," one fan said, "that they've put themselves on the other side of the camera." Billy has himself patiently recited the story of the game and his famous run more times than he can remember.

The game did not start well for the Tigers. Four fumbles, including one by Billy, either extinguished a drive or gave the Rebels good field position. An Ole Miss field goal in the opening quarter put the Rebels up by three, a lead which they jealously guarded into the fourth quarter. The Tigers played brilliant defense as well, but were unable to score. After Billy intercepted a pass and returned it to the Rebels' 36-yard line, Ole Miss Coach Johnny Vaught shut down his team's throwing game. He refused to take any unnecessary offensive risks. It was a damp, muddy back-and-forth battle on the ground. Vaught believed he could win with his aggressive and superior defense. So confident was Vaught in his team's ability to stop the Tigers that deep into the fourth quarter he had his quarterback and kicker, Jake Gibbs, punt on first down.

"They kept punting the ball, sticking us back in a hole," Billy remembered, "and I thought, 'If I can get my hands on this one, I'm going to take it back.'" Billy waited at the 5-yard line as the ball descended. Gibbs's 47-yard kick hit the turf and took a high bounce. As Billy recounted that crucial instant, "We had a rule that we weren't supposed to field a punt behind the 15-yard line, and so I hesitated for an instant. It's hard to believe now, but I thought about letting it go." But the football practically bounced into his arms, and he couldn't resist going for broke. When Billy started running with the ball at the 11-yard line, Dietzel, who had set the 15-yard punt return limit, responded with an anguished "No, no, no!" But, as Billy began to sail past and through defenders, Dietzel changed his cry to an ecstatic "Go, go, go!" "It was," Dietzel said simply, "one of the greatest efforts in the history of college football."

While many have memorialized the run in praise as lofty as Dietzel's (Peter Finney described it as "superhuman"), Billy Cannon told the story of his amazing run with his usual wry understatement. "After I caught the ball," Billy recounted, "the first person looking me in the eye was [Ole Miss linebacker] Larry Grantham. I knew how good he was. I wanted to go to the left toward the open field, but there he was, so I cut back to the right, and he missed the tackle. I started down field, following the sideline, picking up a few blocks, and some guys missed their tackles. Finally, I broke into the open, and there was nobody left but me and Jake Gibbs. Gibbs thought I was going to the wide side of the field, so I gave a little head fake." Billy looked up and grinned. "Now I've got to give Jake great credit on this: That was the only tackle he had missed in his entire career to that point. Of course, with the team he had around him, that was the only tackle he tried to make in four years. After I had the clear sailing to the goal line, it was a question of was I going to make it, was the referee going to beat me there, or was the cameraman gaining on both of us going to outrun the whole bunch."

The often-viewed film of the run shows Billy breaking five tackles before the camera loses sight of him. When it catches up with him again, Billy has, in spite of his telling, left behind all but an official and a cameraman who race to keep up with him as he crosses the goal line, exhausted.

Billy has heard countless fans retell the run from their own perspectives. "It's kind of like Kennedy's assassination," said one zealous fan. "Everybody remembers where they were when it happened." One of Billy's favorite stories was told to him at a party years after the run.

> The man told me he'd bought two tickets up in the second tier of the south end zone. His wife had the flu all week, and her brother was hoping she'd stay that way so he could go. Well, it wasn't until Saturday afternoon that she decided she felt well enough to go (and of course the brother-in-law went off to sulk and listen on the radio at home). About midway through the third quarter, the wife started

to feel faint, and the man took her down to the first-aid station which was right on the back side of the stadium. They laid her on a stretcher and took her blood pressure, and they put some cold towels on her face. He was kneeling there beside her on the stretcher, holding her hand when he heard this roar. The man told me as this roar went up, and got louder and louder, he stretched his wife's arm out as far as it would reach, but he still couldn't see into the stadium, so he dropped her hand and ran to the portal, and saw the last fifty yards of my run, the last missed tackle, and saw me score.

Incredulous, Billy asked the man, "'You don't mean you left your wife on a stretcher to see a play?' About this time, his wife walked up to where we were having our conversation. She heard me ask that question, and she answered for him, 'Yes, the s.o.b. did!'"

Peter Finney, in *The Fighting Tigers II,* describes the tumultuous aftermath of the run. "Oblivious to the tremendous roar during his 89-yard journey, Cannon became conscious of an exploding Tiger Stadium as soon as he crossed the goal line. 'I seemed to hear everything at once,' [Cannon] said. 'I don't think I got hit much harder in the game than I did by my teammates in the end zone. I was lucky to get out alive.'" Amid the bedlam, Wendell Harris kicked the extra point.

But 7–3 was a precarious lead against a team like Ole Miss, and ten minutes were still left on the clock. With surprising ease, under the leadership of sophomore quarterback Doug Elmore, the Rebels pushed back the Chinese Bandits for four consecutive first downs all the way to the 23-yard line. Dietzel pulled out the Bandits and sent in the White Team. With ninety seconds left on the clock, the Tigers dug in, but four plays later, the Rebels had reached the 7 and yet another first down. Three hard plays later, the Rebels had reached the 2. "As middle linebacker, I was in on every tackle," Billy remembered, "backing up the linemen who were plugging the hole, pushing them." On a fourth down that was essentially the last play of the game, Elmore faked inside and kept the ball as he ran around his left end, only to be stopped on the 1 by Warren Rabb and Billy Cannon.

"I knew in my mind, he was going to roll one way or the other," Billy recalled, "I just didn't know which. I had to wait for him to make his fake before I moved. When I saw the fake, I flew to the outside as fast as I could run. All of a sudden, Warren Rabb had his arms around him. I leaped on him to drive him back. It was a brilliant one-man stop by Rabb, and I got there quick enough so we didn't have to worry about whether he could roll or wiggle forward." When the clock ran out, LSU fans rushed onto the field in a madness of joy.

Fred Russell, veteran sports editor for the *Nashville Banner,* summarized the importance of the game for his readers and for football history: "For its fury, suspense and competitive team performances, Louisiana State's heart throbber over Ole Miss was the fullest and finest football game I've witnessed in 31 years of sports reporting."

The Stop

But the season was not over, and for Billy Cannon and the Tigers, the next game against Tennessee would be as heartbreaking as the Ole Miss game was exhilarating. "Everyone was on a high," Billy remembered. "We knew we could beat them handily, but we weren't taking the Vols for granted. We were focused, and practice that week was good. There was good togetherness among the coaches and players. We studied hard what Tennessee would throw at us." Game day in Knoxville was clear and bright, the temperature somewhere below freezing. "It couldn't have been a better day for football," Billy said. "We were ready."

And the Tigers played brilliantly. Before the afternoon was over, LSU had a 19–9 edge in first downs and 334 offensive yards to the Vols' 112 (Billy and Johnny Robinson each outgained the entire Tennessee team). Unfortunately, the statistics did not tell the whole story.

The first touchdown was LSU's with a 26-yard off-tackle run by Billy. The Tigers' 7–0 lead lasted until the third quarter when a Rabb pass, intended for Robinson, was intercepted by Vols linebacker Jim Cartwright, who raced across the goal line. Within two minutes, Tennessee had scored again; with the extra points, the score was now 14–7. A recovered fumble on the Volunteers' 2 and a subsequent TD put the Tigers back into the game. The score was 14–13. A 2-point conversion would give the Tigers the lead, and perhaps the victory. Billy Cannon was sent in to do the job. "Everybody in the stadium, including people who didn't know anything about football, knew they were going to run me off right tackle," Billy recalled, and when he did run that play, Billy was hit by a succession of defenders.

> I will go to my grave believing I went across into the end zone, but when the play was over, the linesman waved his arms that no, I hadn't. The most sickening feeling I've ever had was after getting hit, fighting through, and knowing I'd crossed the goal line with the ball, albeit by inches or less than a foot, and seeing the referee saying no. The play that you would like to have run—bursting through the line like the superman you were the week before—and now you can't gain three yards. The score never changed after that. We lost our chance for the national championship. We were not number one again. We were fifty guys, coming back tired, disgusted, not pointing fingers but upset about the mistakes we'd made. I think on that trip home, the fire burned out.

Years later, someone mailed Billy a copy of a print by artist and Tennessee Volunteers fan T. J. Sharp. Titled simply, "The Stop," it shows three orange-jerseyed defenders holding the line against Billy Cannon. By this time, Billy was in the pros. He showed the print to his young son, Billy Cannon Jr., better known in the family as "Little Bill." Billy shook his head as he told the story. "Little Bill said he loved the picture, and asked me what it had been like. 'Son,' I told him, 'that's a picture of my greatest failure.'" Undeterred, Little Bill said, "Oh, Dad, can I have it?" Little Bill hung the picture in his room until he left for a college football career of his own at Texas A&M.

"Of course when we got home from Knoxville, there was a huge crowd waiting for us at the airport. It was our first loss, and they had been there for so many victories. Don't get me wrong. It was nice, but I don't think there was anything anybody could have said or done to make anybody on our team feel decent. All you felt was rotten—to have worked that hard, that long, and to get beat—not through what they did well but through what we should have done and didn't." To make things worse, Ole Miss beat Tennessee the next week 37–7.

Sugar Bowl

For Billy, feeling the weight of the Tennessee loss on his shoulders, the season seemed over. There were two more games to play—Mississippi State and Tulane—games easily won by LSU and games in which Billy played well, but he called them "flat, anti-climactic, hollow victories."

Finally, the regular season really was over, and, despite the loss to the Volunteers, LSU would have a chance to play in a bowl game. The Sugar Bowl Committee invited the Tigers to play Ole Miss on January 1 in New Orleans. Coach Dietzel and athletic director Jim Corbett called the team together, so the players were told, to vote on whether or not to accept the invitation. "Corbett knew we didn't want to go," Billy recalled, "and he knew if he tried to force us to go, it would be a wasted trip. We weren't dummies. We'd played the game defensively as well as we could," Billy said of the regular-season Ole Miss game, "and had gotten lucky and won the game offensively."

Billy called the vote a charade. "Corbett was really pushing us, telling us how great the game would be for LSU. We ended up voting on the proposal three times. The first time we voted no. Then Corbett offered us ten tickets each that they would sell for us," a financial incentive for the players, "and when we voted no a second time, they let all the red-shirts [team members not part of the game squad] vote. I stood up and said 'Coach, why don't we go to another bowl game,' and he said 'No, we're going to the Sugar Bowl game or we're going to no game at all.' I sat down and shut up. The third time, Max Fugler and I didn't bother to participate, and it passed by three of four votes."

According to Dietzel in *Call Me Coach,* accepting the Sugar Bowl bid turned out to be a bad decision. "From the beginning, I felt that it was a mistake to replay Ole Miss. As it turned out, agreeing to play in the Sugar Bowl was a serious failure on my part. But I also thought it was wrong for some folks at LSU to insist that we play in that game. We quickly found out that we were not ready to play Ole Miss again." The Rebels beat the Tigers 21–0. "It was a sour note to end a fine year." When all was said and done, LSU concluded its 1959 season ranked No. 3 in the AP and Coaches polls.

The Heisman Trophy

Billy was at home when Dot answered the phone. Coach Dietzel and LSU president Gen. Troy H. Middleton were calling to congratulate Billy on his selection to receive the most prestigious honor in college football, the Heisman Trophy. Billy remembered that he and his teammates knew of the trophy, given annually to "the outstanding college football player whose performance best exhibits the pursuit of excellence with integrity," but gave it little thought. "It was a great honor, of course," Billy said, but he hadn't expected to get it. Dietzel told him that reservations were being made to take Billy, Dot, and Billy's parents to the ceremonies in New York City. Coach Dietzel and his wife, Anne, would also attend. It was an honor Billy was happy to accept on behalf of his team. Billy called it "our trophy."

The presentation ceremonies lasted several days and included gatherings with former trophy winners, press events, and national television appearances. The trophy itself was presented to Billy by Vice-President Richard Nixon. "It was an awkward position to hold the trophy and it's heavy," Billy recalled, "so I had to help him lift it and keep it up." He laughed. "I presented myself the Heisman Trophy."

For all the glamour of the Heisman events, what Billy most appreciated was the way his parents were treated. "Everyone was really, really nice to them," Billy said. "They were treated like southern gentry."

The iconic trophy, which depicts a running back in full motion, ball under one arm and the other arm straight out, stiff-arming would-be tacklers, now resides in a glass case in a Baton Rouge restaurant, T. J. Ribs. Former owner T. J. Moran, a friend of Billy's, asked if he could display it for the opening of a new location. "Everybody liked it there," Billy said, "and they ended up building a special display case for it. Members of our team love to take people in to eat and show off their trophy."

Billy returned to Baton Rouge only to receive more accolades. "Billy Cannon Day" was celebrated with a parade through downtown Baton Rouge. Billy, Dot, Harvey Sr., and Virgie were driven in a brand-new gleaming white Plymouth Fury convertible down Nicholson Drive, Third Street, past the Capitol and on to the Governor's Mansion. Stores emptied onto the streets as the motorcade made its way through town. "Third Street was totally lined and backed up," Billy remembered. "Kids were wearing No. 20 jerseys. I saw my old high school coaches on one corner. The Istrouma marching band played. I saw many, many friends." Billy paused. "Baton Rouge didn't look as big that day." At the end of the route, Paul Dietzel and Troy Middleton made speeches thanking Billy, and Governor Earl K. Long presented Billy with a plaque.

Billy Cannon Leaves LSU

Billy's last game for the LSU Fighting Tigers, the January 1, 1960, Sugar Bowl loss to Ole Miss, was also the beginning of his career in the pros. In the end zone, at the end of the game, Billy Cannon signed a contract to play with a brand-new team in a brand-new league—the American Football League's Houston Oilers. Billy would play professional football for eleven more years and would move on afterwards to a career in dentistry and orthodontics, but he would never forget and would always be a part of LSU.

On October 1, 2010, fifty-one years after his famous run, Billy Cannon spoke before friends and fans at a Friday evening reception at the Jack & Priscilla Andonie Museum of LSU sports. He reflected on his many years as a Tiger fan and supporter. "My favorite thing is to come to the football game and eat at the Faculty Club and have a few cocktails. And then, as the sun is going down just about this time of day, I like to walk to the stadium—across the parade ground where I faked passing out to get out of marching with the ROTC, by the Campanile and through the Quadrangle, in front of the library that was being built when we were here, and on down to the stadium that was made into a bowl while we were here, to remember being part of the team that played the first night that stadium ever sold out. It just brings back a flood of wonderful memories of a group of kids that were fantastic to live with and play with." When Billy finished speaking, his fans, as always, cheered.

7

THE PROS

The Signings and the Suit

In the chaotic aftermath of the January 1, 1960, Sugar Bowl Game, two coaches, one from each side, waded toward each other through the jubilation and dejection of their respective fans—winning Ole Miss coach Johnny Vaught with the spring of vindication in every step, the loser, LSU's Paul Dietzel, with grim self-control—to shake hands, exchange a word, and move back to the locker rooms where their players either slumped exhausted in head-hung silence or reveled, roaring and pounding each other.

For Billy Cannon, it was a disappointing end of a celebrated college career. In his three years as a varsity player, he had amassed 2,389 yards from scrimmage—1,867 yards rushing and 522 yards receiving—and scored twenty-one touchdowns, all this on a team that employed a three-platoon system which kept him off the field roughly half of each game. His long résumé of honors included his election as a consensus All-American and SEC Player of the Year in 1958 and 1959, and in 1959, he was named AP Player of the Year, UPI Player of the Year, and received the Walter Camp Memorial Trophy and the Heisman Trophy.

But Billy couldn't linger for long, thinking about the Sugar Bowl loss or his college stats and honors. Already the photographers clustered around him under the goalpost as an attorney for the Houston Oilers—a new team in the new American Football League—stood nearby holding a pen and a lucrative contract. As the cameras' flashbulbs fired, Billy grinned and signed. He hadn't even walked off the

143

field of his last college game, and he was already one of the high-est-paid players in professional football. Before the decade ended, the AFL would merge with the well-established National Football League, and Billy would still be playing professional ball.

Billy was not unaccustomed to limelight, nor was he a stranger to controversy. Still on the field, reporters peppered him with questions about which team he was *really* going to play for. The AFL contract he had just signed was, in fact, his second professional contract in as many months, and now two leagues were battling to get him. In late November of 1959 he had ridden the train from New York City, where he had been celebrating with other college All-Americans, to Phila-delphia, where he had been chosen the number-one draft pick in the long-established National Football League. Billy had posed for pic-tures there as well, sitting between Los Angeles Rams coach Sid Gill-man and general manger Pete Rozelle. The forty-year-old NFL had been busy recruiting—and successfully signing—some of the best college players, determined to quash the upstart AFL before it could call its first play. Among the many NFL draftees who signed early contracts were George Izo of Notre Dame (the number-two draft pick), Charlie Flowers of Ole Miss, and Johnny Robinson of LSU.

Billy and Dot Cannon were at the Waldorf Astoria, enjoying the All-America festivities (including an appearance on the *Ed Sullivan Show*), when Pete Rozelle phoned their room. He promptly offered Billy $30,000 for a three-year contract plus a $10,000 signing bonus, and, for good measure, a $500 "travel check" to come to Philadelphia. At first, Billy deferred, telling Rozelle there was no hurry, that they could meet later in Baton Rouge, but the more he thought about the offer, the better it sounded. It was, after all, substantially more than his friend Jimmy Taylor was making playing for the Green Bay Pack-ers, and, of course, more money than he had ever known in his life. Billy took the train to Philadelphia.

Later, when Billy showed his checks to Dot, he had trouble be-lieving it. "For a kid from north Baton Rouge, it was a different real-ity. They gave me $500 to cover a $20 train ticket." Rozelle assured him both the checks were good. "You can cash the $500 but not the $10,000," he warned Billy, "and you can't tell anybody about this until after the Sugar Bowl." In later months, Billy would deny that the contract was binding and would return both checks, unsigned, to the Rams.

Billy and other top college players had been hearing rumors about the American Football League, created only the year before by a group of wealthy businessmen, including twenty-seven-year-old Lamar Hunt, the son of Texas billionaire H. L. Hunt, and another flamboyant oilman, Kenneth S. "Bud" Adams Jr. Interested in owning teams, they had approached the NFL to expand the league's franchises, but they were rebuffed; the NFL had no interest, they were told, in expanding. Undeterred and with plenty of money, they started their own league, going after the NFL's first-round draft picks with more money than all but the most experienced players were receiving from the established league.

First on their list was Heisman Trophy winner Billy Cannon. If the AFL could snag Cannon, it would give them instant credibility and nationwide publicity. Sometime in December, as he was training for the Sugar Bowl game, Billy got a phone call from one of the new league's major sponsors, Houston Oilers team owner Bud Adams. "The conversation was amiable," Billy recalled. "He said he wanted me to play for Houston. We didn't talk money, but he wanted to fly into Baton Rouge to meet with me. I thanked him, but I said I wasn't interested."

Back in Baton Rouge, preparing for the Sugar Bowl, Billy had all but forgotten the offer when he got a call from his good friend and longtime trainer Alvin Roy. "I've just talked to Bud Adams," Roy said. "These guys are for real. This is big money. I think you ought to talk to him."

"I've already signed a contract with the Rams, Alvin. You know that."

"Listen to me on this," Roy said. "You're going to want to hear what they have to say."

Billy recalled what happened next. "Alvin and I met Bud Adams and his lawyer in the office of Alvin's attorney, R. O. Rush." Rush had agreed to represent Billy in the negotiations. Adams's offer staggered Billy: a $10,000 bonus plus $33,000 per year for three years, guaranteed, even if he got hurt, and $500 for expenses. "It was probably more than anybody was making in the NFL except maybe Charlie Conerly, quarterback for the [New York] Giants and one of the best in that league."

"What about my contract with the Rams?" Billy asked. Rush and the other attorney explained that the contract in Philadelphia hadn't been fully executed—the NFL commissioner hadn't signed—and that it had been postdated and was therefore not binding. Billy gave the unendorsed checks from the Rams—one for $500, the other for $10,000—to the Oilers' attorney to return to Pete Rozelle. "They told me if a lawsuit was filed, that they would defend it, Bud Adams would pay the cost, and that we would win." In time, all of those predictions came to pass.

"I was green, but I knew I shouldn't just take what they offered," Billy recalled, "so I told them I wanted a Cadillac for my father, the biggest one they made, and I wanted the $10,000 in cash." Billy laughed to remember. "Imagine this Houston oil man who could raise millions on a handshake going to the bank asking for $10,000 in cash." Again, Billy was sworn to secrecy. It was also agreed that the signing would be reenacted for publicity at the end of the Sugar Bowl game.

Harvey Cannon Sr. was, of course, delighted when he got a brand-new white, four-door Cadillac Fleetwood. Billy smiled to remember getting the $10,000 in cash. "It turned out to be one heck of a lot of $100 bills."

Billy Cannon was, in effect, leading interference for many other top players. When word got out that Billy Cannon had signed with the AFL in spite of the earlier NFL commitment, there was a rush of other young players doing the same. Longtime teammate Johnny Robinson, drafted and signed by the Detroit Lions of the NFL, accepted a spot on the AFL's Dallas Texans (later to become the Kansas City Chiefs). Ole Miss standout Charlie Flowers originally went with the New York Giants of the NFL but quickly took a better offer from the Los Angeles (later San Diego) Chargers. TCU lineman Don Floyd signed first with the Baltimore Colts, then with the Oilers. Ohio State fullback Bob White agreed to play for both the Oilers and the Cleveland Browns.

Always the lightning rod, it was Billy Cannon who took the heat as the national media began covering the story. On January 8, 1960, the Rams filed an injunction suit in Los Angeles County, claiming that

Billy was bound by their contract and had no right to sign with Houston. As promised, Bud Adams assembled a team of topflight attorneys to represent the Oilers' interests and Billy's. Billy and the Oilers prevailed. In his ruling, handed down in early June of 1960, Judge William J. Lindberg ruled that two of what were actually three contracts (one for each of the three years) had not been signed or filed with the NFL commissioner. The third contract, Judge Lindberg ruled, though properly executed and filed, was invalid because Cannon hadn't had the benefit of advice from anyone other than Rams general manager Pete Rozelle in their one-on-one negotiations. In his ruling, Lindberg called Billy "exceptionally naive . . . a provincial lad untutored and unwise in the ways of the business world." The characterization amused Billy. Even in an age before players regularly hired agents to represent them, "they were generous to call me naive," Billy admitted. "The truth is I was green as a gourd, but I got more money than I thought there was in the world, and I also helped raise the salary for every football player that's played since."

Finally, Football

The Houston Oilers had pledged over $100,000 to acquire their Heisman Trophy winner and more than $37,000 defending him, but both the team and the league were elevated by the publicity they received in the process. The question now: Was Billy Cannon worth it? That question could only be answered in the months and years to come.

For his part, Billy was happy to walk out of the courtroom and onto a football field, an arena where, even if he was a rookie, he was far from untried or naive. Perhaps not surprisingly, in the first games of the season—and sometimes even in practice with his own team— Billy was the target of jibes and ferocious hits. At the line of scrimmage, one lineman taunted, "You come over this way, Cannon, and I'm going to get a piece of your contract." After an unsuccessful run, at the bottom of a pile of defenders, Billy was told by a helmet, face-mask-to-facemask with his, "Not so good on that one were you, Mr. High Dollar!" Billy understood and expected the early treatment he got, and held it against no one. He was making more in a year than some of the veteran players would make their whole career. And, of course, trash talk was then, as it is now, a part of the game.

Football was played differently in the pros from how it had been in college, so there was plenty to learn. It was a more wide-open style of offense with much more passing—especially in the AFL, which was offering a more exciting variety of the game to draw new fans. Also, professional players were more specialized. "You had to have a talent and sharpen it to be effective at this next level," Billy said. The speed and the power of his running had always been Billy's gifts, and they remained so. "All I really had to do was adapt to new plays and blocking patterns. I was a quick study. By the end of that first training camp, I was set."

Four Years, Three Coaches, Two Championships, 3,374 Yards, and One Injured Back

The AFL and its eight teams were brand new, thrown together in intense but hurried negotiations involving players, coaches, stadiums, and media time. Many early skeptics wondered if the league would last. Billy too thought more than once that he might have to go back to the NFL, hat in hand, to find a place to play, but then, as he said, "my checks never bounced."

From the beginning, Billy didn't get along with his coach, Lou Rymkus. Nicknamed "the battler," for his toughness as a tackle in the NFL, the six-foot four-inch, 240-pound Rymkus had helped the Cleveland Browns win five championships. Although he had worked several times as an assistant, Houston was his first head coaching job. Billy called him "unpleasant, confrontational, with a nasty disposition and an oversized ego. It was obvious he didn't like me either. I was making more money than he was, and he would allude to it in front of others in a sarcastic way. And it wasn't just me. If he had a problem with someone, he would make snide remarks about them in team meetings. It was unprofessional."

Nor did Billy agree with Rymkus on an overall strategy for the team. "We had ended up with a talented but raw group," Billy said, "a combination of high-paid rookies and veteran NFL players. It was a group you could have molded into a winning team for years to come, but Rymkus's total emphasis was on winning now—not down the road, not next year, but now." Billy contrasted Rymkus's style with that of Al Davis, who would later coach Billy at Oakland. "Davis took the long view and slowly built a program that held up, that was successful for many, many years."

One of the veterans on the Oilers was quarterback George Blanda. Billy credited him with the team's first successes. By the time he signed with Houston in 1960, Blanda had already played eleven years with the Chicago Bears. An outstanding kicker as well as a passer and strategist, Blanda would play professional football for twenty-six years, the longest career of anyone in the sport, finally retiring in 1976 at the age of forty-six.

Billy's first pro season was one of learning and success. He led his team in rushing with 644 yards, but he was a leading receiver too: five of Billy's seven touchdowns were pass receptions. He was also returning kickoffs and punts. "During that early era, we'd throw forty to forty-five passes per game," Billy recalled, "way beyond what college teams were doing."

The emphasis on passing was reflected in the statistics. Wide receivers Bill Groman and Charley Hennigan led in receiving with 1,473 and 722 yards, respectively. Billy was fourth with 187 receiving yards, but after a great running game and scoring on an 81-yard pass from Blanda to seal the victory in the AFL championship game, Billy was voted Most Valuable Player.

Under Blanda's leadership and with Billy Cannon running and receiving out of the backfield, the untried Oilers ended their inaugural season with a 10–4 record, earning the AFL Eastern Division title and defeating the Los Angeles Chargers 24–16 for the AFL Championship at Houston's home field, Jeppesen Stadium.

In spite of the success of his first season as head coach (he was named the 1960 AFL Coach of the Year), Lou Rymkus would not last his second season at Houston. "His award made him even crazier," Billy remembered. "Now he knew everything about everything." After the Oilers lost two of the first three games in 1961, Rymkus boasted of their next opponent, "I'll shoot myself if we lose to Buffalo." When the Oilers lost that one too, Rymkus didn't keep his promise.

The Oilers played the Patriots next in Boston. Players were beginning to hear rumors that Rymkus was going to be fired. As was his custom, Rymkus talked to his players after a pregame meal. Aware of what was at stake for him, he did his best to get his team motivated. The atmosphere was tense. "The more he talked," Billy said of Rymkus, "the more emotional he got. I was looking down at my plate. It was embarrassing. I didn't want to make eye contact with him. We were just suffering through it." As he coached the punt team to extend its defensive coverage evenly across the field, Rymkus found a metaphor that he liked: "We've got to spread the net." Billy remembered how Rymkus kept repeating the phrase: "We've got to spread the net, spread the net." Billy was sitting next to wide receiver Bill Groman, who was also looking down, his forehead resting on his fist. Groman said it quietly, but everybody heard. "Dammit, we forgot to bring the fucking net!" Billy and the others struggled not to laugh.

The night before the game against Boston, Billy got a call from a friend, Sid Adger, an influential Houston oilman who had played basketball at LSU and was close to the Oilers' owner, Bud Adams. Adger told Billy that the decision had been made to terminate Lou Rymkus. "He told me not to worry, to play as hard as we could, because they were going to fire Rymkus, win or lose," Billy said.

The Oilers did play hard, and so did the Patriots. The two teams traded touchdowns and field goals through three quarters of play and into the fourth. In the final minutes, with Houston trailing 28–31, the Oilers faced a fourth-down decision—to go for a first down and risk losing the game or to tie the game with a field goal, a virtual certainty with Blanda kicking from the Patriot's 24-yard line. In the huddle, Blanda looked over at Billy. "He didn't say a word," Billy remembered, "but he was asking me what I thought." Billy told Blanda his inside news in a few short words, "Kick it. They're going to fire the son-of-a-bitch anyway." Blanda kicked, and the Oilers ended the game with a 31–31 tie. The next day Rymkus was fired.

Wally Lemm stepped in as head coach. Lemm had left his position as the Oilers' defensive backfield coach at the end of the 1960 season. "Everybody was glad to see him back," Billy recalled. He described Lemm as "low-key, intelligent, likable." But the new head coach had the sudden and unenviable job of salvaging a losing season. Lemm did more than salvage the season, Billy said. "He totally turned us around." The Oilers won ten consecutive games which included their second AFL championship.

It was an astonishing comeback, and Billy Cannon, ending the 1961 season as the AFL's leading rusher with 948 yards, was a major part of it. In one game alone, a 48–21 victory over the New York Titans, Billy rushed and received for 373 yards, setting the record for single-game all-purpose yards, and scoring a total of five touchdowns—three rushing and two receiving. Once again, Billy was named the MVP of the AFL championship game, a 10–3 victory over the Chargers, and for the first time, he made first team All Pro. It was a heady time, and the future seemed limitless for Billy and the Oilers alike. But it was not to be for either.

In February of 1962, Billy got word from a teammate, fullback Dave Smith, that Wally Lemm was not coming back as head coach of the Oilers. After making a verbal commitment to Houston for the coming year, he had taken the top coaching job with the St. Louis Cardinals, so he said, because of its proximity to his home in Lake Bluff, Illinois. Strangely, Houston's replacement, Pop Ivy, had just left as head coach of those same Cardinals, and with only a mediocre record. Sports-writer Mickey Herskowitz, described Ivy as "tall, soft-spoken, shy . . . more like the corner grocer than a coach. He did not communicate well with his players and was not public relations conscious." Billy called him simply "very bland."

The Beginning of the End at Houston

In spite of the rapid turnover of coaches, the Oilers were at the top of the league, and Billy was at the top of his game. In 1962, the Houston Oilers were primed for another successful season. Although Billy was not a fan of his new coach, Pop Ivy, the team had won two consecutive league championships, and the roster was loaded with talented players such as George Blanda, Charlie Tolar, Bill Groman, Charley Hennigan, Bob Talamini, and Dave Smith. "Pop used a different offensive set," Billy said. "He had us in the wing, which I was used to from college. He took me off the punt return team, but I was still returning kickoffs, and I was catching more passes. Our defense was playing extremely well."

Houston won its first game 28–23 in Buffalo against the Bills, then lost to the Patriots 21–34 in Boston the next week, but it was the third game against San Diego that would change Billy's life as a football player forever. He described the play.

I was running from left halfback to off right tackle, a play I'd run maybe a thousand times in my career. We didn't have a hole. The linemen had made their blocks but the hole was jammed up, just a pileup. I'm flying because I'm anticipating breaking through, but bodies are stacked up, so I hurdle over the pile. In my hurdling, one of the defensive guys who was blocked and down, reached up and grabbed my back foot. Now I'm ass over teakettle. It was an awkward fall, since I wasn't expecting it. I'd never fallen like this before (and I haven't since). I fell forward, flat onto the ground, with the ball to the side. Emil Karas, a linebacker with the Chargers came in and dropped both knees on my back. He hit me right in the middle of my lower back. I didn't skid or turn. There was nothing to give but the body. I never felt pain like that in all my playing career.

The trainers came out and helped Billy, dizzy with pain, to the sideline. "I was hurting bad. But it's the old story, you sit there and you feel a little better, and a little better. So I told Ivy, 'I'm ready to go in.'" Billy conceded it was a mistake. He took a handoff from Blanda, but made it only four or five steps before his back shut down. "I slowed, went down to both knees, then fell over." Because no one had tackled him, the ball was still in play. "The first guy on the scene was the Chargers' Ernie Ladd, a six-foot nine-inch, 310-pound defensive tackle who had played at Grambling. He was a huge man. He could have drilled me the way the other guy did—I couldn't do anything to protect myself, I was in utter pain, I couldn't even roll over—but he just tapped me on the shoulder, and the play was over. Years later, in a Pro Bowl game, I thanked Ernie for not killing me. He told me, 'Old folks, I knew if you hadn't been hurt bad, I couldn't have caught you.' And we both had a big laugh."

Billy wondered if his career in football was over. "The doctor looked at me every day, I continued stretching and rehab, but I couldn't help thinking I might have played my last game." Billy had never enjoyed watching from the sideline. "I wanted us to win, and I didn't want to be a distraction, but I wasn't doing anything but watching. It scared the hell out of me."

Billy doesn't remember in which game he returned to the lineup, but when he did, even with the injury healed, Billy experienced a loss of confidence in his body. "I still had speed, but I couldn't cut as well. My movements were a little more tentative, I'd lost something off my edge. I was playing well but not the way I'd played in '61 and not the way I felt I should be playing."

But Billy's 1962 season was by no means a waste. He finished the year with thirteen touchdowns and 925 yards from scrimmage, second only to Charlie Tolar. He returned eighteen kickoffs for an additional 442 yards (an average of 24.6 yards per return), and he even completed two passes for 46 yards.

The Oilers ended the regular season with an 11–3 record, good enough to win the East Division title and to earn a trip for the third time to the AFL championship game, this time against the Dallas Texans. Played in a muddy Jeppesen Stadium, the game was dubbed by one sportswriter as "the longest day" since it went into double overtime. It turned out to be one of the longest games in the history of the sport. Billy and Charlie Tolar did much of the running from a double wing formation. Tolar, in the off-season an oil-well firefighter, lived up to his nickname of "the human bowling ball" by repeatedly running over Dallas defenders. As the game progressed, Blanda threw the ball more, connecting with Billy and Charley Hennigan. But when the fourth quarter ended, Houston and Dallas each had seventeen points, sending the game into a sudden-death overtime.

Near the end of the first overtime period, the Oilers were easily within Blanda's field-goal range. "In the huddle," Billy remembered, "I told George, 'kick that ball through there, and let's get this thing over with and go home.' But he said, 'No, I want to run this play first.' We ran an off-tackle play action. George faked the ball to me and did a short roll to the right. When he threw it, this kid with Dallas [Bill Hull] made a great interception and took it the other way." The game continued without a score well into the second overtime period before Dallas kicked its own field goal and won the game 20–17. "With that loss," Billy said, "on top of the injury, the lost playing time, and struggling to recover enough to play decent football again, what an empty feeling after that game."

Billy Leaves the Oilers

Exasperated after the disheartening championship loss to Dallas, Billy told his teammates that he would never again play for Pop Ivy. The prediction turned out to be mostly true. Team owner Bud Adams was enthusiastic enough about Ivy to make him general manager as well as head coach, and though Billy stayed on board for awhile, more troubles with his back and new leg injuries kept him out of play for much of the 1963 season. Adams's confidence in Ivy turned out to be ill-founded—the Oilers ended the 1963 season third in the Eastern Division with a 6–8 record. Adams fired Ivy, and Sammy Baugh became the Oilers' fourth coach in five seasons.

Although he knew and liked Sammy Baugh (eight years earlier, Baugh had been a coach for the East-West Prep All-Star game in which Billy and Max Fugler had played), Billy had had enough of the Oilers. When the new general manager asked him what was needed to bring the Oilers back to top form, Billy said, "Get rid of me and get you some good offensive linemen." Not long afterwards, Baugh told Billy directly that his suggestion had been taken. "I left the team with good feelings and a lot of good friends," Billy later recalled. "It was just time to go."

Raising a Family in the Car

In 1964, as he planned his transition from the Oilers to another team, Billy decided it was also a good time to begin his education for a career as a dentist, a dream he had nurtured since high school. Even before he left Houston to play for the Oakland Raiders, he enrolled in the University of Tennessee School of Dentistry, a program that allowed him to take classes during his off-seasons.

At home, Billy's family had grown. Joining the three Cannon girls, Terri, Gina, and Dara, was the first boy, Billy Abb Cannon Jr., born on October 8, 1961, the Sunday his father had played against the Buffalo Bills. "Little Bill" was the first birth Billy missed, but when the game against Buffalo was over, he managed to get to Baton Rouge, hold his baby, and still be back to Houston in time for practice on Tuesday.

The Cannons were a family in motion. For the next several years, Dot and Billy moved three times each year. Whether it was for training camp in Oakland in August or dental school in Memphis in January, Billy would leave a little early to secure an apartment or rent a house for his family. Back in Baton Rouge, the Cannons built a beautiful new home on Sherwood Forest Boulevard, across the street from a country club, where they would enjoy brief summer respites and major holidays.

"We raised our kids in a car," Dot Cannon said of the years of Billy's combined pro career and postgraduate studies. "We had a station wagon. I would put the seat down and lay out a pallet for them and our little white poodle, and off we'd go. Each girl got the same size box, and they could bring whatever they could fit into that box. We all became master packers." Dot and the four kids would make a vacation out of their trips to Oakland, taking a different route each year and stopping along the way to see the major sites. Billy's oldest child, Terri, remembered, "We'd leave Baton Rouge saying 'y'all' and come back saying 'you guys.' We got to see a lot of things our classmates hadn't, and we'd come back from California with the latest styles that hadn't yet reached the South."

The Raiders: A Slow Build to Glory

Billy was twenty-six when he was traded to the Raiders. From the beginning, he admired Al Davis, his new coach. "It was an enlightening experience to get with somebody who knew what they were doing," Billy said. Davis not only knew football, he was passionate about it. As an undergraduate at Syracuse, he had repeatedly tried and failed to make various college varsity teams, but he became a serious student of the game of football, taking classes in strategy attended mostly by the team's players. Davis remains to this day the only figure in the game to have been an assistant coach, head coach, general manager, league commissioner, and team owner.

Davis knew he wanted Billy; he just wasn't sure what to do with him. In his memoir about the early Oakland days, *Tales from the Oakland Raiders Sideline: A Collection of the Greatest Raiders Stories Ever Told,* quarterback Tom Flores remembered that Cannon "fit in, yet he didn't fit in. He was a cross between a fullback and a halfback."

Davis tried him first at fullback. Billy bulked up from 200 to 240 pounds in order to block for Clem Daniels and the other running backs. "I did my best as a blocker, but it's not what I did best," Billy said. What Billy brought to the position that not all fullbacks possessed was his ability to catch the football—and to beat defenders to the goal line once he'd caught it. "He had great hands," Flores remembered. "Obviously his speed down the field was a weapon too." The coaches decided to alternate Billy's assignments so that he had plenty of opportunities to catch passes from quarterbacks Flores and

Cotton Davidson. Billy ended the season with thirty-seven catches, totaling 454 yards. He scored eight touchdowns for the year, as many as Clem Daniels, and second only to wide receiver Art Powell, one of Oakland's all-time leading receivers.

For his part, Billy respected the players around him, most of whom he'd competed against for the last four years. Billy was particularly taken with quarterbacks Flores and Davidson. Davis used them both. "They roomed together," Billy recalled, "and were great friends. There was a great interchangeability between them as players, and they pulled for each other as much as they did for themselves."

Davis's second year with Oakland, 1964, Billy's first, ended with a record of 5–7–2, all the more disappointing because the team had done so well the year before. "It was not fun," Billy recalled, "being on a team that loses five games in a row. It's basically unacceptable for a pro." But Billy's confidence in Davis and the team remained strong. "Davis was still bringing in new players, and he was trying out people in different positions to find the best configuration of players on the squad. We won five of the last eight games, including the last game. Everybody knew the organization was getting better. He was gathering the pieces and putting the puzzle together. What made it fun to be part of the team wasn't that we had a great year but that we were building, improving. Next year, with a little help, we'd be better."

But Billy didn't think he was contributing from the fullback position as much as he could, so he was not surprised when Davis called him in after practice near the end of the season and told him he was moving him "to the outside," that is, to either tight end or wide receiver. "Billy, you're not a fullback," Davis said. Billy laughed. "Why didn't you just ask me when you hired me? I could have told you that!"

As the 1965 season opened, Billy assumed that he'd be named as a wide receiver on the right side since the great Art Powell, "as good a receiver as there was in either league," was on the left. The position suited Billy. He called a wide receiver "a running back with a defensive back mentality," and he had repeatedly proved himself on both sides of the line of scrimmage. Davis told Billy he'd need to trim down for his new position. "It was the first time in my career I'd been told to lose weight," Billy said, but he happily spent his summer working out with weights, playing handball, and denying himself his usual second and third helpings at the dinner table, in the process slimming down from 240 to 196 pounds. Billy returned to training camp in August fit and ready to play.

New Kid on the Block

Between the time Davis talked to Billy in the spring and August training camp, Davis drafted a young player named Fred Biletnikoff, an All-American receiver from Florida State University. "The first time you saw him run a pattern," Billy said, "you could tell he was going to be a ten-year player." Biletnikoff, in fact, played for the Raiders for fourteen years and helped coach the team after that. An inductee into both the College Football Hall of Fame and the Pro Football Hall of Fame, Biletnikoff was ranked number 94 on *The Sporting News* list of the "100 Greatest Football Players." A pro receiving award was created in his name. Billy described him as "a fierce competitor, tough as a boot, and one of the hardest-working receivers outside of Charley Hennigan I've ever been around."

Despite the appearance of the newly recruited receiver, Billy was surprised to be called in to see Davis before the second game of the season. Davis was direct. "I'm moving you to tight end." Billy's response was immediate. "'You're not moving me anywhere.' I told him. 'I'm not playing tight end. Put me on waivers [cut from the roster and allowed to be a free agent], I'll find a job, I can still play. I'm not going to play tight end.'" Billy smiled as he remembered the moment. "And I may have cursed him a little bit in there too."

Davis was unperturbed. He assured Billy the new position would be temporary, three games maximum. "Just play there for me until I get some other players."

At the next practice, Billy got the ribbing he expected. It was too good for his teammates to resist—the one-time Heisman Trophy-winning running back had been relegated to blocking and running decoy patterns and short-yardage routes—but he took it in the good-natured spirit in which it was intended. As he described their jokes, "they put that needle in my ass many times that week." But for Billy, the disappointment opened up a possible new way to play the position. He knew he wasn't a great blocker, but how, he wondered, could he use not only his catching ability but his speed to excel as a tight end?

The learning curve was steeper than Billy expected. Linemen constituted a team within a team, and he was now part of it. "We went over to work on the seven-man blocking sled. It was the first time I had lined up as a tight end. I was on the left side. I was going to hit the dummy with the six other guys and move this big sled—with two coaches standing on it—about five yards. The quarterback gave the count, the snap was on two, and I fired out into the dummy. I realized in an instant that my start was a lot quicker than those big linemen, but I couldn't pull back. I hit the sled one count before anybody else touched it, and it knocked me on my ass." Again, the team got a good laugh at Billy's expense. Lesson learned: "I never beat them to the punch again."

In general, Billy adapted quickly to his new position, blending in with the rest of the line and, for the first time, giving the team a deep threat at tight end. Billy was twenty-eight, but he still had plenty of speed. He could get in the open, catch the ball, and then widen his distance from linebackers and safeties. But the transition was not without its frustrations, especially early on. His first game at tight end was against the San Diego Chargers. From the right side, he faced off against six-foot-five-inch, 260-pound Earl Faison at defensive end. Billy had already started trying to regain some of the weight he'd lost over the summer, but at about 200 pounds, he was much the smaller player. Faison easily kept Billy in check, unable to get in the open. When the game was over, Billy was walking off the field, disgusted, when Al Davis came up, wanting to talk. "I turned and started cursing him," Billy said. "I kept cursing and kept walking. He stayed with me step for step from about the forty-yard line to the twenty-yard line. You could see the other players scattering in every direction. He never got to say a word, and finally, he turned around and walked off. Of course I knew I was way out of bounds, and I assumed I'd be on waivers by the next morning. But to his credit he let it go, and I never heard another word about it."

Billy funneled his frustration into mastering the skills and techniques of the tight end position, an assignment which, in spite of Al Davis's promised three-game limit, Billy occupied until he left Oakland in 1970. He honed his blocking skills. He learned to work as a member of the line, especially in coordinating with the offensive tackle to double-team defenders (big, quick, square-bodied Harry

Schuh was Billy's favorite). And he learned to split out slightly and utilize his starting speed to more quickly get around defensive ends like Earl Faison.

Throughout the 1965 season, Coach Davis continued to bring in younger players and to recycle or cut older players, each change intended to produce a more efficient organization and a balanced, dynamic team. And the Raiders were steadily becoming such a team. The 8–5–1 record was a clear improvement over the previous year. Despite its second-place finish in the Western Division, the team was poised to continue its upward movement. "Coaches, players and fans could all sense it," Billy remembered. "We were going somewhere."

Personally, it was a humbling year for Billy. He caught only seven passes for 127 yards, none for touchdowns. "The offense just didn't use the tight end much," he said. But he too was in tune with the direction of the team as a whole. "Art Powell and Fred Biletnikoff both had great years. You could see Freddy coming on stronger and stronger. We were running lots of deep patterns." It reminded Billy of his sophomore year in high school. "My job was to be patient and keep improving."

One Step Closer to the Super Bowl

Before the 1966 season began, Al Davis left his coaching spot at Oakland to become AFL commissioner. The league decided it could use Davis's prodigious recruiting skills in the continuing war with the NFL for players. He focused on picking up NFL quarterbacks such as Roman Gabriel of the Los Angeles Rams and John Brodie of the San Francisco 49ers, whose contracts had expired. The bidding war pushed salaries ever higher (Gabriel received a $100,000 bonus), luring the best players from the weaker NFL teams and ultimately forcing a merger between the leagues.

Fearful of Davis's poaching and the escalating player salaries it was producing, the NFL (not the AFL as is sometimes assumed) initiated merger talks, held in secret without the knowledge of the new AFL commissioner. The merger was announced in June 1966 but wouldn't be fully consummated until 1970. Until then, the two leagues would maintain their regular schedules and would play an annual AFL-NFL World Championship Game, which would eventually become America's annual extravaganza of media saturation and its holiest of holy days: the Super Bowl. When the merger was complete, each of the old leagues would become a conference in the new merged league, to be called the National Football League. Davis returned to the Raiders as general manager, appointing his offensive coordinator, Johnny Rauch, as the new head coach.

In spite of his apprenticeship at his new position and his having to alternate with a rookie tight end named Tom Mitchell, Billy had a better season with the Raiders in 1966. He doubled his number of receptions from the previous year, totaling 436 yards, an average of 31.1 yards per reception, and he contributed two touchdowns (two more than the year before).

And Billy remained a fan favorite. "I was basically splitting time with Tom Mitchell," Billy remembered, "but when he'd get into trouble, they'd put me in. One day we were playing in Oakland and they called me off the bench. They told me they'd throw to me in the corner, they gave me the number of the play, and I jogged in. It was third and eight. I split out a little at the line of scrimmage, went down and around the corner past the safety. It was about a twenty-yard completion. When I made my catch, and jumped up into the stands, fans were slapping my back and helmet. All the way back to the bench, the fans were leaning over, and I was slapping their hands. Before I sat down Rauch started swinging his arms and yelling at me, 'Go back, damnnit, get back in the game!'"

The Raiders' 1966 record of 8–5–1 was a duplicate of 1965, but that didn't discourage Billy or his teammates. "Again," Billy said, "great new players were coming in all the time, and you could feel the team building and getting better." Over the next three years, Rauch added three talented linemen to the roster to join the team's anchor, center Jim Otto. Billy knew, when he watched them play, the impact they would have. "From the day these guys walked onto the field, they had 'All Pro' written all over them. That's when we knew the corner was turned and that we were heading to the top of the heap." The three newcomers were tackles Harry Schuh and Art Shell, and guard Gene Upshaw. Upshaw and Shell would be voted into the Pro Hall of Fame, and Shell would twice be head coach at Oakland.

By 1967, Al Davis was very much at the helm, not only as Oakland's general manager but as one of its three owners. That year, Davis acquired two new quarterbacks who would complete what would become the 1967 AFL championship team. Billy was instrumental in the acquisition of the first, George Blanda, his old teammate on the championship teams in Houston. By now, Blanda was 39, still a reliable placekicker, but would likely have been considered a risk by anyone but Davis. "Al asked me if he should get Blanda," Billy recalled of a conversation with Davis. "Would he fit in with the young kids, he wanted to know. 'He's crotchety and crusty,' I told him, 'but he'll play for you.' 'I just want him to kick,' Davis said. 'No,' I insisted, 'he'll *play* for you!'"

Acquiring Blanda was an inspired move. Still one of the best kickers in either league, Blanda was, as Billy argued, still very much a player, and he would serve as an ideal mentor for the second quarterback the Raiders acquired—Daryle Lamonica. Early in his career, Lamonica had been a backup for Jack Kemp on two AFL championship Buffalo Bills teams. He became a star at the Raiders. Under the mentorship of George Blanda, who became known as "The Grand Old Man," Lamonica acquired his own nickname, "The Mad Bomber," for his ability to connect long passes under almost any situation. Lamonica led the 1967 Raiders to a 13–1 record and a 40–7 victory over Houston for the AFL Championship.

The team Davis had labored to build was now complete. "Everything fell into place at the right time," Billy recalled. "The line, which was already rock solid, was rejuvenated by Schuh and Upshaw, providing running room for Clem Daniels and Hewritt Dixon, and great pass protection for Lamonica to set up and reach the deep receivers." Billy marveled at the way Blanda and Lamonica complemented one another. They were very different from the former quarterback duo of Cotton Davidson and Tom Flores who, as players, were in many ways much alike. "Lamonica could put the ball in a martin hole at a hundred yards," Billy said, "but George could read a defense like no one else. When Daryle got in trouble, Blanda would step in and take us down the field—and he was still a great passer." Oakland had receivers too. "Art Powell was gone," Billy recalled. "but Warren Wells came in from Kansas City and was a perfect bookend to Fred Biletnikoff."

For Billy, the AFL championship victory over Houston was particularly sweet. It was played the last day of the year in the Raiders' new venue, the Oakland–Alameda County Coliseum. Oakland took a 10–0 lead in the second quarter on a Blanda field goal (one of four he would kick that day) and a 69-yard run down the left sidelines by Hewritt Dixon. Lamonica faked a field goal and passed to Dave Kocourek to close the half at 17–0. Houston did not score until the fourth quarter, when they already trailed 30–0. The Raiders kept scoring, finishing the game with a 40–7 win.

Super Bowl II

The win against Houston meant a place in the Second AFL-NFL World Championship game (known retroactively as Super Bowl II), where the Raiders would meet the NFL champions, the Green Bay Packers, at the Orange Bowl in Miami. Even without Green Bay legends Paul Hornung and Jim Taylor, the Packers won the NFL Central Division with a record of 9–4–1 and postseason victories over the Los Angeles Rams and the Dallas Cowboys.

"We had a couple of weeks to get ready for the game," Billy recalled. "We had a good game plan, we looked sharp in practice, and we thought we could win. The Packers had won Super Bowl I the year before, and we looked at many of their films. When we got to Miami, there were lots of people and lots of excitement." Dot and Billy's parents came down for the game.

Billy conceded that the press coverage didn't compare to later Super Bowls, "but it was still a media circus. Everybody was scheduled for an interview, and reporters were throwing out statistics and questions by the bushel. The Packers were favored, and we kept getting asked, 'Do you think you have a chance?' We thought we could win, but I wasn't ready to make predictions this time."

And for good reason. Quarter by quarter, Green Bay steadily accrued field goals and touchdowns while Oakland was able to score only once in each half, both times with a pass from Lamonica to wide receiver Bill Miller. Later Billy reflected on the game: "Were we in over our heads? I don't think so. Nobody had his best day, but we were in the game the whole time. George Blanda was great, but the rest of us were not."

Billy described his lowest moment of the game: "Early in the fourth quarter, we had the ball and were in good field position. It was third down. Lamonica called a crossing pattern for the tight end. And I couldn't wait because that was one of the few patterns that I knew we could catch and move the ball a good distance and maybe even score. Once I cleared the linebacker and started across, I knew I was going to be in the open, and I had a chance to score and get us back in the game. We needed something to happen. As he delivered the ball—perfectly—my head was up the field, I was already making the cut back up the sidelines to score, and I dropped the damned ball. I think that was the clumsiest drop of my career. It was not a good day for me or the black and silver." The Raiders lost the game 33–14.

But overall, it had been a great year. Billy's own contributions to the championship season were substantial. Once again, he more than doubled his offensive stats from the year before, receiving thirty-two passes for 629 yards and adding ten touchdowns. He led the league as a tight end and was named an AFL first-team All-Pro.

A Long Farewell to Football

As the Raiders entered the 1968 season, Billy was thirty-one years old. He had no illusions that he was the same player who entered the pros in 1960, but he also had no intention of quitting football. The disappointing end to the 1967 season was mitigated not only by the Raiders' winning record but by confidence that the team Al Davis had taken so long to assemble was still together and poised to win more games. "Everybody was looking for another great season," Billy recalled. "Like the rest of the team, I was thinking, 'we'll win it next year.' We were a solid football team. We were just not solid on that given day."

Davis had, in fact, patiently and painstakingly constructed a team and an organization that was built to last. Between 1967 and 1969, its last three years in the AFL, Oakland led the league, compiling a 37–4–1 record. After Billy left the Raiders in 1970, the team's success continued into the next decade with six division titles and six AFC championship games. In 1976, the team captured its first Super Bowl championship by defeating the Minnesota Vikings in Super Bowl XI.

Billy's pass receptions declined with each of his last two years with the Raiders. In 1968, he caught twenty-three passes for 360 yards and six touchdowns. His 1969 totals were twenty-one completions for 262 yards and two touchdowns. He believed those statistics didn't reflect what he wanted to do and could do. He was frustrated. "We were three or four games into the '69 season. I was running decoy routes up the middle. Nobody was close to me, and Lamonica continued to throw the long ball into double coverage. It was giving me a bad case of the red ass. We were in practice one day, and I ran the pattern, and for some reason, on that day, he threw it to me. I made a less than half-hearted attempt to put my hand up and catch the ball. And I came back to the huddle with the red ass even more because he'd throw it to me in practice but wouldn't throw it to me in a game." John Madden, starting his first year as head coach, came up to Billy and asked him what was wrong. "'Not a goddamned thing!' I told him, and I stormed off. After practice, I went by to see Al Davis [then the general manager] and we had a long talk. I never mentioned it again, and to Madden's credit, he didn't either."

Billy's frustrations were compounded the next year when the Raiders picked a young tight end named Raymond Chester in the first round of the draft. "If Al would have called and told me we were going to go with this young kid, I would have retired and finished up dental school. But I worked out, got in good shape, and reported to training camp."

Later, Billy said that he would have liked to have mentored the rookie. Over the years, he had seen older players pass on their experience and expertise to young players, most recently George Blanda's tutoring of Kenny Stabler, a quarterback who joined the Raiders the same year as Chester. "He had good speed," Billy said of Chester, "but he needed some pointers—to help him get off the line of scrimmage quicker, how to run patterns against this particular guy, things like that. All he needed was a little polish and not much. Unfortunately, he didn't want to take any of my suggestions. In his mind, and to his credit, he was trying to earn the job on his own. I quit trying to help him. He turned out to be a good tight end."

And, of course, Billy *was* on the way out. "It was my time to go," he said. "I had outlasted all my former roommates, and I was rooming with Ben Davidson, a defensive end. We went into a meeting, and I noticed that I wasn't on the special teams positions list as left wing for field goal and extra points. I was second behind Marv Hubbard.

That was the first sign, and I told Harry Schuh I was gone. And then I heard Al Davis wanted to meet with me.

"I walked in and Davis was on the phone—he was always on the phone. When he got off, he said, 'Well, Billy, I guess you know why you're here.' And I said, 'Yeah, you're going to move me back to wide receiver like you promised seven years ago!' After we laughed, he told me what I already knew, he was going to let me go. I thanked him."

Word that Billy was leaving quickly spread, and many teammates and coaches came by to see him and wish him well. He was thirty-three years old. He had been playing football—at Istrouma High School, LSU, and the pros—for eighteen years. Within three hours of his meeting with Al Davis, Billy was on a plane to Baton Rouge.

One Last Run

Alvin Roy had been a friend and mentor to Billy nearly his whole life. He had made Billy and a few other select players part of his first elite weightlifting group at Istrouma High when Billy was a junior. He had continued to train Billy throughout college and even during the summers of his pro years, never charging him a penny. Roy even bought the suit Billy wore when he married Dot. Roy had been instrumental in getting Billy into the AFL with the Oilers, and it was Alvin Roy who gave Billy his final run at football.

Roy had had a groundbreaking career of his own in professional football. Once the game finally got the message that Roy had been preaching in vain for so long—that weights should be a fundamental part of football training—he was in high demand. He was the NFL's first strength coach, working for the San Diego Chargers, Kansas City Chiefs, Dallas Cowboys, New Orleans Saints, and Oakland Raiders. He called Billy from Kansas City and put him in touch with Chiefs head coach Hank Stram, who reached Billy by phone in Chicago where Billy was making arrangements to start postgraduate studies in orthodontics at the Loyola University School of Dentistry.

"'When can you be here?' Hank asked me. I told him tomorrow. 'Okay, be here at eleven.'" Billy drove down from Chicago and stayed with his friend and former Oakland teammate Tom Flores, now a quarterback for Kansas City. Because Billy was still being paid under his Oakland contract, he couldn't practice until the Chiefs "deactivated" that contract and "activated" its own. "We'll get you set up to play by the next game," Stram told him. While he waited for the paperwork to get done, Billy kidded his new coach, "I'm loving this: Al Davis is paying me to play for you." Billy watched from the sidelines at practice and began to learn yet another offense. When he put on his Kansas City uniform for the first time, Stram looked him up and down and said, "Boy, I like you better in red."

At thirty-three, Billy's most productive years were behind him, but he was grateful to get to play, to be in the game, to contribute, to continue to live his philosophy of "individual excellence within a team concept." And in fact, in the 1970 Kansas City season, his last year of football, Billy did get to play. He helped the Chiefs to a 7–5–2 season by catching seven passes for 125 yards and scoring two touchdowns.

Billy's last game of football came near the end of the season. "We were on around the fifteen-yard line. They called a sweep to the right, and I was the right tight end. I was supposed to block the linebacker, and I fired out and got a good hit, catching him off guard and knocking him straight back two or three feet. But in the process I fell facedown, flat, with the bottom of my legs kicked up. Ed Budde was the pulling guard—a perennial all-leaguer, as good as there was in the game—and as he came around, leading the ball carrier, he hooked my right leg and bent it over to the ground. The pain ripped through my knee. I said to myself, 'This ain't good!'"

An orthopedic surgeon agreed that Billy was clearly out for the rest of the year. "When I asked him if I could play another year, he said 'Oh, no! But get the money!' I asked him, 'How will I do as a dentist?' He said, 'Fine.' I told him, 'Doc, you just snapped my suitcase.'"

In *Tales from the Oakland Raiders Sideline,* Tom Flores ponders the legacy of Billy Cannon: "There are heroes, and there are legends. Billy was a legend in the state of Louisiana and in the whole South. In fact, he is still a legend.... Billy was the first real rookie superstar who came into the AFL.... In his first couple of years in the AFL, he was one of the league's foremost running backs." When he became a tight end, Flores says, "Billy set a precedent for what tight ends were going to be in the future because he was one who could go deep.... He was the guy who could catch the ball down the field—30, 40, 50 yards—and then go in for the score."

8

THE PRACTICE

The Dream

The unlikely but lifelong connection between football and dentistry introduced itself to Billy Cannon with several hard hits to the mouth. In the fall of 1955, the Istrouma High varsity squad had just moved up to plastic helmets with a single-bar facemask. These new helmets allowed for good vision and afforded much better protection, but, as Billy discovered, there was still plenty of room left for an elbow or foot to get through to the face. For some reason, Billy kept getting hit in the same tooth—his right lateral incisor. The tooth had grown in slightly back from the other front teeth. "I never knew whether to call it my unlucky tooth—since it kept getting hit—or my lucky tooth—since it seemed to spare the rest of my teeth from getting clobbered too."

After the first hard hit on his "lucky" tooth, Billy went in to see dentist Dr. Carl Baldridge. He had passed Dr. Baldridge's clinic countless times since he and his family moved to Baton Rouge. It was located on one of the main streets in the Istrouma neighborhood, Plank Road. An investor and a member of the board of American Bank, right down the street from his clinic, Dr. Baldridge was known as an excellent businessman, a philanthropist who had made generous donations to the LSU School of Dentistry, and a prominent leader in the community.

Billy already knew Dr. Baldridge, not as a dentist or a community leader, but as an Istrouma football supporter. Dr. Baldridge held the down marker at Friday night games. The dentist was known to be scrupulously honest, which is what made the jokes about him so funny. The Istrouma fans used to kid that, after an incomplete pass on first down, Istrouma would somehow go from first down and ten yards to second and eight. After Billy became the school's most famous running back, people kidded Dr. Baldridge that he had made more yards as a down marker for the Indians than Billy Cannon had as a fullback. It was said that the Istrouma games needed an extra official—someone to keep an eye on Dr. Baldridge. The dentist took the ribbing gracefully.

Dr. Baldridge owned a farm north of Baton Rouge on the way to Alexandria, and once a year, he would butcher some of his calves and throw a barbecue for the Istrouma football team and their families. Billy attended these events, held in an open yard behind the clinic, first with his parents, when Harvey Jr. was a player, and later when he was playing himself.

But now Billy needed to see Dr. Baldridge as a patient. After a severe blow, his "lucky" tooth had abscessed and was extremely painful to touch. He was afraid he might lose it, but the dentist gave Billy a shot and started on a root canal. "It got better, and I was able to go back to practice," Billy remembered, "but he had me come back so he could fill four or five cavities I had."

During one of those follow-up visits, Dr. Baldridge invited teammate Luther Fortenberry, who had driven Billy for his appointment, to take a seat in the exam chair. "He looked at Luther's teeth," Billy said, "and told him to come back the next week. Over a couple of appointments, he filled Luther's cavities. Somehow, before we knew it, one by one, he had fixed the teeth of every player on the team—and never charged any of us a nickel."

Billy was not only grateful; he admired the dentist's generosity, and the success he had achieved that made such generosity possible. "He had his practice and investments," Billy said, "and his wife had a floral shop. He would have these cookouts for the team or for the church [Istrouma Baptist] and you'd always see prominent people there—politicos and community bigwigs. Everybody had a great time. You were served a huge beef steak on a platter with potato salad. People mingled and enjoyed themselves."

As early as high school, Billy had set his sights on a professional football career. That he was also able to envision a life beyond football was extraordinary. Dr. Baldridge was, for Billy, the inspiration and model for that post-football career. "I liked the way he handled himself in the community," Billy said. "I liked that he could afford to give his services away when he wanted to. I liked the way he lived. I liked him. Did I know anything about dentistry? I had one root canal and a handful of fillings. I knew nothing about dentistry, but I wanted to be a dentist."

Asked about what became of his lucky tooth, Billy smiled. "It got kicked out later when I was at LSU."

First Steps

With two years of pro ball behind him, Billy began to plot a course for his second vocation. Unfortunately, he had managed to graduate from LSU without one of the principal science courses—organic chemistry—required for dental school. "I'm not sure what my academic advisor was thinking," Billy said. "I graduated from LSU with an elective course in astronomy, thirteen hours in Spanish, and even a class in music appreciation when what I needed to get into dental school was organic chemistry." LSU, like most universities, offered the course on a semester basis—an amount of time which would have consumed one entire off-season period for Billy, so in 1963, he began looking for schools that worked on a quarter system; there he could make up the chemistry course and still get in one quarter's worth of classes of dental school before having to go back to the Oilers training camp in August.

Billy first heard about Jones County Junior College from a friend whose brother, in much the same situation as Billy, picked up a final course at Jones to get into optometry school. Once Billy had secured his chemistry credit, he would be able to start immediately at the University of Tennessee College of Dentistry in Memphis, which also operated on the quarter system.

In March of 1964, Billy drove up with his transcripts to the campus in Ellisville—a south-central Mississippi town between Hattiesburg and Laurel—to meet with the college president. Billy described him as a "southern gentleman educator," who had already checked into Billy's academic record. "I see you've done well in school," he told the running back, and he assured Billy that the University of Tennessee would accept the chemistry credit when the course was completed. "They were very gracious," Billy said, "to let me come in a little after school had started. After we chatted for about thirty minutes, he told me, 'They're in class over there right now.' He brought me over and introduced me to the chemistry teacher—his brother."

In fact, Billy was treated as a celebrity in Ellisville. He was invited to share a ramshackle apartment house with T. Terrell Tisdale, the dean of men. "T. Terrell was about my age," Billy remembered, "and not married at the time. He was as country as you could get, but he was smart and had earned his PhD in a short time. He was from that part of the country, and had gone to the college at Jones, walking to school and wading across the river every day to get to classes." In time, Dr. Tisdale and Billy became good friends. They would go out together to one or another of the few places in Ellisville to eat. "He introduced me to everyone."

Before long, Billy had settled into a routine. He would drive up from Baton Rouge on Monday morning, go to school all week, and leave for home after class on Friday. "It was easy," Billy recalled. "I went to class from eight to ten-thirty and had the rest of the day to study. There wasn't a lot else to do."

Opposite Ends of the Rainbow

Junior college may have been a light lift for Billy, but dental school was not. It was, in many ways, the academic equivalent of professional football. "For the next several years, I alternated between two kinds of pressure," Billy reflected, "Half of my year was football. Half was dental school. Back and forth between the two—it was like opposite ends of the rainbow."

Billy was long accustomed to one end—the physical grind of sports. "I had trained my whole life for it. It was intense, yes—the chase, the hunt, national television, three games in a row, then the looming playoff games, always trying to make an outstanding play that will give your team the chance to make it to the next level. Play all out but with control so as not to make a mistake. It was pressure but one I was used to. It was fun pressure."

The other end—the demands of dental school—Billy called "a mental game" that took some getting used to. "I really had to dig hard, harder than I ever had in college. There didn't seem to be enough hours in the day to do it and do it well. Back and forth I went: six months of football, six of the school. The real connection between the two was striving to be the best you could be, and to do that, you had to deal with the pressure."

Billy wasn't the only professional football player studying to be a dentist at the University of Tennessee. Another was Gary Cuozzo, an undrafted quarterback from the University of Virginia, hired by the Baltimore Colts as a backup for Johnny Unitas. During Cuozzo's ten-year career, nearly as long as Billy's, he also played for the New Orleans Saints, Minnesota Vikings, and St. Louis Cardinals. The other pro was Louis Guy, a wingback at the University of Mississippi turned defensive back in the pros, who played with the New York Giants in 1963 and with Billy for the Oakland Raiders in 1964.

The three football players shared a lab table—and a cadaver—in first-quarter anatomy. Billy recalled how difficult a task dissection was to master. "The anatomy text books were beautiful, brightly illustrated, showing the arteries in blue going one way and the veins in red going the other, but in a body that's been pickled, everything is the same color. Muscles, arteries, nerves, all mashed together in this poor body. Our first quarter we worked on the head and neck, and after that we got into the torso and the arms. I had no idea how many muscles and nerves you have just in your face. We struggled through it as a group."

In spite of (or perhaps because of) the rigors of dental school and his age, twenty-six, Billy's penchant for clowning hadn't diminished. An extracurricular anatomy-class activity in which he had a part almost got him and his group kicked out of school. The students were well into the second quarter. Billy described their professor as a top scientist, well published in his field, who needed a teaching income to support his research. "Dr. Fitzgerald was a brilliant man and a very nice man but straight-laced, by the book." It was a stifling day in the lab with no air conditioning. "We were so tired we were starting to get goofy," Billy remembered. "In this class was the first woman dental student in the history of the school. Some of the male students came up with this idea to run a string around the penis of one of the cadavers. I had some string in my locker and offered it. Somebody else rigged it so that when she came by, the string was pulled, and the penis went erect. Everybody got a big laugh out of this—until we saw this hand come across and jerk the string away. It was Dr. Fitzgerald. He stormed out, totally upset."

Before the next day's lecture, Billy entered his professor's office to apologize. "I told him, 'I didn't have anything to do with the planning, but I did supply the string that was used. If there are any repercussions, and I hope there aren't, I am as much to blame as anyone. It was juvenile, irresponsible, disrespectful of our fellow student and of you. I accept my punishment, whatever it may be.'" Dr. Fitzgerald listened carefully. "Mr. Cannon," he said, "I'm glad you came in to see me today. If you hadn't, this class would have been a lot smaller than it was yesterday." Dr. Fitzgerald began his next lecture with an invitation. "Gentleman, Mr. Cannon has paid me a visit to discuss what happened yesterday. If any of you would like to do the same, I'd be happy to see you."

Carving Teeth

Learning to carve by hand is an important part of dental school—hours, weeks, semesters of it—in order to achieve the manual dexterity that will be required of a successful dentist. The hands as well as the mind must be trained for "operative dentistry," and the training begins with carving precise wax replicas of each of the individual human teeth, and, over time, making typodonts (models of the oral cavity, complete with teeth and palate), crowns, bridges, and, finally, creating complex dental casts and molds for various materials.

Billy's large hands and lack of artistic training were impediments to precision carving, especially at first. "It was a cross between anatomy and sculpture," Billy remembered. "You started with a wax block and used a carving knife to make each one—bicuspids, molars, incisors, cuspids, and on and on. Each had to be carved according to the dimensions in the text or exactly like the dried tooth they gave you, and each had to be approved by the professor. You went in for three hours at a time, three times per week, and it took about a week for each tooth." The stifling classroom during the summer quarter (May–July) in Memphis—even with the windows open—didn't help either. "It was a perfect formula for frustration."

Having to leave for a season of football and then return to school was in many ways a distinct disadvantage. The endless lists of definitions and identifications associated with each course were easily forgotten and, to some extent, had to be relearned each time Billy returned to Memphis. And because it was taking twice as long to complete the curriculum, Billy could only watch with envy as full-time students moved ahead, graduated, and started their practices. On the other hand, being able to take a break from the relentless study was a relief. He relished the first days of each new football season—the familiar stretching, warming up, putting on his pads, and trotting out onto the practice field. He loved preparing for games, and he loved the games themselves, slicing past a defensive end with a feint of head and body, past a safety in a burst of speed, catching a long, well-thrown pass, striding into the end zone. The full-bore physical pressure of football relieved the tedium and frustrations of dental school. And when the season was over, bruised and sore from fourteen or more professional games, he was ready again to go back to school.

Family Life in Memphis

When Billy first arrived in Memphis for dental school, Dot and the kids came with him. They rented a rambling two-story house, and Dot enrolled the kids in a nearby Episcopal school. "It made it so much easier for me having them there," Billy said. "The kids loved going up and down that big old staircase, and I had my own place to study."

But one day the kids came home with tales of a girl bullying them in a nearby park. "This girl was older than mine," Billy remembered, "and she was giving them the devil. She would hit on the youngest—Dara and Bill. I got them together for a talk. 'All right, girls, from now on, if she hits one of y'all, she's hit all of you. If she picks on any of y'all—including Little Bill—and y'all don't beat the hell out of her, then you're going to get a whipping from me. And if all of you don't get into it, I'm going to whip the one who doesn't participate. You might get in a fight out there, and you might lose, but if you don't get in a fight, you're going to lose when I get you.'"

The next morning, Dot looked out the window to see Little Bill, still in diapers, dragging a tree limb across the yard. "He'd heard every word I told the girls," Billy said, "and he was getting ready for the fight. And they had the fight. The oldest, Terri, led the charge, and they whipped the little girl, and she ran home and never bothered them again. They prevailed. I came home and told them how proud of them I was."

Later that evening, as Billy left home to do some lab work at school, he met two policemen coming up the stairs. "They told me they had come to see about an altercation with a child down the street. 'Well,' I told them, 'you need to talk to the children's mother. She's inside. Y'all walk right up these stairs and talk to her. Good seeing you,' I said, and left." Billy collapsed in laughter as he told the story. "When I got back home about 10:30 that night, I had a fight of my own. But we were proud that the kids stuck together."

The Human Factor

Among the many challenging courses at the dental school, there was no course in human psychology, a course Billy believed would have been very useful. "When you got out of the mechanics of dentistry and started dealing with live patients, you realized there was a whole other factor to deal with—the human factor." As in many dental schools, senior-year students started working with real patients in the school clinic for low rates, and so Billy began to learn on his own about the human factor.

Among Billy's first patients was "a wonderful little lady named Annie. She'd worn out her old set of dentures and needed a new one." When she took out her old set, Billy had to call for a professor to help him identify what they were made of. "They were vulcanite, used by dentists after the war, a step up from previous materials and very gentle on the tissues in the mouth. But these had worn completely down." Billy explained to Annie the process of fitting her for a new set, then worked with her carefully through each step: precise measurements, "bite blocks" to gauge lateral jaw movements, an impression, setting the teeth first in wax, then in plastic, and polishing them to a luster. When the day came to put in Annie's new dentures, the professor was there to observe. Billy slipped them into her mouth, took a deep breath, and told her to bite down. Looking at him with wide eyes—and a wide-open mouth—she told him, as best she could, "I *am* biting down." With more work and several follow up visits, Billy got them to fit perfectly. "They looked great. They were brighter than the teeth she'd worn for the last twenty-five years, and they gave her a beautiful smile. To me it was a miracle." The problem was, Billy discovered, that Annie wasn't wearing them. "I'd gone to school for dentistry, and now I was learning something about people. It turns out she had a roommate, a seventy-five-year-old lady who also wore dentures, and the roommate told Annie the new ones 'didn't look right' because they weren't exactly the same as her own. I ended up having to get Annie and her roommate in together and explain that they had different shaped faces and all the other reasons for the differences in the two sets of dentures. When I got done, Annie put them in her mouth and beamed. 'Dr. Cannon,' she told me, 'I'm so relieved to know that these are just for me.'"

Orthodontics and Monkeys

In his final months of dental school, Billy thought his next step would be an advanced certification in pedodontics, children's dentistry. The Tennessee dental school was about to confer on him a doctor of dental surgery degree, but if he wanted to practice a specialty, he would need more education. He had enjoyed working with young patients and discovered he was good at it. He was named the outstanding pedodontics student of his class. "I liked the kids," Billy said. "Having my own and having seen their fears of the dentist or the doctor, I found I could put them at ease." He had been particularly moved by a class trip to St. Jude Children's Research Hospital in Memphis to look at cancer in the mouths of the young patients there. "If you want your heart broken by ten in the morning," Billy said of the trip, "that is the place to go." Nevertheless, he thought he had found his specialty.

But his friend, Gary Cuozzo, talked Billy into joining him at Loyola University School of Dentistry in Chicago to pursue an MS degree with a certificate in orthodontics. Loyola was willing to structure a program similar to the one at Tennessee, allowing the two pros to play football in the fall and to attend school in their off-seasons. Billy was thirty-three. Still with the Raiders, he knew his athletic career was winding down, but he thought he might have a few more seasons left in him. He could continue to make the excellent money that football afforded and keep going to school. And orthodontics would certainly give him the chance to work with young patients since a typical practice was mostly about fitting youngsters with braces. He decided to do it.

Loyola's program was rigorous, and, as Billy discovered, exhausting. Each student attended lectures by faculty and outside orthodontists, took on a running caseload of one hundred patients, and was required to research and write a thesis on an original topic.

Billy's thesis tested a surgical procedure designed to improve the alignment process after an extraction. He used three of the macaque monkeys in the school's animal facility, kept in cages for research by professors and students. He had to tranquilize each of his animals periodically, at first to extract a tooth from each quadrant of the animals' mouths and install orthodontic braces, later repeating the process to measure the movement of teeth and to adjust the braces. He utilized a "squeeze cage" with an adjustable block to trap and hold the animals while they were anesthetized for the operations.

It was not a maneuver designed to endear the researcher to the monkeys. "They fought you at every step," Billy remembered. A friend who was living in Chicago at the time, Ted Flora (he had played with the old Baton Rouge Red Sticks baseball team), agreed to help.

"The monkeys seemed to especially dislike me," Billy said. "When I came in, they would go crazy." He performed a simple experiment to test his theory. Billy gave Ted Flora his white lab coat, a possible trigger for the animals' reactions, but when Ted came into the lab with the white coat on, the animals remained calm. "All I had to do," Billy said, "was peep around a corner and they would go bonkers."

By the end of the 1970 season, Billy had retired from professional football and was able to go to school full-time. It had taken him the first two quarters of the academic year to design his project and to outfit his monkeys with braces. Before he left at Christmas for Baton Rouge (Dot had decided against a move to Chicago), he checked a final time to make sure the braces were tight. But when he came back to Chicago after the holiday, the braces had disappeared. "I had spent six months getting to this stage, and the monkeys had easily taken out the braces and, I suppose, eaten them. There wasn't a trace. All this time was completely wasted. I had to start over."

Billy had to figure out how to keep the monkeys from getting their hands on the braces. A waitress at the restaurant where Billy and Ted had breakfast suggested an inverted cone. Billy designed and made one. "It was brilliant," Billy said. "It looked like an Elizabethan collar but the cone had to start at the elbows to work. When they came out from the anesthetic, you had three drowsy monkeys who looked like a cross between Shakespeare and grand dragons of the KKK. I caught a lot of flak from staff and fellow students about my 'upside down dresses,' but, hey, they worked!"

Dr. Billy A. Cannon, DDS

With his dual career of student and pro athlete finally at its end, Billy stepped gracefully into the practice of orthodontics in his hometown of Baton Rouge. Eleven years in professional football had provided very well for the Cannons: Billy, Dot, and the children lived in a new and beautifully decorated home on a treelined boulevard, far from the smoking stacks of the refinery and in a good school district. Since leaving LSU, Billy had remained a Baton Rouge favorite son as a running back for the Houston Oilers and a tight end for the Oakland Raiders; his status as a hometown hero and football legend was undiminished. He would have no trouble attracting patients for his new practice.

But as the Cannons began this new phase of their lives, Dot had concerns of her own. "Tell me this," she asked Billy, "am I going to have to go to all those luncheons and teas that those other doctors' wives do?" Always the kidder, Billy told her, "No, mamma, because if you do, you'll cost me too many patients." She was happy not to go.

Billy began his new career assisting Dr. Murry Decoteau, an experienced orthodontist with a thriving practice, while he built a clientele of his own. When a pedodontist's office on Lobdell Avenue became available, Billy bought it, along with the small shopping mall in which it was situated. Near what was then the downtown airport, now Independence Park, Billy remodeled the office and opened his own practice.

Billy's experience as a father, along with his many observations about the "human factor," were put to good use in treating his young patients. He kept a treatment log in which he jotted notes from his conversations with the children and their parents. "I would fish for some bit of information that would help me get inside the child's world, help me gain his trust. Every kid had a key. If you could find it, he would work with you. You had to keep the child wanting to come back and to keep wearing the braces. If you learned that the little girl had a dog, you'd ask her about how Tuffy was doing. Another child might be doing ballet or soccer. Whatever it was, you'd get them talking, and your worries were over." Billy added, "Of course all the boys—and their dads—wanted to talk about football."

In this, his post-football life, Billy found great satisfaction in his practice. "Nothing in orthodontics happens in a day," he said, but you can help change the way a kid feels about herself, and that changes everything. "I've gotten so many pictures from patients over the years— they want to show me what they've done or how good they look—or they'll see me when I'm out and come up to me to ask if I remember them. It's a great feeling to get involved with a kid and get the result that you want and that the mom wants."

Not all of Billy's patients could easily pay for the expensive regimen of treatments. Remembering his own sometimes difficult childhood, he would often work for an adjusted fee, sometimes for nothing at all. "A little girl came in with horrible teeth," Billy remembered. "There wasn't a straight tooth in her jaw, top or bottom. When I went through what we could do and how much it cost, the mother broke down in tears because they couldn't afford it. I asked her what they could afford and we agreed on that amount." Billy pulled four teeth, fit her for braces, and eventually operated to sever fibers that, without braces, would gradually pull the teeth back to where they had been. "It was a gorgeous result," Billy said, "and the mom paid faithfully until the girl got her own job and finished the payments." On occasion, Billy's friend and former teammate Johnny Robinson would call him for help. Robinson ran a group home for indigent boys in Monroe, and over the years, Billy fixed the teeth of several of "Johnny's boys" at no cost.

At its peak, Billy's practice had as many clients as he could handle. At any time, he had a caseload of as many as 500 patients and was seeing 150 per week. "I wouldn't just run them in and out," Billy said. "You were guiding them through a challenging time, and I took the time to talk to them, get to know them. You had to get personally involved in their lives to get them through the process as painlessly as possible. Lots of days, I'd come from the office after the last consultation, totally whipped. Physically I hadn't worked enough to eat—not one pound of physical labor—but I was flat worn out."

The Cannons of Baton Rouge

The last of the Cannon children, Bunnie Rene Cannon, was born August 4, 1969. Her oldest sister, Terri, was twelve, Gina eleven, Dara ten, and "Little Bill," as he was known in the family, was eight. The older siblings had known extended stays in Memphis, Houston, and Oakland, following their father to football or dental school, but Bunnie was spared the traveling life and grew up in the family's Sherwood Forest Boulevard home in Baton Rouge.

All the Cannon children performed well academically, attending the same neighborhood schools and eventually graduating from Broadmoor High School, but sometimes school seemed like an afterthought. "I grew up at the ballpark," Bunnie remembered. "My older brother and sisters were always playing something and, as much as we could, the family went to everybody's games." That Billy and Dot Cannon would have five athletic and competitive children was hardly a wonder. From neighborhood games to team sports (football, basketball, track, and baseball for Bill, basketball, track, and softball for the girls), the Cannons were in it for the long haul; they were a family in motion.

"Some of the hardest times Dot and I had were when we had to split up to see who went to whose games," Billy remembered. The girls were stair-stepped in age so sometimes they were not always able to be on the same team at the same time. As Little Bill grew up, more games were added to the Cannon schedule. "The girls would play two or three afternoons a week, and Little Bill would play two or three," Billy recalled. "One night, Dot was complaining, 'I'm just worn out. Do you realize we've been at the ballpark every night for two weeks?' I said, 'Dot, where else would you rather be?' That stopped her. She said, 'Oh, I never thought of it that way.' By the time Little Bill was a freshman, he was playing football, and Gina and Dara were in the marching group, all at Broadmoor High, and again we were able to see three of them in one night. We enjoyed that."

The Cannon household was a happy place, but it was not without turmoil. "With four girls down the hall, there was a crisis of some sort before school every morning," Billy said. "This one wore some-body else's something. That one did something to the other one. At first I thought it was just us, but I came to find out from other par-ents that we were all going through this. It was universal." Dot found an outlet for her artistic talent in the ornamental decoration of eggs, eventually becoming a teacher of the craft. She also loved to do yard work. "I was very happy to make sure she had every tool she needed," Billy said.

According to the Cannon women, it was Billy who wanted every-one to stay busy. "Billy didn't want lazy children," Dot said. "Every-body had to be doing something. He would bring home a bushel of peas, and if it looked like you were just sitting around, he'd make you start shelling." Dara remembered when Little Bill wanted to sit out a season of basketball. "Daddy got him up early the next morning to go find a guitar instructor. Little Bill went straight back to basketball."

Billy encouraged his children to strive beyond others' expecta-tions of them and their own expectations as well. "If you wanted to be a nurse," Terri said, "he'd ask you why you didn't want to be a doctor." For Billy, education was the key. "You were expected to go to college," Bunnie said. "Your only choice was which Division 1-A university you would attend. Gina partied one semester and flunked out. Daddy made her earn her own money for the next semester." Eventually, the five Cannon children collectively earned nine academic degrees.

Yankees, Tigers, and Aggies

All the Cannon children were good athletes, but Little Bill was ex-ceptional. By the time he was in high school, the six-foot-four, two-hundred-pound star lettered in four sports, earning All-America status in baseball and football. Fans, who loved to compare Little Bill with his dad, were amazed when he replicated his father's most famous run: on Halloween night of 1979, exactly twenty years after the original, Little Bill, playing for Broadmoor High, returned a punt against Istrouma (Billy's alma mater) 89 yards for a game-winning touchdown.

Understandably, Little Bill was considered a likely early-round pick in the 1980 baseball draft, and was also being fiercely recruited by many college football and baseball teams, including, of course,

LSU. Baton Rouge fans hoped Little Bill would suit up under the lights of Tiger Stadium, establishing a Cannon dynasty, but Little Bill's first choice was baseball. As Little Bill approached his 1980 high-school graduation, his father, understanding the process well and wanting the best deal for his son, became heavily involved in steering him through the upcoming ordeal.

"Professional baseball recruiting was not as well organized a system as football," Billy recalled. "One major-league team might have two minor-league squads, and another team only one. Everybody wanted Little Bill, and they were after him to commit before the draft took place, but no one would tell me definitively that he would make the major leagues, and no one would give us a firm offer."

That is, until the New York Yankees called. "The Yankees organization had a rookie league," Billy recalled, "a triple-A team and four other teams at different levels. They had a system to bring a kid up the right way. . . . I told [a Yankee scout] that if the team would recommend Bill as their number-one draft pick, we'd talk."

Not long afterwards, Yankees owner George Steinbrenner called Billy at home. "We want your boy," Steinbrenner said. "I told him I had an idea to get Bill to him in the draft," Billy said. "'If you don't like it,' I told him, 'just don't do it, but if you'll treat Little Bill as well as you did that kid from Oklahoma last year [in 1979, the Yankees had drafted a first baseman out of Oklahoma City, Todd Demeter, paying him a bonus of $208,000, a record at the time], I promise Little Bill will be available for the draft.'"

After he hung up with the Yankees' owner, Billy got busy. He obtained the addresses of every major-league baseball team from Ted Castillo, a sportswriter for the Baton Rouge *Advocate* who had covered Billy in high school. Billy sent the same telegram to each team. "It said that Little Bill was going to play college football and baseball," Billy remembered, "that he wasn't going to sign if drafted, and that they shouldn't waste a draft pick on him." And nobody did until the Yankees got their first pick sometime in the third round. They picked Billy A. Cannon Jr.

It didn't take long for other teams to file grievances. They claimed that they had been misled by the telegrams, and that secret contract negotiations had been held between the Cannons and the Yankees. After hearings and delays, baseball commissioner Bowie Kuhn vetoed the contract on June 25, forfeited the Yankees draft pick, and called for a special draft for the younger Cannon. Billy and the Yankees both fought the ruling and lost. The Cleveland Indians selected Cannon in the special draft, and Little Bill declined.

Father and son were both disappointed. Billy was quoted in the *Advocate*: "The boy's let down. . . . He's going through a period of adjustment. I'm just trying to let him go at his own pace." Billy told reporters his son would choose a college "in a few weeks."

Much to the disappointment of LSU Tiger fans, Billy Cannon Jr. announced on July 30, 1980, that he would be playing football and baseball at Texas A&M. He explained to reporters that it had been a hard choice between A&M and his hometown university, but various factors had led him to become an Aggie. "Getting out of town was one factor, but I like the state and area, plus I really liked their coaching staff," he said. Little Bill went to great lengths to express approval and support for the LSU program and its coach, Jerry Stovall. "There's not much difference [between the two programs], and I hated to say no to LSU."

Billy Sr. was less circumspect. "The LSU program under Jerry Stovall will be outstanding in time," Billy said at the same announcement, "but at this time I think Billy Jr. made the right choice. It's no disrespect for any other coach, especially Stovall, but there were situations that figured in the choice. If he stays here, every time he touches the ball on a kickoff or punt return, people are going to expect an 89-yard punt return." Later, Billy admitted that he had been unhappy about Stovall's insistence to use Little Bill as a defensive end.

Little Bill played baseball his first three years and football for all four years in College Station. By the time he was a senior, he was six-foot-five, 240 pounds, and ready to play professional football. Like his father twenty years earlier, he was a first-round draft pick of a Texas team, the Dallas Cowboys. The Cannons happily celebrated the announcement, but Billy Sr. was not at home to enjoy it. He was in prison.

9

THE CRIME, THE TIME

Race Horses and Real Estate

There's a faded black-and-white photograph on the wall in Billy Cannon's office in which he and his older brother, Harvey Jr., are standing on either side of their father. Behind them are the spires of Churchill Downs, the famous thoroughbred racetrack that hosts the Kentucky Derby on the first Saturday of May. It was 1941, the boys were four and eight, respectively, and the Derby had been held only the day before. Billy's mother, Virgie, hoped to get a look at the winner, Whirlaway, and to take a picture of her family standing next to the now famous horse, but it was already on its way to the second test of the Triple Crown, the Preakness Stakes in Baltimore. Billy smiled. "It was my first connection to a racehorse, and I never even got to see it."

Billy's love of horses began when he was playing for the Houston Oilers in the early 1960s. There were no tracks in Texas at the time, so he and Dot and one or two friends would drive to the Fairgrounds in New Orleans or to Evangeline Downs in Lafayette, Louisiana. "We'd go with a group," Billy remembered, "and sometimes there would be somebody with us who owned a horse that was racing. That was especially fun," Billy said. "It made a race more exciting."

Billy gambled a bit on the horses, but he denied being a heavy bettor. "Contrary to what the news media have reported over the years, I have never bet a lot of money. I worked too hard for it." He told of a July 4 outing to Evangeline Downs, a typical day at the races and one that encapsulated his philosophy of betting.

It was an afternoon card of nine races and an evening card of nine races. Between them was a buffet dinner that knocked your eyes out. Every dish was good, I can tell you, because I tried them all. I got lucky with a couple of races on the first card, and I was up a hundred dollars. When the night session came, I put twenty bucks on a horse in the first race. He jumped out on top, and going into the turn he was fifteen links in front—he was flying. Then all of a sudden, he started wobbling and staggering, and he finally went down, slid to within about a yard of the finish line, and died. All the other horses had passed him, and my twenty dollars was lying there on the ground, dead. And that was my omen for the night because it took the next eight races for me to lose my other eighty dollars in winnings. It was a wonderful day at the track. I didn't win any money but didn't lose any either.

Billy continued to go to the races in California when he moved to Oakland in 1964 to play for the Raiders. He was twenty-seven years old. Santa Rosa, the site of the Raiders' training camp, offered horse racing at the county fair, and the Bay Meadows thoroughbred track in San Mateo was just across the bridge. "I found out our team trainer, George Anderson, was a pretty good handicapper," Billy recalled, "and I'd get his handicaps for the day at Bay Meadows, go to the track and bet my six-dollar combinations. Pretty soon, people started coming with me, and it got to be a regular outing." The group would go on Mondays, the team's day off. "I really enjoyed the racing aspect," Billy said. "We always had a great time." Sometimes an old LSU teammate, the renowned kicker Tommy Davis of the San Francisco 49ers, would join him. Other times it would be fellow Raiders, often wide receiver Bill Miller, who knew a lot about racing and the horses.

Billy purchased his first horse for $2,500 at a "claiming race," in which all the horses running are up for sale. The buyer pays the asking price, and the transaction is made shortly before the race begins. Billy's new horse was named Edie's All. "She was a good race filly in her class, and she kept getting better and better until she advanced up to a $20,000 claiming race." Billy kept her in the Bay Meadows stables, under the care of a trainer and friend. "Dot and the girls would come to watch 'Daddy's horse' run," Billy said. "She ran well and did win a number of races, but she never got claimed." By the time Billy retired her, Edie's All had earned $35,000 in winnings. When

Billy moved back to Louisiana, he kept Edie (as his children called her) in Thibodaux, Louisiana, at the farm of Donald Peltier, a sugarcane farmer and horse breeder whose father, Harvey Peltier Sr., had been a Louisiana state senator and had managed Huey Long's campaigns for Louisiana governor and the U.S. Senate.

Although Billy bought another Bay Meadows thoroughbred, a gelding, he lost the horse to a claim within four weeks. "Turns out he had all kinds of problems I didn't know about when I purchased him," Billy remembered, "and I was lucky when somebody took him and I got my money back. That was a lesson learned."

It was when Edie foaled back in Louisiana that Billy knew he wanted to stay in the racing game and in what manner. "I liked the racing itself, the competitiveness of it, trying to get your horse in the right spot, to get the best jockey available, and so forth, but what I discovered I really enjoyed were the babies. Once you're there at a birth, helping the foal out of the amniotic sac, putting the iodine on its navel, and then to have one of those come along and really run! It's your horse. You're the doctor, you're the veterinarian, you're the paymaster, you're the feed man. To see it progress and grow and then bring it to the track—one that you bred the mare and delivered. It's a tremendous feeling. It's a way of competing without getting beat up."

Eventually, Billy bought a piece of property in West Feliciana Parish and built a bunkhouse with the barn and stables adjoining. "When a mare goes into labor," he said, "I can check on her by looking out my back door. When it's time, I just step out and help with the delivery." Over the years, Billy raised and raced many thoroughbreds. Some have done well; some, as Billy put it, "couldn't outrun a fat duck. But I have never raised the big horse," he said, "the one that everybody is looking for. But you know the next spring is coming. There's going to be another little crop born, and of course, they're all going to the Derby!"

From Strip Mall to the Hard Times Plantation

When Billy opened his orthodontics practice in Baton Rouge, he discovered another passion: real estate. He had taken out a loan to make his first purchase: the office in which he practiced and its adjoining buildings. Included were a convenience store, a beauty shop, another dentist's office, and the Hawk's Nest, a restaurant and lounge that Billy insisted had the best shrimp remoulade in town. It was a good investment: He paid no rent for an office, there was rental income from the other businesses, and he could claim depreciation on the buildings. And Billy enjoyed stopping by the Hawk's Nest after his final consultation.

This was the early 1970s. As Billy's practice grew, he began to salt away extra money, and the success of his first purchase gave him borrowing power at the bank. It was a perfect time to buy more real estate. "I bought two or three little pieces of property," Billy said, "in areas I thought were going to grow. Baton Rouge was expanding, everybody was working, and I turned these little pieces over at very good profits."

Billy fell in love with real estate. "It's the mental picture you have for that piece of property," he explained about the allure of buying and developing raw land. "With a baby horse, it is what it is. It's going to have the same markings throughout its life. It's either going to be a runner or it's not, and you'll eventually find out, but there's nothing you can do about it. With land, it's what you can do with it to make it more valuable."

But real estate and horse racing were alike in one important way: they were both competitive, and Billy loved the thrill of competition. "It was an excellent game," Billy said, "and I was playing with some of the best." Billy played the game well. With each new successful investment, he bought more property and eventually began diversifying into developed property and even businesses. "It was typical Billy Cannon," he said, "everything had to be more and bigger."

Billy began to put together partnerships to finance larger purchases. "I would take half, and I would piece out the rest to doctors or friends," he said. One early venture was a raw 2.5-acre tract on the busy intersection of Florida Boulevard and Airline Highway in Baton Rouge. Billy developed, subdivided, and sold it in parcels to several different businesses. "We tripled our investment on that one."

Already admired for his football heroics and his successful orthodontics practice, Billy, now in his late thirties, widened his circle of wealthy and influential friends through his growing real estate business. He became part of a group known as the "Chinese Inn crowd," named after their favorite place to eat. It included politicians, judges, and businessmen.

With continuing success and a growing economy, Billy bought more and larger tracts of land with ever-increasing amounts of borrowed money. He worked easily with Capital Bank and Trust of Baton Rouge and its chief lending officer, Allie Pogue. "With my financial statement and my practice," Billy said, "I don't think that Capital Bank or Allie ever turned me down."

Billy's initiation into the world of business came at a good time. The late 1960s and early 1970s were years of prosperity—not just in Baton Rouge but in the country—and had been since World War II. But starting in the 1970s and continuing into the 1980s, the economy began to falter. Economists called it "stagflation," the coincidence of high unemployment and high inflation. Exacerbated by a 1973 oil embargo by the Organization of Arab Petroleum Exporting Countries (OAPEC), interest rates more than doubled from an annual 3.2 percent postwar average to 7.7 percent. By 1975, interest rates spiked above 9 percent and continued to edge higher. Corrective efforts by Federal Reserve chairman Paul Volcker only pushed rates higher until the prime rate reached 21 percent in June of 1982.

"The early '80s were a rough time for real estate investors," remembered Paul Burns, a longtime Baton Rouge realtor, "so you saw a lot of creative financing to try to move things along. Banks would offer 'buy-down' loans with more affordable rates on the front end so sellers could turn their property, and buyers could weather the storm. But not everybody weathered the storm."

Billy was holding a lot of notes—on condos and apartment complexes as well as undeveloped land, in New Orleans as well as Baton Rouge. Nothing was moving, but the interest payments on his loans kept coming due all the same. Like many others heavily invested in real estate, Billy knew that if something didn't change, he was facing catastrophe. "I was over-extended for the time. The market had gone to hell in a handbag. Lenders were charging up to 22 percent. Capital Bank never jacked me to the highest—18 percent was the most I paid—but if I didn't sell some property, everything I'd worked for was going to crash."

Up until this point, Billy's life had been a series of hard-won successes, sometimes improbable but never easy, always achieved by perseverance and the power of his will. He might run around an obstacle, or he might run over it, but one way or the other, he would put it behind him. His real-estate strategy was adopted from his running—fast forward movement—but for the first time, this strategy wasn't working. In fact, he couldn't even see the way forward. He struggled to sell what he could to pay off what he couldn't, but it was never enough, and he continued to fall further and further behind. During the closing months of this difficult period, lenders began to sue Billy and his partners for nonpayment.

One large property promised at least temporary relief from his troubles, 142 acres of Mississippi River frontage with deep-channel access. A sale of this property could buy him time to juggle his other investments and possibly find a way through the morass. A group of buyers expressed interest, a purchase agreement was signed, but the property's levee collapsed the day before the scheduled closing, and the buyers backed out. As Billy rifled through the unsigned closing documents, he noticed for the first time since he'd bought it the name of the tract on the river. It was called the Hard Times Plantation. Billy looked back on this moment as an omen of things to come.

Buried Treasure

One of Billy's investments was a Baton Rouge T-shirt printing company, and one of its employees was a former LSU boxer named John Stiglets. Known as "the Gulfport battler," for his hometown of Gulfport, Mississippi, Stiglets twice won the Sugar Bowl Boxing Tournament in New Orleans. Billy, six years his junior, had seen him box in the mid-1950s. The two men became friends. Billy learned that in the early 1970s, Stiglets, then the owner of a Baton Rouge print shop, had been convicted and sentenced to six years for counterfeiting about $1 million in $20 denominations. As Billy's financial situation worsened, what started as idle curiosity about printing money and light-hearted jesting about making some of their own over a period of about a year became for the two men serious and directed planning. Billy would later tell a federal court how gradually, almost imperceptibly, the jokes became reality: "It's a funny thing; the more you talk about something, the easier it becomes. Why it changed from something I

wouldn't normally do to something I would do, I can't answer that."
Many years later, Billy acknowledged that the unrelenting financial
strain he'd been under was the primary motivating factor. "Over a period of a year or so," Billy said, "I got to thinking how much I needed a
boost to get over this hump until the economy got better. Until somebody paid me realistic prices, I was going to be in a bind and possibly
bankrupt."

Through the spring and summer of 1980, the unthinkable became
reality. Billy and Stiglets met at one of Billy's tracts of land, an isolated parcel off Jones Creek Road, to work out a plan. They decided
to counterfeit $100 bills—lots of them. Billy would provide Stiglets
with the front money—$10,000 in cash—and Stiglets would do the
printing. In order to be less conspicuous, Stiglets set up his operation
in the small town of Cleburn, Texas, fifty miles southwest of Dallas.
Using the cash from Billy, Stiglets bought the press, photographic
equipment, and other supplies he needed, and rented a warehouse
to manufacture the money. As a cover, Stiglets got a job in the area,
working at a power plant.

According to the original plan, once Stiglets made the phony bills,
he would sell or destroy the equipment used to make them. To help
insulate them from detection, another confederate would be brought
in to take the bills on consignment, paying Billy and his partner their
share after the counterfeits had been sold. Stiglets told Billy he already had someone lined up to handle the sale and distribution of the
bills. Beyond his original $10,000 investment, Billy's involvement
was to be limited to collecting his share of the profit.

Weeks, then months, dragged by as Stiglets set up shop in Texas,
periodically informing Billy of progress—the offset printing machine was up and running, the right inks were in, some early runs
were promising and adjustments were being made—but Billy didn't
want the details. It was 1981 by then, interest rates were at record
highs, and his investments were not moving. What Billy wanted was
enough money to pay off his loans and stay in business.

Another accomplice in the plan was William Glascock. Glascock
had purchased the T-shirt company from Billy in 1979, and the two
were involved in other business dealings. Glascock agreed to distribute the counterfeits outside the United States. Glascock set up a front
business, Asian International, Ltd., in a building on Stanford Avenue

across from the LSU lakes, as a place to transfer the bills. By the time he finished the printing runs, Stiglets had made some $6 million in counterfeit money. Together, the three men hoped to make $1 million in profit. In the end, Billy never saw a dime.

Billy remembered the day Stiglets told him the person he had lined up to sell the counterfeits was "out of business." "I asked him what he meant by 'out of business.' He said, 'I mean he's in jail. He won't be out for another twelve or fifteen years.'" Billy shook his head. "He tried to assure me he had an excellent replacement, someone with a good reputation. 'Right,' I told him, 'a good reputation in the world of counterfeiting!'" At this point, Billy seriously considered walking away. "I could have bit the bullet and lost my $10,000 . . . but I didn't."

Instead, Billy became a hands-on participant. "Stiglets brought a half million dollars counterfeit in a sack to my office," Billy said, "and told me to hold it until this guy from Alabama showed up for it. I'd never seen or heard of this person in my life. Now I'm walking on a tightrope. I've got a half-million dollars in counterfeit bills hidden in my clinic storeroom—along with some dental molds—none of the doors inside my office are ever locked, and I'm waiting for someone I've never seen to pick it up."

Again, Billy considered getting out. "I thought about starting a bonfire with the stuff and walking away. I had ample opportunity to quit, and I didn't." By the time he got a phone call from the new distributor—the "guy from Alabama"—Billy had moved the bills into an ice chest. The guy's name was Herbert "Jack" Jessup, and when he showed up at the office with his wife, Billy gave him the ice chest and told him, "No matter what you do, don't tell anyone I had anything to do with this." Jessup promised to keep Billy's name out of it. As he later told the story, that promise was broken by Jessup, Glascock, and others who became involved with Billy in the scheme. As part of his eventual plea agreement, Billy would testify against them all.

Everybody would later agree that Stiglets was a true artist in his criminal tradecraft. "When I saw the first bills," Billy said, "I held one up to the real thing, and I couldn't tell the difference." Billy knew about Stiglets's 1971 conviction for counterfeiting; what he didn't know was how much the Secret Service admired his partner's work. Agents later told Billy that when the first of the Cannon-Stiglets hundred-dollar bills surfaced and made their way to the Secret Service analysts in the home office in Washington, DC, investigators were advised, "Find John Stiglets and you'll find the rest of this money." Agents told Billy that they rated most counterfeit bills at about a three or four on a ten-point scale. Stiglets's best runs, they said, were rated at an eight or nine.

By 1982, Stiglets had quit his power-plant job in Texas and come back to Baton Rouge, moving into a house in a subdivision close to Billy's family residence in Sherwood Forest. The counterfeit money he brought with him was now packaged neatly in zipped plastic bags. Again, Billy agreed to hold the bills until they could be picked up by those who were to pass them into the currency stream. Billy purchased more ice chests for the phony money and buried them, two larger chests between his office and the drainage ditch, and four smaller chests on his Jones Creek Road property. Jessup and other confederates kept coming by for more.

"Soon, the bills started turning up," Billy said, "the first one at the World's Fair in Knoxville, Tennessee." Those caught passing them were questioned, first by local police and then by Secret Service agents who specialize in financial crimes. Agents began the painstaking process of following the chain of possession to those who knowingly profited from the counterfeits, linking them to someone higher up the chain, searching ultimately for the makers of the bills. As the weeks passed, the counterfeit bills appeared across the Southeast—Georgia, North Carolina, Alabama. "Every week it was a new article about a new arrest," Billy said. "I told John [Stiglets] that it was over, that it was only a matter of time before the trail led back to us." Billy's fears were realized when he heard from a friend that his name had been mentioned by federal investigators pursuing the case. Stiglets confirmed for Billy what he knew from experience: "Once they've got your name, they never forget it."

The following months were for Billy a time of diminishing hope and growing anxiety, but he couldn't help but appreciate the absurd humor of it. He felt sure his phones had been tapped and that he was under surveillance. "A friend from the courthouse took me out to the Holiday Inn on Seigen Lane and showed me which floors about thirty Secret Service agents were on. I began to recognize their cars and to recognize them." After work one night, Billy stepped into the Hawk's Nest lounge to find several agents sitting together at a table. Another time, he and Dot were pulling into Phil's Oyster Bar on Government Street. "At first it was a stand-off as we tried to maneuver into the last two parking spots." Billy smiled. "We worked it out like gentlemen, and pulled in next to each other. They were so close to us, Dot couldn't get out of her door." Since Dot knew nothing of Billy's crime, he couldn't share the joke with her.

The Bust

As law enforcement closed in, Billy began to try to divest some of his properties, even if it meant taking lower prices. He knew his arrest would come any day; he just didn't know which day. "The only thing I didn't cut back on were two or three [racing] mares," he said.

On Saturday, July 9, 1983, Billy went to the Fairgrounds in New Orleans. He had a horse that was ready to race, but he needed to renew his license to be able to run it. "I had just finished renewing the license when I got a phone call from Dot. The Secret Service had raided the house. They came in over the back fence, though the side door and the front door. I told Dot to let them know I was coming straight home. My daughter, Terri, drove over to pick up my lawyer, [Robert L.] 'Buck' Kleinpeter."

When Billy walked through the front door, Dot, Terri, Buck Kleinpeter, and three Secret Service agents were waiting. The agents advised Billy of his rights and pronounced him under arrest. The arrest was the end of a year-long federal investigation, tracing counterfeit bills from street-level purchases up through various levels of distribution, back to the men whose idea and product it was. It was a complex trail that began with various leads and ran through men involved in other illegal activities such as drug smuggling. Agents had already recovered ice chests buried on the Jones Creek Road property and arrested two accomplices, Charles Whitfield and Timothy Melancon, who had gone for money there. Billy told the agents he had more buried next to his clinic, and he told them were to find it.

"Buck didn't know about any of this," Billy said. Nor did Dot. "She had no idea what was going on. She was beside herself."

Dot went back to the bedroom crying. Billy wanted to go to her, to try to explain what had happened, what was happening, but the agents stopped him. "I don't know if they thought I was going to get a gun or try to escape," Billy said. Kleinpeter, a graduate of Istrouma High School, was a seasoned attorney and had been an FBI agent early in his career. "He told them to ease up and let me go, that I wasn't going to do anything stupid. Buck was my champion in this whole thing."

"Overall," Billy said, "the Secret Service agents were very nice people. They asked lots of questions, but they'd also answer questions. They said people had been telling them that Billy Cannon would never do this kind of thing, that he didn't need the money. Well, I did need the money. I did do it. I made my first mistake when I gave Stiglets the $10,000."

Billy and Kleinpeter drove with the agents to the federal courthouse in downtown Baton Rouge for an arraignment. It was a Saturday afternoon. U.S. District Court Judge Frank J. Polozola was called. While they waited for the judge to arrive, Kleinpeter had time to get a clearer understanding of what Billy had done in order to help him fashion a plea. "Buck asked me if I did it," Billy recalled, "and I told him, 'Yeah, I did it. I put up the money, I passed it, and I've got a lot more of it buried.' He asked me if any of my friends were involved. I told him, 'Buck, I wouldn't let my friends get involved in something like this.' He didn't laugh. He told me the best thing I could do was to plead guilty, give up my fall partners [accomplices], and we'd make the best deal we could. I didn't have any trouble giving them up." Referring to the number of times his accomplices had broken their promises not to use his name, Billy said, "They gave me up."

Once Polozola arrived, the arraignment itself took only minutes. Billy stood before the judge, confessed to his crimes, and agreed to cooperate with authorities in catching and prosecuting the others involved in the scheme. Polozola said he wanted to be sure Billy had time to think about what he was doing. "I want to make sure this is what you want to do," Polozola said. He gave Billy until the following Friday to reconsider his plea and released him on $100,000 bond.

When Billy returned home from the courthouse, he turned off the lights, sat on the living-room floor, and tried to fathom what had happened. "The house seemed very empty," he said. He knew that word of his arrest and plea was quickly spreading across town, and that his life would never be the same. What had he gotten himself into and why? Later that evening, Dot answered a knock at the front door. It was Boots Garland, LSU track coach and Billy's longtime friend. He was one of only a handful of people Dot would have let in the house. "When I looked in the living room," Garland remembered, "Billy was sitting on the floor, his elbows on his knees, his head hanging down. I told him, 'Billy, I'm not going to stay, but I wanted to see if there was anything I could do for you.' There was only the slightest pause. 'Yeah, Boots,' he said, 'you got change for a hundred?' Now who in a million people has a sense of humor like that and on a day like the one he'd just been through? It was good to know he wasn't too low to laugh." Questioned by the press after his meeting with Billy, Garland said simply, "He'll pick up and go on."

By the time of his rehearing on July 15, new developments in the case had been appearing in the news media every day, and Billy was pursued by reporters on his way in and out of the courthouse. Inside, he stuck with his plea, telling a packed courtroom, "What I did was wrong, terribly wrong, and I have done everything in my power to correct my mistake, and I will continue to do so."

At the end of a series of trials to follow, several other men associated with the counterfeit bills and their distribution were eventually prosecuted and served time in the case. Besides Billy, Stiglets, and Glascock, the convicted included Jack Jessup, Charles Whitfield, and Timothy Melancon.

The Fallout

Garland wasn't the only friend to encourage and support Billy. Johnny Robinson, his good friend from playing days who had since become a minister, called, as did other old teammates and friends. Many who knew Billy, including Robinson, were contacted by reporters for comment. "Billy was always generous with his success," Robinson told the *Times-Picayune*. "Those who played with him always shared in his rewards. . . . He's going to need the same qualities that made him a great football player. . . . I'll stand behind him and do what I can to help him." Former high-school rival and college teammate Warren Rabb described Billy for one newspaper as a hard worker and a good family man who had never lost his hero status. Billy's old LSU coach Paul Dietzel described him in his prime as a fierce competitor who could single-handedly turn a game around with his talent and determination. "When I heard the news," Dietzel said, "I couldn't believe it. I felt so bad. You never know what's going on in someone's mind unless you walk in their shoes."

Many others were not so generous and were happy to turn on the one-time hero. Jokes circulated around the city. One asked how you could identify a Cannon counterfeit; the answer: Ben Franklin had braces. Another described the counterfeit $100 bills as having Billy's face in the middle and in place of "In God We Trust" was the slogan "Go to hell, Ole Miss."

Old friends and associates condemned Billy and distanced themselves quickly. A political candidate for sheriff, Mike Barnett, had his campaign signs removed from Billy's yard. Billy had donated office space for Barnett's campaign in the small complex near his clinic. Barnett began to pay $1,000 per month for the space that Billy had been letting him use for free—and the candidate made sure the press knew about it.

For the next weeks and months, the Billy Cannon counterfeiting story made daily news in Baton Rouge and was the talk of the town. Supporters and detractors alike had one thing in common: shock. No one could understand why he had done it. Billy was a man who seemed to have everything, above all prestige in a community that worshipped him. How could he put at risk what to others seemed a perfect life?

At the time, Billy himself didn't seem to understand why. In testimony against Jack Jessup, one of those involved in the scheme, Billy told the court that he couldn't explain why he (Billy) had become one of the nation's biggest counterfeiters. In answering an attorney's question from the witness stand, Billy said, "If you think you are asking me why I did this . . . I still don't know why."

Billy's own family didn't know why, and he never told them. The Cannons' oldest daughter, Terri, speculated that it was the many pressures he was under. "All this real estate, four kids in college, and interest rates at 21 percent. He was trying just to keep his ducks in a row. But we don't know the story," she admitted. "None of us knows that story."

Bunnie, the youngest Cannon child, in high school at the time, remembered a father in constant motion, moving from his busy orthodontics practice to one real estate deal after another. "All those deals, and there was lots of drinking that went with each one. I don't think he was making the best decisions." Dot agreed. "He was drinking too much, and I believe it impaired his judgment." Bunnie added, "and he trusted the wrong people. There were always hangers-on, always somebody putting together some deal and always wanting it financed by him. He would do anything for people. That's the one thing I'd change. He'll give it all away. He'll give you the shirt off his back."

Judge Frank Polozola sentenced Billy to five years in prison and a $10,000 fine. Billy and Buck Kleinpeter tried to negotiate a lighter sentence that would allow Billy to stay in the area and do free dental work on underprivileged children. Polozola refused, insisting that he would not be swayed by Cannon's fame and standing in the community.

With the time reduction allowed for good behavior, Billy served a little over half of his five-year sentence. When he got out of prison, he was no longer the public figure he had been. Many described him during those days after prison as a recluse, socializing with only his most trusted friends. He quit talking to reporters and turned down several lucrative offers to tell his story.

To no one's surprise, it was an extremely difficult period for the Cannon family. "How do you love somebody and want to kill him at the same time?" Dot asked. "It wasn't about me; I was angry because it hurt the kids." Little Bill was playing football for Texas A&M at the time, and Dot recalled how opposing players would razz him during games about being a prisoner's kid. "It was hell, pure hell," Bunnie said of the period of her father's arrest and incarceration. "He'd always made us do what was right, so when he did something wrong, it was hard. But the whole thing also helped us sort things out. We'd had so much of everything, all these friends and all this stuff. And then all of a sudden we were down here, and we had to decide what was really important and figure out who our real friends were."

What was most important for Dot and the children was that they continue to love and support Billy. Yes, he had been abandoned by those who once adored him, but his family closed ranks around him. "The whole city of Baton Rouge thought he'd done something to them," Bunnie said, "but the truth is they never knew him." Terri agreed. "People had all these ideas about who he was, and they idolized him, but they didn't know him. All of a sudden they were bad-mouthing him, and they still didn't know him." When, after many years, Billy told his family he was going to allow a biography about him to be written, they were cautious. "In a way," Bunnie said, "it was good because he was going to be able to tell his story." Terri added, "But we all want to protect him."

The Wasted Years

With only three weeks left before he began serving his sentence at the Federal Correctional Institution in Texarkana, Texas, Billy scrambled to put his affairs in order—salvaging and protecting what he could of his assets and preparing for prison and its consequences. His life as he had known it had disintegrated quickly, and he was picking up what pieces he could. He sold his practice to another Baton Rouge orthodontist, Dr. John Harbour, and he sold what he could of his real estate to pay outstanding debts. Much of what he couldn't sell was foreclosed and sold by his lenders.

During such a painful period, other members of the Cannon family soon became aware that everything they said and did was being observed and judged by others. They had always been a close family; they became closer, drawing strength from one another and their most trusted friends. When a girl at school made a cutting remark, one of Bunnie's friends jumped on her instantly and had to be pulled off.

Billy knew that his poorer patients wouldn't be able to afford their treatments under the care of most other doctors. They had paid Billy when they could, sometimes taking years to close their accounts. He asked a young friend, Dr. Tommy Kiebach, to take them into his practice. Billy smiled to remember. "After he'd seen one or two of these patients, he asked me how many like these I had in my practice. 'Kiebach,' I told him, 'If I hadn't treated these patients, nobody would have.' He told me, 'Billy, you are a terrible businessman but you're a good guy, and they sure do love you.'"

On September 2, 1983, Billy walked into the federal prison in Texarkana, Texas. Billy called these "the wasted years, a total waste of time, but something I had to do." He jokingly called himself "a good convict. I made my bed perfectly. As my rehabilitation, I did 'landscaping,' which meant I cut the grass. I didn't tell them that Dot did all the yard work at home—and I certainly didn't tell Dot about my new training." He took a course in horticulture, taught by a professor from a local junior college. "It was a good course," Billy said, "and the professor that taught us was a good guy."

Possession of Roast Beef with Intent to Distribute

From time to time, Billy had to remind himself that he was in prison. There were no perimeter fences in the complex of the facility where Billy lived, and inmates there were free to move about the grounds. Prisoners had access to handball and basketball courts, and wide-open fields in which Billy liked to walk. Adjacent to the prison was a high school, and inmates would walk over together to watch Friday night football games, coming back in time for the evening prisoner count.

Once, Billy witnessed an escape. As he was playing handball, Billy hit a volley out of bounds. An inmate who ordinarily stood by and shagged loose balls walked over to it but didn't stop to throw it back. "He just kept walking and walking," Billy said, "and he never even turned around. It struck me, 'he's escaping.' We got our ball and went in. Security officers questioned us later that night about the escape."

Like other inmates, Billy lived in a dorm room with a roommate. "Because most people were serving short sentences, people moved out, and you changed roommates a lot." One of Billy's fellow inmates was from the Texarkana area, and occasionally a neighbor or friend would drop off home-cooked meals and sandwich makings in grocery bags near the road. "This was against the rules, of course," Billy said, "but it got to be where we'd put in orders with him. We'd take turns going to the road to pick up the contraband groceries and then bring them back into the laundry where we could split up and warm our food. Well, somebody saw us. As another guy and I were coming around the corner with the groceries, we got arrested." Billy laughed. "I pled guilty to possession of roast beef with intent to distribute."

Billy had one other, more serious, infraction. As his release date got closer, time seemed to move more slowly. "It became what they call 'hard time,' or 'slow time,'" Billy said. "Your aggravation level goes way up, and it's easy to get into trouble." A bank of telephones was hung in a wide hall that separated two units of men. There were four phones for 250 men. When the evening count cleared—indicating that all prisoners were accounted for—there was always a race from both sides to get to the phones. It was the custom for men from each unit to share the two phones closest to their side of the building. Billy had less than ninety days before his release, and he was anxious to talk to Dot. Before the count had cleared, he was already working his way down the hall—only fifteen or so yards to the phones—but when the count was completed, men raced in from both units, and Billy found himself without a phone. Worse, one of the men from the other unit had taken the very phone Billy had planned to use, one of the two on his side. When the man laughed at Billy and turned to make his call, it was all Billy could do to keep from assaulting him. "Why would he do something like that?" Billy asked. "I grabbed the cord and jerked the phone off the wall." Thirty years later, Billy doubled over with laughter as he told the story. "Do you know how many little wires there are on the other side of the wall? Good God, I thought, what a mess! And he's standing there, and the whole phone box and a chunk of the wall is on the floor at our feet. What a commotion. The guys who weren't involved started running to get away from us, and here comes the security officer."

When questioned, Billy lied and claimed the other man had lost his temper and pulled the phone off the wall. As he recalled the story, Billy laughed again and shook his head. "Here I am, a grown man, playing a fourth grade game." Years later, as the chief dentist at the Angola state prison, Billy would advise inmates to watch themselves carefully as their time got short. "I know from experience what can happen. I tell them if they feel themselves getting uptight, to come and see me. Some of them have, and we talk and joke around for ten minutes or so to relieve the tension, and I help get them out of the danger zone."

Halfway Home

On August 4, 1986, Billy was released to a halfway house in Baton Rouge. A front-page photograph in the *Morning Advocate* shows Little Bill escorting his father into the Salvation Army on Airline Highway where the program was then housed. (Billy was later moved to an alternate location on North Street.) He stayed there for about four months, checking out at six in the morning and checking back in by ten at night.

Billy's small circle of trusted friends noticed how much he seemed changed by his prison experience. Virgil Davis, a used-car dealer and longtime friend, told a reporter, "Before it was go, go, go. It was let's make this deal, let's make this deal. . . . He seems to be adjusting. He shows no bitterness. He blames himself. He just wants it to be a thing of the past and get on with his life."

Little Bill was solicitous and protective of his dad. The newspaper photo shows him leading interference through a knot of photographers and reporters as Billy makes his way into the halfway house. A friend sat with the Cannon father and son at a Baton Rouge restaurant when another patron made a sarcastic remark about Billy. Little Bill had to be restrained by his father. "He wanted no more trouble," the friend said of Billy. "He wanted only to get his life in order."

At the same time, Billy was determined not to let the counterfeiting and prison experiences define who he was. "He's going to stand tall," said another friend, a Louisiana legislator named Donald Ray Kennard. "He's going to get his train back on track."

10

THE DENTIST, THE WARDEN, AND THE PRISON

The Slow Pull Up

One of Billy's fondest memories of childhood was a day he spent with his Grandpa Will on the farm in Neshoba County, Mississippi. His grandfather had hitched a wagon to a pair of mules and, together, the old man and the boy dropped into the bottomlands to load sheaves of hay, pulling up and out of "the bottoms" with each fresh wagon-load until, at the end of the day, they hauled the last load back up to the barn. The path into the bottom pasture was steep and the descent exhilarating—the mules had to race at top speed to keep ahead of the wagon. But the return up the hill was slow and difficult. Billy had marveled at the strength and determination of the mules with each ascent as they lost and recovered their grip in the red clay, persevering until they mounted the slope. It was an image that had motivated him through twenty years of athletics and through the hardest challenges of his life.

Billy's descent from football legend and hometown hero to an object of ridicule and disgrace had been precipitous, but he was as determined as his grandfather's mules to make his way back up—not to the high-flying life that had led him downhill in the first place, but to roles he was sure of and loved—husband, father, provider, and a doctor who could help shape for the better the lives of his patients.

Settling Accounts

Before he reported to the prison in Texarkana, Billy put his finances in the care of a financial advisor, giving him a power of attorney and instructions to sell his remaining properties and hold the earnings in a trust account until Billy was released, since he would need a nest egg to restart his practice, his businesses, and his life. "I trusted him," Billy said simply, "and it was a big mistake." While Billy was in prison, the advisor sold the properties, generating substantial earnings. But when Billy got home from prison, the advisor informed him that the money had been "lost on bad investments." The account was empty, and Billy believed the money had been squandered. "There were no real investments," Billy said. "I think he stole it all, but there was nothing I could do. I'd given him power of attorney."

To make matters worse, the advisor claimed that he had paid the capital gains taxes due on the real estate income, but the taxes weren't paid. "As you might expect in a money situation with me coming out of jail, the IRS was already all over me." Government revenue attorneys requested a meeting. "Of course they had all the numbers since they'd been waiting for me to get out. They told me how much I owed. I laughed and told them I didn't have a penny."

The IRS representatives told Billy they would go after whatever he did have. "All I had left was my home, my cars, and three mares," Billy said. "When they asked me how much the mares were worth, thoughts of strangling somebody went through my mind. I took a couple of deep breaths and told them, 'It's too late today, but first thing in the morning, I'll get a lawyer and declare bankruptcy.'" He did.

The License

Billy had a retirement income from his days of professional football, but it was hardly enough to keep him and Dot going. If he was to survive, it was imperative that he resume his orthodontics practice. At the time he pled guilty of counterfeiting, he had voluntarily submitted his license to the Louisiana State Board of Dentistry in the hopes of getting it back when he had served his sentence. And with his jail time finally behind him, he did reapply. Through friends, he learned that a small group of dentists was actively opposing him on moral grounds. A convicted felon, they argued, even one whose time has been served, shouldn't be allowed to practice. But Billy wasn't about to let critics discourage or stop him.

In Louisiana, there is only one license issued for those in dental practice; specialists such as orthodontists and oral surgeons must receive extra training and be certified by professional organizations in their field in order to practice. Billy still had his orthodontics certificate, but to practice, he needed his dental license. As quickly as he could, he submitted the forms and scheduled a meeting with the state board. It was a professional but not unfriendly meeting, Billy remembered. "After I made my case, they took a break to meet in private, and when they reconvened, they told me I could have my license back if I would take additional training to make sure I was up to date in my field. They were fair. It was a good decision."

Billy completed his additional training over a period of several months in 1987 at the Orthodontics Department of the LSU Dental School in New Orleans. "There were a few techniques that had been added," Billy said, "but the biggest changes since I had practiced were dental materials—which were much improved." With his license in hand, Billy reopened his office on Lobdell Avenue.

Billy didn't have the time or desire for retribution against the dentists who had opposed him, but he was not sad to read that one of them who had led the effort against his licensure was caught giving his patients nitrous oxide, fondling them, and photographing their private parts. "Of course he lost his license," Billy said. "I could hardly believe it when he called to ask me the best way to get it back. I told him I'd get back with him, and somehow it keeps slipping my mind."

Help from a Friend

Murrell "Boots" Garland had been a friend of Billy's since 1957. They met on a ride back to Baton Rouge from the Southwestern Relays in Lafayette, one of the larger college track meets at the time, in which Billy had just competed. They struck up an easy friendship. Both were garrulous and funny, and each tried to outdo the other with a better story. Boots, like kicker Tommy Davis, had spent time in the Army before coming to LSU (Boots had been an editor of the *Stars and Stripes* military newspaper in Japan). He took a job as a dorm proctor in Broussard Hall, the athletic dorm, in the spring of 1958, long after Billy had married and moved out. On game days, the team's married players were required to come to Broussard Hall, and often ended up in Boots's dorm room talking.

Garland had been a coach since he was a young man growing up in Shreveport, and over the years he had worked in different sports and at every level, from little league to head coach of LSU's track-and-field program. As a speed specialist, he later worked for professional football and baseball teams. Boots even played the role of a high-school coach in a movie about his friend and LSU basketball great, Pete Maravich.

In the late 1980s, as Billy struggled to get his practice up and going, Garland regularly visited him at his office. The group of dentists who had objected to Billy's licensure continued to oppose him, discouraging others from sending any patients his way, intent, it seemed, on driving him out of business. "Lots of times, it was just me and Billy," Garland said. "He couldn't even afford a dental assistant." Many in Baton Rouge refused to forgive Billy's crime, and even after Billy began to attract a few patients, his practice was never the same as it had been before prison. Billy avoided public appearances, spending many of his extra hours at home. Garland and other close friends did what they could do keep his spirits up.

But Garland did more than keep him company; he helped Billy find meaningful work. "Would you work for the state?" Garland asked him one day. Billy answered, "Whatever it would take." Garland drove Billy down to Franklin, Louisiana, to introduce him to Pres Foster, the brother of then Louisiana governor Mike Foster. It was a productive visit. Pres agreed to talk to his brother on Billy's behalf. A new warden at the Louisiana State Penitentiary north of Baton Rouge was facing the enormous challenge of getting America's largest prison—and one of its most notorious—out from under judicial oversight and two lawsuits. The men talked of the possible need for dentists at Angola.

The Reformers

Burl Cain, warden of the Angola prison, got the call one night at home in 1995. His boss, Richard Stalder, secretary of the Louisiana Department of Public Safety and Corrections, wanted to know if there were any openings for dentists at Angola. "He told me Dr. Billy Cannon was looking for a job," Cain said. "Of course I knew about Billy Cannon—everybody knows about Billy Cannon—but I didn't know him."

Cain had only recently taken the job as warden of Angola, the nation's largest prison, inheriting two lawsuits, one of which claimed that the prison's medical care was so bad it violated inmates' constitutional rights. "I told him if we didn't have a job for him, we'd make one. I wanted him because he was who he was, because Stalder was asking, and because Governor Foster's brother was trying to help him. I also realized he'd be a great asset here [at Angola]. For one thing, he'd had his trials and tribulations, and he'd come out the other side. He would be able to relate to the inmates, and they would respect him. And I needed help with the dental and medical programs."

Cain wasn't sure what to expect when Billy came to the prison for their first meeting. "He could have been pompous the way some doctors are or because he was a football legend," Cain said, "but he wasn't. He was humble, he was grateful, very appreciative—not because he needed to be but because that's the way he is."

And, of course, Billy was funny. He also remembered his first meeting with Cain. "Warden Cain started out by telling me, 'I hear you've got a lot of experience.' 'Yes, sir,' I responded. 'Which side of the razor wire do you want it on?' Burl said, 'They told me you were crazy.' That was our kickoff."

At their second meeting, Cain described the 1992 lawsuit and explained that the prison's medical program was facing tremendous stress. Inmates with AIDS had increased by 50 percent between 1992 and 1994, tests showed that about 20 percent of inmates had been exposed to tuberculosis, and of those, 10 percent had the disease. In addition, because of the great number of life sentences at Angola, the percentage of elderly inmates continued to grow. The dental clinic was backed up with long waits, and Cain had a stack of inmate complaints about the poor quality of dental care.

Billy's first assignment was not to practice dentistry at all but to assess Angola's medical program. Cain initially hired Billy as a part-time contractor (Billy was still seeing a few of his own patients) to observe and make recommendations that would satisfy the list of demands in the suit. He even made Billy an interim hospital administrator for several months during a vacancy at that position.

Billy remembered the warden's instructions. "'All I want you to do is fix it,' he told me. 'Take your time. If you need my help, let me know.' I told him, 'Burl, I'll have it fixed in two years, maybe a year-and-a-half.' But I underestimated how bad it was. After the first year, I went back to him and said, 'Burl, I lied to you. There's no way we can fix it in that amount of time, but we can fix it.'"

Today, Cain credits Billy's work as vital to restoring a constitutional level of medical care for the Angola inmates, though it took not two but four years. On March 26, 1999, U.S. District Court Judge Frank Polozola dismissed the suit against the prison. A major part of the solution was a contract allowing LSU Medical School leadership in the prison's medical program. According to Corrections Secretary Stalder, the contract more effectively utilized money the prison system was already spending on medical care. In the process, Angola's hospital was changed to a treatment center to stabilize patients before sending them elsewhere for more serious medical conditions and providing patients with recovery units when they returned.

With the lawsuit behind him, Cain told Billy, who had since become a full-time employee, that he could concentrate on upgrading the dental program. Billy described the lamentable state of things.

All they had was one small x-ray machine, an antique that must have been bought when the facility was built during the [Governor Robert F.] Kennon administration [1952–56]. The scheduling system was a pad. When a doctor worked on an inmate, the inmate would sign the pad for a follow-up visit. There were multiple doctors, but the clinic was only seeing about ten patients per day. A patient would get his initial exam, but somebody else might do the filling. If a dentist pulled a harder case, he might put it back into the rotation and hope he didn't pull it when it came up again. It was tailor-made to dodge work, to kick the more difficult cases down the road. It was a haphazard system, hardly a system at all. It was so bad, one inmate had his teeth cleaned, was rescheduled, and finally got the work he needed a year later.

Billy called it "total negligence."

Billy was glad to get work where he could make a difference, and he appreciated that Cain let him do his job without interference, giving him support when he needed it. "He enjoyed watching us turn this dental program totally around," Billy said of Cain, "but what we were doing for the dental and medical programs the warden was getting done all across the prison. He's an innovator who is constantly thinking of ways to make this place better and safer. When we got here, you had lawyers coming in to sue us. Now you have busloads of penologists and wardens from other states coming down here to see what he's doing and how he's doing it." Billy so admired Cain's work that he helped to set up a website (wardenburlcain.com) to showcase the warden's reforms.

After carefully observing the department's operations, Billy replaced slacking or inefficient dentists and staff. He instituted a rigorous method of accounting for patient care which included, over time, designing and implementing his own computer program to make sure each patient was getting the care he needed in a timely manner. He kept the clinic in the main prison complex, but he also opened clinics in the prison's many "out-camps," autonomous prison units, sometimes miles apart, on the huge Angola property.

"When I got here, dentists were pulling teeth," Cain said. "When Billy came, it was about repairing the tooth, fixing the tooth, saving the tooth." (Billy began to use chrome crowns to save unnecessary extractions.) "He brought a level of care to this prison that you find in clinics in the free world. I'm sorry I can't go to him."

What did the prisoners make of Dr. Cannon? "I remember when he first got here," said William Kissinger, serving his fortieth year of a life sentence at Angola, "there was a lot of buzz about him: 'That's Billy Cannon, he's the one that did such and forth.' But when people met him, he was down to earth and funny. He always gives you these little pearls of wisdom. The positive approach that he has towards us is what really helps. They say laughter is the best medicine, and he's going to make you laugh."

The inmates at Angola weren't the only ones to take note of Billy's way of doing things. "He was serious about his work," Cain said. "He was holding people accountable. It helped change not just our medical and dental facilities but the whole prison, the whole culture. This man was all about doing the right thing. It was contagious—it changed the way people were doing things all over the prison. If you saw the movie *Brubaker* [about a prison reformer, played by Robert Redford, in an Arkansas prison], he was Brubaker. He filled the role right here."

For his part, Billy believed his own prison experience made him a better doctor—especially for the patients he treated at Angola.

"Sometimes I catch flak from people," Billy said. "They hear about what I do, and they think I'm soft on convicts. They're misunderstanding the difference between sympathy and empathy. I'm not soft on criminals. I treat them like human beings. I've been where they've been. I can empathize."

When the rare Angola inmate has served his term and is ready for release (some 80 percent of Angola inmates are serving life sentences and will never get out), Billy does a final check on their teeth and gives them a warning. "I get to talk to them when they first come in," Billy said, "and when they leave. I tell them, 'You can make it.' They say, 'You made it, Doc. We got a shot, don't we?' And I say, 'Yeah, you got a shot. Don't waste it!'"

The Return of Billy Cannon

Boots Garland had been a faithful friend to Billy during those most difficult years of his arrest and incarceration, and afterwards, as the one-time football hero struggled to get back on his feet and resume a normal life in his hometown, Garland had been instrumental in getting Billy the job at Angola. Many had been quick to condemn and distance themselves from Billy, but even those who wanted in some way to reach out to him found it awkward. Without planning to, Garland became something of a point man, a way to get in touch with Billy. "For a long time, Billy didn't want to be out in public," Garland said. "He refused to go to the functions he was invited to." Billy had bought twelve acres in West Feliciana Parish, an easy drive to and from work at Angola, where Little Bill helped him build a house and stable for his race horses. He avoided the Baton Rouge traffic—and possible unpleasant encounters. Dot would come up for the weekends with a fresh load of laundry. It was a much quieter life than the one he had lived as a younger man, but he liked it.

One day, Garland called Billy at his office to pass along another invitation, this one to speak at the Gridiron Club, a Tiger football boosters organization started in 1995 by then coach Gerry DiNardo. As usual, Billy declined, but this time, Garland insisted. "It was around the time of the Ole Miss game," Garland remembered, "and people wanted to hear from Billy. The meeting was at a restaurant in Baton Rouge, and I told Billy, 'I'm going to pick you up, we're going to go, and you're going to talk.' After a little back and forth, Billy said, 'Okay, I'll go, but I'm not going to talk.' I told him, 'We're going, and you're going to talk. Billy, it's time!'"

Billy was not prepared for the reception he received—nor was Garland. "Word had got out that Billy was going to speak. When we drove up to the restaurant, there wasn't a parking place within two blocks. It was packed with fans and old friends—even some guys from Ole Miss whom Billy had played against. When I introduced him, all I said was, 'I know two things about this man. One, he made friends with my three-year-old grandson faster than any person I've known, and two, [as an orthodontist] he gave my daughter a beautiful smile. Ladies and gentlemen, Dr. Billy Cannon.' I'm telling you, they jumped to their feet roaring. The hair on my arms stood up. They nearly tore the place down."

Billy may not have been prepared for the warmth of his reception, but as always, he was quick with a one-liner. He stepped to the microphone with a grin. "Thank you, Boots, for that kind introduction. You said it just the way I wrote it."

The Run Plus Fifty

Others also helped to bring Billy back into the public eye. Billy's youngest daughter, Bunnie, was working for the LSU Sports Information Department during the years after Billy's release. She remembered how the athletic director, Joe Dean, quietly introduced Billy back into the university community. "He'd bring my dad back for an event," Bunnie said. "Then he'd wait a year and bring him back for something else. Gradually he brought Daddy back into the spotlight where he could feel good about himself. I love that man for doing that. Slowly, slowly he came back into it. It took ten or fifteen years."

One successful outing led to another. Billy began appearing at charity and social functions as well as sports events. Wherever he went, he was besieged for autographs. Wherever he was asked to speak, he left his audience laughing. One writer reported, "He seemed to be enjoying his fame instead of needing to hide from it. . . . It was almost as though he was desperate to make up for all that lost time."

A number of acquaintances noticed that Billy had changed during his years away from public view. One of those was his old coach, Paul

Dietzel. The two men often shared the head table at galas and con-
ferences, and while Billy didn't mind taking shots at the coach who
once irritated him so badly, it was all in good fun. "I really like him,"
Dietzel told a reporter. "I like him a whole lot more than I did when
he was younger. He's much more friendly. He is a lot more humble
than he used to be. I've been to several signings with him. He carries
on a very pleasant conversation with everyone who comes up. I can't
imagine the Billy Cannon of yesteryear doing that. He's just become
a more genuine person." Even Boots Garland was surprised at Billy's
changes. After watching him sign autographs for an entire evening,
listening to one story after another about "the run," Garland found
himself waiting for Billy to lose his patience. But he didn't. "That's
when it dawned on me," Garland said, "how well he'd adjusted to
being Billy Cannon, and the obligation" that came with it.

   Billy was himself at the center of a series of charity events. Longtime friends Shorty Rogers and Bobby Olah asked Billy to speak to a
private gathering at Shorty's Ribs and Seafood Restaurant in Ham-
mond. Billy suggested they sell tickets to raise money to support
the home for wayward boys started and run by his LSU teammate,
Johnny Robinson. Billy entertained a packed crowd with stories of
his college and professional careers while Rogers and Olah collected
a sizable donation for Johnny Robinson's Boys Home in Monroe. The
three friends turned the fundraiser into an annual affair, each year
moving to a larger venue, featuring more LSU star athletes, and raising more money.

Four events in recent years solidified the public acceptance and forgiveness of Billy Cannon. One was when he was named to the College Football Hall of Fame—for the second time. In 1983, the National
Football Foundation revoked its first invitation to be inducted, only
weeks after his arrest. Twenty-five years later, in December 2008,
Billy traveled with his family to New York for the long-delayed ceremony. Surrounded by other honorees, sports celebrities, fans, and reporters, he anticipated—and dodged—the inevitable questions about
his past. "I don't look back," Billy said, then added with a smile: "They
might be gaining on me." But after the ceremony, he was candid with
an Associated Press reporter. "You heard all about guidance, leadership, doing the right thing [at the induction ceremony]," Billy said,

"and there's a convicted felon sitting in the middle of them. One of the reasons I'm here today: I did the crime, I did the time, and I haven't had a problem since. Not even a speeding ticket."

Three weeks earlier, on November 22, 2008, there was a tribute closer to home. Between the first and second quarter of the LSU–Ole Miss game, announcer Dan Borne directed the fans' attention to the southeast corner of Tiger Stadium. A black veil was slowly lowered, revealing Billy's name and his famous number 20, long since retired, displayed on a permanent stadium installation. Billy walked onto the field and waved to 90,000 cheering fans.

A year later, on October 31, 2009, exactly fifty years after his famous run, Billy stood again on the Tiger Stadium field. This time he and the fans watched together the grainy film as it was replayed on the stadium's new video screen. The excited voice of J. C. Politz, who called the game so many years before, swelled ever higher as the young Billy Cannon took the first bounce of the Ole Miss punt and made his glorious way upfield for the touchdown. The ghostly mix of the cheers of those long-ago voices with the roar of the crowd that night was deafening.

Billy was once again honored by his alma mater in 2010 when he was named Alumnus of the Year by the LSU Alumni Association and inducted into its Hall of Distinction. At the award ceremony, Billy, dressed in tuxedo, with his thinning gray hair brushed back, charmed the audience, as always. He closed his remarks with thanks, telling them what he has told many people many times: "The people of Louisiana are quick to love, and they are also quick to forgive."

Legacies

One day in 2015, Billy leaned back at his desk in the small office of the Angola dental clinic. During the last several months of this, his seventy-seventh year, he had recounted many stories from his past for a book about his life. As he thumbed through a manuscript of the book, he asked the writer why so many of his stories had been left out. The writer tapped his own copy of the manuscript as he answered. "Because if I included every good story you told, the book would be a thousand pages long."

The writer asked Billy a question, "What do all the stories—told and untold—add up to? What is the impact, the meaning of your life?"

"I would judge anyone's legacy the same way I'd judge a coach's stay at a university," Billy said. "Did he leave it better than when he got there? Players come and players go. Coaches come and coaches go. But the great institutions endure. I've been associated with two great institutions in the state of Louisiana—LSU and LSP [Louisiana State Penitentiary]. Each is great in its own way. Both are much needed and much underfunded. But you don't judge a coach until his days are done. He might have had good years and bad years, but did he leave his institution better than when he came to it? I would like to think that all the places I've been—on both sides of the razor-wire—were better for my having been there." He paused. He had been serious longer than he could take it. "Now the telephone at the prison in Texarkana may not feel the same way!" He shook his head, remembering the time a fellow inmate beat him to the phone, and he had responded by ripping it out of the wall. "I didn't know those things had so many wires!"

What about the people who contributed to your success, the writer asked. Billy smiled. "Well, then the book would have to be two thousand pages long." He paused and tilted his head back in thought. "But I know I couldn't have achieved what I did without the help of" (he used his fingers to remember) "Alvin Roy, Ralph Moran, Marty Broussard, Ed Partin, Tickie Saia, Buck Kleinpeter, and Burl Cain." All of these men have a place in the book about him.

What about future plans, the writer asked. Billy motioned to the clinic around him, where he has spent the last twenty years working with men and women, most of whom have been with him nearly that long. "I'm going to keep working as long as Burl Cain is warden," he said. "And I'm going to keep raising race horses. If I can stay with it long enough, I'll eventually get a Kentucky Derby winner! And I'm going to keep watching LSU football on my three TV sets. If the Tigers are doing good, I'll get to see it three times at once." He pauses for effect, "and if they're not doing so good. . . ."

The Person, the Player, and the Long, Long Run

As a youngster and the son of LSU's track-and-field coach, Al Moreau, Doug Moreau had watched Billy on track and football fields many times. He idolized Billy. It was an era when the Tigers were finally beginning to win in football, and game attendance was picking up. "It was a thrilling place to be," Moreau remembered of the last half of the 1950s, "and Billy Cannon was right in the middle of it, and people were rightly attributing [LSU's] success to the fact that he was there."

Doug Moreau would become an LSU Tiger hero in his own right, a wide receiver and placekicker who earned All-American status in 1965, and who moved into the pros as a tight end for the Miami Dolphins.

When Moreau returned to Baton Rouge to go to law school in the early 1970s, he reestablished his connection to Tiger football by becoming a radio color analyst for LSU broadcasts. It's a position he has held ever since, even as he moved up in the legal profession from city judge to district court judge to district attorney, and even after he stepped down as DA.

In July of 1983, Moreau was on vacation with his family in Tennessee when he heard the news of Billy's arrest. "I can remember thinking about the irony of my being there," he said. "Tennessee was where Billy was stopped at the goal line in the Tigers' first loss in two seasons, right after the big game against Ole Miss in 1959."

When he got home, be heard more details—tapped phone lines, co-conspirators, ice chests stuffed with counterfeit money and buried in a field. "It was big news. My first reaction, probably just like everybody else, was why did he do it. Here's a guy who had great athletic ability, very famous, everybody knew who he was; he had a whole lot more to lose getting caught for something like this. What made him think he was going to win? And I don't know. I still don't know. What I do know is he handled it like a man. He got caught, and he paid his penalty. He has once again become a very productive member of society. You wouldn't know from talking to him that he's let it affect the rest of his life."

In his career as a judge and district attorney, Moreau has seen many varieties of human fallibility: "Doing what I did legally, I learned that people are prone to make mistakes, to make stupid judgments. There are some people who do evil things, who do it intentionally. [These kinds of] things, the very fact that you did them, are sufficient to be condemned. But that's not most of life. Most of life, people make mistakes, they make bad judgments, they decide things on the spur of the moment. Had they chosen to think about it reflectively, they would have made a different decision."

Moreau, like many in Baton Rouge, chose to focus on the good in Billy's life. "When you consider everything," Moreau said, "Billy Cannon is one of those guys who has been a real positive for our civilization. And I think the good things he has done in life are much more important for people to hold up, look at, and model their conduct after than the bad things."

In Moreau's estimation, Billy is one of the greatest athletes in LSU history, arguably the greatest. "He had the ability to do so many things physically and mentally that so few have the ability to do. He was fast, strong, tough, relentless, relatively injury-free, and when you line that up . . . he stands out. It's the same way that Pete Maravich stands out. There are some people who are so much better than other people. He was one of those. And I think he handled it very gracefully. I never saw him be braggadocios—cocky yes—but I never saw him hang it over somebody's head. I never saw that part of him, which could easily have been a part and does become a part of some people who don't know how to handle the fact that God gave them some gifts that other people don't have."

In 2010, *Tiger Rag,* a Baton Rouge sports periodical, compiled a list of athletes, coaches, administrators, politicians, journalists, and others considered to be "The Top 150 Most Influential People in LSU Athletics History." Maravich is near the top, of course, as are many of the school's greatest coaches and players: Skip Bertman, Shaquille O'Neal, and Paul Dietzel. Moreau himself has been placed at number 49. Number one on the list is Billy Cannon. "You can debate about that, of course," Moreau said, "but I believe Billy deserves to be right there at the top."

Moreau remembered Billy's famous run, the 1959 punt return late in the game against Ole Miss. "You can look at it over and over again," Moreau said,

> and you never stop marveling at what an extreme human feat it was for him to have broken so many tackles at that stage in the game— after having played both ways, on a wet night when people were tired, and uniforms were weighing fifteen pounds. If back then there would have been all the modern-day technology that you have

now, with all the cameras from different angles, all the slow-mo, it would have been more famous today because it was so spectacular. That play at any time in history was one of the greatest, and it would have been greater if it had been memorialized with all the cameras, the high-definition, the color. All you have is that grainy film from a distance. But it shows what it shows, that one guy, one giant, knocking down all the pawns, finishing in the end zone.

NOTE ON SOURCES

Many hours of interviews with Billy Cannon and his family constitute the major source of information for this book. In addition, I interviewed classmates, teammates, friends, journalists, attorneys, and others knowledgeable about one or more aspects of his life.

I relied heavily on Peter Finney's *The Fighting Tigers, 1893–1993: One Hundred Years of LSU Football* (1993) for details of individual games. Finney's accounts were supplemented by newspaper and magazine articles. *The Perfect Season: LSU's Magic Year—1958* by Bud Johnson (2007) provided background and detail on LSU's national championship season, and Bud was himself generous in providing me with additional information. Paul Dietzel's memoir, *Call Me Coach: A Life in College Football* (2008), was an important perspective on LSU's glory years of the late 1950s and early 1960s, and the documentary *Ole War Skule: The Story of Saturday Night*, directed by John Darling Haynes (2011), provided excellent film and commentary on LSU football history.

Numerous sources were useful in researching the Houston Oilers and the early days of the Oakland Raiders. These included *Houston Oilers: The Early Years* by Kevin Carroll (2001); *From Cannon to Campbell: An Illustrated History of the Houston Oilers*, edited by Mickey Herskowitz (2007); *Tales from the Oakland Raiders Sideline: A Collection of the Greatest Raiders Stories Ever Told* by Tom Flores with Matt Fulks (2012); and *The Good, the Bad, and the Ugly: Oakland Raiders: Heart-Pounding, Jaw-Dropping, and Gut-Wrenching Moments from Oakland Raiders History* by Steven Travers (2008).

Among the sources I used in the chapter on the Louisiana State Prison and its warden, Burl Cain, were Mark Carleton's *Politics and Punishment: The History of the Louisiana State Penal System* (1971); *Cain's Redemption: A Story of Hope and Transformation in America's Bloodiest Prison* by Dennis Shere (2005); *God of the Rodeo: The Quest for Redemption in Louisiana's Angola Prison* by Daniel Bergner (1999); *In the Place of Justice: A Story of Punishment and Deliverance* by Wilbert Rideau (2010); and *Conviction: A True Story* by Peter D. Tattersall (1980). Of several excellent documentary films about Angola, two were especially helpful: *The Farm: Angola, USA,* directed by Jonathan Stack, Liz Garbus, and Wilbert Rideau (1998); and *Serving Life,* directed by Lisa R. Cohen (2010). In addition, I conducted personal interviews with Warden Burl Cain and several inmates at Louisiana State Penitentiary. A special thanks to Kerry Myers, editor of the *Angolite* magazine, for information concerning Billy Cannon's work at the prison.

I relied primarily on two books to write the chapter on Baton Rouge: *River Capital: An Illustrated History of Baton Rouge* by Mark Carleton (1981), and *Historic Baton Rouge: An Illustrated History* by Sylvia Frank Rodrigue and Faye Phillips (2006).

INDEX

Rabenhorst, Harry, 96, 111
Rauch, Johnny, 160
Rice University (Owls), 6, 92, 102–3,
115, 116
Robinson, Johnny: as Cannon friend,
178, 194, 210; on LSU team, 3, 86, 88,
92, 94, 105, 108, 109, 113, 116, 120, 123,
128, 129, 131, 132, 133, 137–38; signing
with NFL, 144, 146
Robinson, W. T. "Dub," 88
Rockefeller, John D., 31
Rogers, Shorty, 210
Roosevelt, Franklin, 31
Roy, Alvin, 11, 67, 68, 99, 100, 107, 145,
165, 212
Rozelle, Pete, 144, 146, 147
Rush, R. O., 145
Rushing, Samuel A., 12, 95
Russell, Fred, 138
Rymkus, Lou, 148–50

Sachse Electric, Inc., 106–7, 111
Saia, Butchy, 96–97
Saia, Frank Tickie, 106, 119, 120, 212
San Diego (Los Angeles) Chargers, 146,
149, 151–52, 158
San Mateo, CA, 184
Santa Rosa, CA, 184
Savell, Willoughby Henry "Papa Will"
(grandfather), 26–29, 42, 201
Schuh, Harry, 158–59, 160, 161, 165
Schwerner, Michael, 21
Sharp, T. J., 139
Shell, Art, 160
Smiley, Jim, 52
Smith, Dave, 151
Smith, Don "Catfish," 74–75
Solvay Process Company, 26, 47
Southern University (Baton Rouge), 5,
42, 58
Stabiler, Wayne, 66
Stabler, Kenny, 164
Stalder, Richard, 204, 205, 206
St. Aloysius school (New Orleans), 60,
70, 76
Standard Oil Company, 5, 12, 25–26,
30–31, 32, 34, 84
Steinbrenner, George, 181
Stephens, Collins "Cossie," 37

Stevens, Paul, 60
Stiglets, John, 188, 189, 190–91, 193, 194
St. Jude Children's Research Hospital,
175
Stovall, Jerry, 90, 182
Stram, Hank, 165–66
Strange, Bo, 114
Strange, Clarence "Pop," 87, 89–90,
93, 94
Sugar Bowl, 109, 129–30, 140
Suire, Ronald, 64
Sulphur High School (Golden Torna-
dos), 65, 74
Super Bowl, 160, 162–63

Talamini, Bob, 151
Tanner, Mrs., 54
Taylor, Howard, 8–9
Taylor, Jimmy, 60, 99, 100, 144, 162;
as LSU player, 80, 82, 88, 97, 102,
103–4, 107
Teamsters, 99–102
Tennessee, University of: School of
Dentistry, 154, 169–75; Volunteers
football team, 138–39
Terrebonne High School (Houma), 65,
75–76
Terry, George, 118
Texarkana, TX, 197–99, 212
Texas A&M University (Aggies), 10–11,
182, 196
Texas Tech (Red Raiders), 103
Thibodaux, LA, 185
Thompson, Richard, xii–xiii
Tiger Stadium (Baton Rouge), xi–xii, 4,
42, 65, 76, 81–82, 87, 95, 102–3, 119,
123, 137, 181, 211
Tinsley, Gaynell "Gus," 82
Tisdale, T. Terrell, 170
Tittle, Y. A., 92
Tolar, Charlie, 151, 153
Tubb, Ernest, 27
Tucker, MS, 20
Tulane University (Green Wave), 93,
104, 127–29
Turner, Win, 82

Union, MS, 20
Unitas, Johnny, 171